A KEY SECTOR OF INDIAN ECONOMY

A KEY SECTOR OF INDIAN ECONOMY

Systems View of Steel Industry

RAJESH CHADHA

CONCEPT PUBLISHING COMPANY, NEW DELHI-110059

ISBN 81-7022-034-3

First Published 1989

Rajesh **Chadha** (*b*. 1954 -

Published by
Ashok Kumar Mittal
Concept Publishing Company
A/15-16, Commercial Block, Mohan Garden
NEW DELHI-110059 (India)

Lasertypeset by
Microtech Advance Printing Systems (P) Ltd.
H-13 Bali Nagar
NEW DELHI-110015

Printed in India by
D. B. Offset Works
B-218, Naraina Ind. Area
DELHI-110028

DEDICATED

TO

PROFESSOR PREM VRAT

PREFACE

Steel plays a crucial role in the economic development of a nation. There is an urgent need for long term planning in steel industry of a developing economy. The present study takes a systems view of Indian steel industry and attempts to analyse and forecast the important elements of this system, viz. steel consumption requirements of Indian economy, demand for various inputs for the production of steel and the production function in Indian steel industry with the help of an econometric simulation model. The primary aim of the study is to help the planning process by supplying the input information in advance as to what are the likely annual needs of steel consumption in Indian economy up to the year 2005 A.D. and how much of each of the various inputs shall be needed every year to produce the desired quantity of steel at the minimum possible cost.

The context and the problem along with major objectives of this study have been identified. The existing relevant literature has been critically reviewed. The variables used in the system's study have been identified and specified.

A steel consumption function for Indian economy has been estimated by using the global method with GNP as the explanatory variable. A GNP function has also been estimated in case of India.

The cost minimising input demand functions and the relevant cost function in Indian steel industry have been estimated. The corresponding production function has also been derived.

The sub-models of consumption and production of steel have been dovetailed into a simulation model of the system of Indian steel industry. The model so developed has been validated by using graphical and statistical methods. The forecasts of various endogenous variables have been computed upto the year 2005 A.D.

The results of the present study have been extensively analysed along with a sensitivity analysis of various forecasts. The need for a dynamic follow-up of the study has also been emphasised.

At the end, the summary of major findings and the significant contributions made by this study have been discussed. The limitations of the present research and suggestions for future extensions and modifications have also been given.

RAJESH CHADHA

ACKNOWLEDGEMENTS

With deep sense of gratitude I wish to express my sincere thanks to Dr. Prem Vrat, Professor of Industrial Engineering, Department of Mechanical Engineering, Indian Institute of Technology, New Delhi, for his valuable guidance, continuous support and sustained encouragement throughout the period of this research. But for his keen interest, highly penetrating observations and stimulating discussions, this study would not have taken its present shape. I shall always remain obliged to him.

I am grateful to Dr. K.L. Krishna, Professor, Delhi School of Economics, University of Delhi for having spared some of his precious time to go through and critically comment on some of the econometric models of this thesis.

I am obliged to Mr. V.K. Vasal, Dr. B.N. Goldar and Mr. R.N. Bhardwaj for their useful suggestions and comments.

Thanks are due to various officials of the Steel Authority of India Ltd., New Delhi for extending valuable help during my visits to their office. Special thanks are due to Mr. M. Usman, Deputy Manager, SAIL, New Delhi for always providing help with a smile.

Owing to my pre-occupation with the priorities of this research project, my family members, in particular my son, Master Rajat, remained deprived of the privileges and prerogatives that nature and society have bestowed on them. I am very much indebted to them for their patience and cooperation during the period of this study.

Finally, I would like to thank the Concept Publishing Company for bringing this book out in a very neat and efficient manner.

RAJESH CHADHA

CONTENTS

LIST OF FIGURES

LIST OF TABLES

Nomenclature

The necessary descriptions of the symbols/notations used in this thesis are given wherever these appear. Unless otherwise specified, the major system variables are described as follows :

- Y : GNP of India at factor cost at constant (1970-71) prices (Rs. crores)
- S : apparent consumption of steel in India in terms of crude steel equivalent (thousand tonnes)
- Q : production of steel in terms of crude steel equivalent (thousand tonnes)
- L : labour input (lakh man-hours : all employees)
- K : capital input (gross fixed capital in Rs. lakhs at constant 1960 prices)
- F : fuels input (lakh tonnes of coal replacement equivalent)
- M : raw-materials input (Rs. lakhs at constant 1960 prices)
- P_L : price of labour input (Rs. per man-hour)
- P_K : price of capital input (Rs. per rupee of capital input)
- P_F : price of fuels input (Rs. per tonne of coal replacement equivalent)
- P_M : price of raw-materials input (price index, 1960 = 100)
- Rs. : Indian rupees

Note : The terms 'lakh' and 'crore' have the following numerical values :

1 lakh = 10^5
1 crore = 10^7

ONE

INTRODUCTION TO THE PROBLEM

1.1 GENERAL INTRODUCTION

Steel is the foundation of the complex structure of a typical present day economy. The speed and the strength with which this foundation is laid play a major role in determining the rate and level of economic development of a nation. The developed economies have already strengthened their steel base and the developing ones need to follow this precedent. A thorough analysis of this industry is required in order to plan its future in the best possible interests of a nation's economic development.

The present study is an attempt to analyse Indian steel industry as a system. This is a study at macro-level which takes a simultaneous view of steel consumption requirements, input demand requirements and production function in this industry.

The present chapter describes the set up of Indian steel industry and its relationship with planned economic development of the nation. The aims and objectives of the present study and its plan have been briefly discussed.

1.2 A BRIEF HISTORY OF INDIAN STEEL INDUSTRY

India is considered to be the centre of origin of the iron and steel industry in the world. It has been estimated that the technique of making iron and steel has been known to India nearly for past three thousand years (22).*[1] The famous iron pillar near Qutab Minar in Delhi is a standing testimony to the level of sophistication in metallurgical know-how in ancient India. Though, this pillar is nearly fifteen centuries old, it has not shown any tendency to rust.

A start in the development of Indian steel industry based on modern technology was made in 1907 with the launching of Tata Iron and Steel Company (TISCO) at Jamshedpur in Bihar. It was followed by the commissioning of Indian Iron and Steel Company (IISCO) at Burnpur, West Bengal in 1919. The first unit in the public sector, Mysore State Iron Works (MISW), started functioning at Bhadravati, Karnataka in 1923. Now it is a joint undertaking of the Central Government and the State Government of Karnataka and is known as Visvesvaraya Iron and Steel Works Limited (VISL).

The first Five Year Plan (1951-56) recognised the basic importance of iron and steel industry in all round economic development of the nation (78). It was only during the Second Plan (1956-61) that the development of modern steel industry was accelerated. The work was started to set up three integrated steel plants in public sector at Bhilai, Durgapur and Rourkela, each with one million ingot tonnes capacity. these plants became operative in stages between 1956 and 1962. The capacities of two private sector plants TISCO and IISCO were doubled to two and one million ingot tonnes, respectively, during the same period. The total ingot capacity rose from one million to six million tonnes during the period 1947-62.

The capacities of the three public sector plants were further expanded during the period 1962-73. The capacity of integrated steel plants rose to 8.9 million ingot tonnes by 1973.

The Bokaro Steel Plant was commissioned in 1978 in Bihar. The total installed ingot steel capacity stood at 11.4 million tonnes as on 31st March, 1980.

Alloy Steel Plant, Durgapur, produces alloy and special steels. It started its production in 1965. Its current ingot steel capacity is

---

1. * Numbers in parenthesis indicate references at the end of the book.

160,000 tonnes which is proposed to be increased to 260,000 tonnes in future.

The Salem Steel Plant, Tamil Nadu, started its operations during 1981. It has a capacity of 32,000 tonnes of cold rolled stainless steel sheets and strips. It shall have an ultimate capacity of producing 2,20,000 tonnes of stainless, electrical and other special steels.

The Bhilai and the Bokaro Steel Plants are presently under expansion to a capacity of four million ingot tonnes each. The expansion programme is likely to be completed by 1987-88 without further slippages.

The work has already begun to set up Visakhapatnam Steel Project in Andhra Pradesh. It shall be under the management of newly formed Rashtriya Ispat Nigam. The work shall be completed in two stages and it shall have an ultimate capacity of 3.4 million tonnes of liquid steel. The first stage of 1.2 million tonnes is scheduled to be over by 1988-89 with a likely delay of 2-3 years.

Daitari in Orissa and Vijaynagar in Karnataka have been chosen as the locations for new steel plants. The preliminary reports on both the plants are under study by the government.

In early 1970s, government issued lincences to more than 200 mini steel mills. During the second half of 1970s, mini mills were hurt by acute power shortages and inadequate availabilities of important inputs such as ferrous scrap and graphite electrodes. By the end of 1970s most of these mills were operating at low utilisation rates and many had closed. The government, then, came forward to help these mills and allowed them to diversify into alloy steel production and integrate forward by constructing finishing capacity. There were 165 mini steel plants with licenced capacity of 4.1 million tonnes during the year 1982-83. Out of these 144 units were in operation with an ingot capacity equal to 3.32 million tonnes.

Plans were drawn up for the expansion of steel making capacity during the 1980s. A three pronged strategy has been worked out to achieve this expansion, which includes expansion of the existing plants, setting up new capacity and modernisation and upgradation of technologies in existing plants to result in higher productivity (147). The public sector is expected to have 13.6 million tonnes of ingot steel capacity equivalent to 10.9 million tonnes of saleable steel. Besides, TISCO and secondary producers are also expected to contribute to steel availability in the country. Fig. 1.1 shows the major steel plants located or proposed to be located in the country. Table 1.1 mentions the present and/or proposed capacities of these steel plants.

TABLE 1.1
Existing and Proposed Capacities of Major Steel Plants in India by the year 1990

Name of the Plant	Capacity: Million Tonnes of Ingot Steel	
	1982	Proposed by 1990
Bhilai Steel Plant	2.50	4.00
Bokaro Steel Plant	2.50	4.00
Durgapur Steel Plant	1.60	1.60
Rourkela Steel Plant	1.80	1.80
Indian Iron and Steel Company	1.00	1.00
Visakhapatnam Steel Project	-	1.20
Tata Iron and Steel Company	2.16	2.30
Total	11.56	15.90

1.3 ORGANISATION OF INDIAN STEEL INDUSTRY

At present there are five integrated steel plants in public sector, namely, Bhilai, Durgapur, Rourkela, Bokaro and IISCO. The first four are directly under the control of Steel Authority of India Limited (SAIL) while IISCO is a wholly owned subsidiary of SAIL. The management of IISCO was taken over by the government in 1972 and its ownership in 1976 with a view to improve its working. The Alloy Steel Plant (Durgapur) and Salem Steel Plant are two special steel plants in public sector.

Fig. 1.1 Major Steel Plants of India

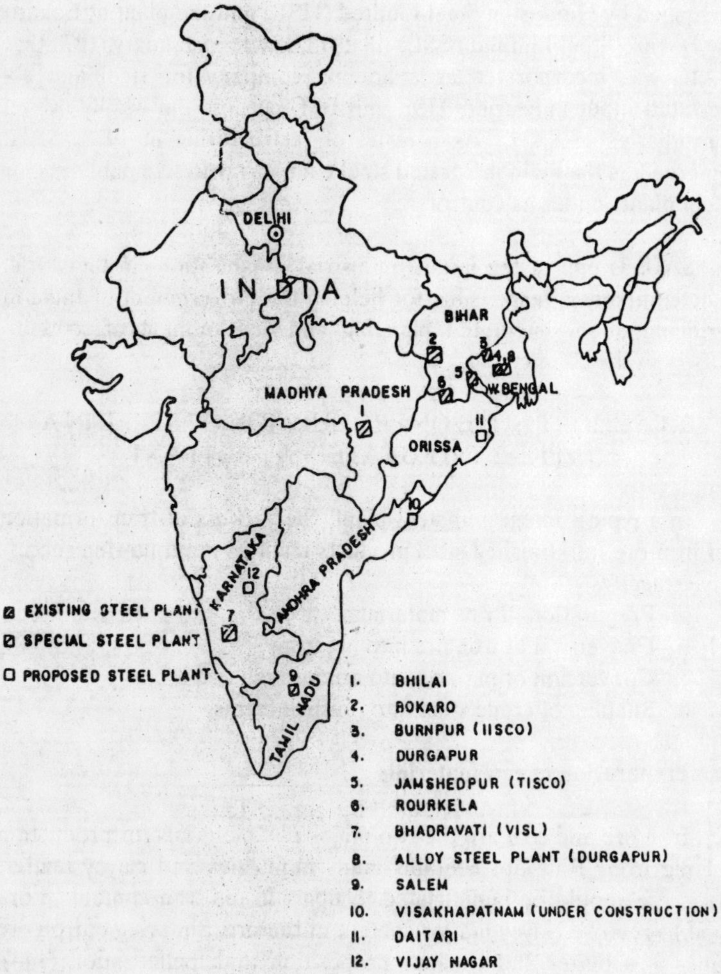

TISCO is the only integrated steel plant in private sector. Besides, there are about 144 licenced mini steel plants that are operative.

The plants at Bhilai, Durgapur and Rourkela were owned and managed by Hindustan Steel Limited (HSL) and the plant at Bokaro by Bokaro Steel Limited (BSL) till 1973. It was in January, 1973 that SAIL was incorporated as a holding company for steel and associated input industries. HSL and BSL became the wholly owned subsidiaries of SAIL. As a result of restructuring in 1978, SAIL emerged as the main integrated steel company with five public sector steel plants under its control.

SAIL is one of the largest industrial organisations in the world. The company is responsible for helping the Government of India in bringing about integrated planning and development of steel industry in the country.

1.4 A SHORT NOTE ON PRODUCTION OF STEEL IN A TYPICAL INTEGRATED STEEL PLANT

In a typical integrated steel plant, the process of transformation of iron ore into finished steel products involves the following successive stages :

a. Preparation of raw materials;
b. Conversion of iron ore into pig iron;
c. Conversion of pig iron into crude steel; and
d. Shaping of crude steel into finished forms.

a. Preparation of raw materials

Iron ore and coal are the two major raw materials for production of pig iron. Raw ore contains many impurities and clayey matter. Iron ore should be beneficiated to upgrade the iron content in ore and to remove clayey matter content of the ore. Sintering of iron ore fines is a better and cheaper proposition than pelletisation (143). Scrap steel may also be used as a raw material along with iron ore.

The quality of coking coal is an important factor while making iron by blast furnace. The quality of coking coal is deteriorating and its reserves are dwindling in India. The high ash content of coal adversely affects the production of iron by blast furnace. It is important that the ash content in the washed coal should be within the 18 per cent limit.

b. Conversion of iron ore into pig iron

Sintered ore is charged into a blast furnace along with limestone and coke and is subjected to a blast of hot air to separate out the iron content from its impurities. Liquid iron is drawn off from the base of the furnace and is solidified into shapes called pigs. Pig iron has a high carbon content with only 93 per cent iron in it.

Blast furnace continues to be the most popular technique of making iron and it contributes nearly 90 per cent of the total world iron production (143). Sponge iron or directly reduced iron is the latest commercially developed technique of making iron which does not require the use of coking coal.

c. Conversion of pig iron into crude steel

The molten or solid pig iron is charged into a furnace for refining. The purified liquid steel is then poured into ingot moulds. In case of a direct casting method, the purified liquid steel is directly put into shapes (billets, blooms, slabs, etc.) for use in rolling mills. Continuous casting is gradually replacing the conventional method of casting liquid steel into ingots.

The open hearth furnance process of steel making has gradually been replaced by the basic oxygen converter process over the last two decades. Basic oxygen process is becoming quite popular for large scale integrated steel plants. For small and medium capacity steel plants, electric arc furnace is the obvious choice (143).

d. Shaping of crude steel into finished forms

This is the stage of transforming crude steel into various final products by rolling, pressing, forging and boring. The semi-finishing mills convert ingot steel into slabs, blooms, billets and tube-rounds.

Fig. 1.2 Process Flow-Chart of a Typical Integrated Steel Plant

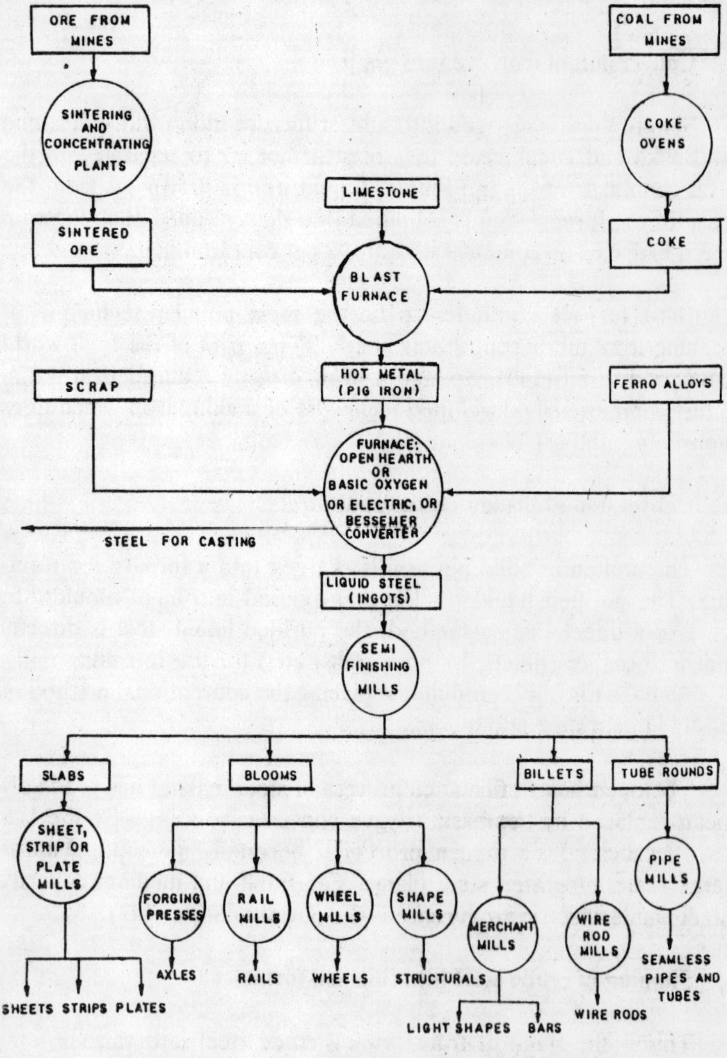

The finishing mills process the semi-finsihed forms into still finer forms. Slabs are turned into sheets, plates, skelp, etc. Blooms are processed to get axles, rails, wheels, structurals, etc. Billets are used to make bars, wire rods, wire products, etc. Seamless pipes and tubes are made out of tube rounds.

The process flow-chart of a typical integrated steel plant is shown in Fig. 1.2.

1.5 ROLE OF STEEL IN ECONOMIC DEVELOPMENT

Development of steel industry is very crucial for the overall economic development of a nation. In the early stages of economic development the consumption of steel is expected to increase at a faster rate than that of industrial production because huge quantities of steel are needed to build the basic infrastructure in the form of bridges, dams, railways, power plants and transmission capacity, etc. Steel is used as a basic material to manufacture metal products, electrical machinery, textile and other machinery. Almost every industry in the economy as well as agriculture require equipment made of steel. Steel is an important input in the construction activity as well.

Hirschman (68) studied the interdependence of industries in Italy, Japan and the USA. A measure of the degree of interdependence is defined by computing the total output of each industry that goes to the other consuming industries and not to the final demand. This measure is indicative of the 'forward linkage effects'. The 'backward linkage effects' indicate that proportion of the output of an industry which represents purchases from other industries. These two measures show the extent to which one industry interlocks with the others. The industries with high linkage effects provide greater growth stimuli in relation to the industries with which they have the linkages, either forward or backward. The iron and steel industry was found to have the highest combined linkage score. It has been pointed out by Hirschman that the great importance given to this industry by the developing countries is, thus, not completely prestige motivated.

1.6 NEED FOR LONG TERM PLANNING IN STEEL INDUSTRY

The growth of agriculture and the production of consumer goods depend on the progress made in the industrial sector in an economy. The investment made during a period of time in the economy may be divided into two components, one goes to augment productive capacity in the investment goods sector and the other in the consumption goods sector. It has been pointed out by Mahalanobis (96) that if a large proportion of investment goes to the consumption goods sector, the economy may enjoy a higher consumption in the early stages of development but the rate of growth of consumption shall be low in the long run. But, if the goal is to achieve a higher rate of growth of consumption in the long run, a large proportion of investment should go to the investment goods sector. This is shown in Fig. 1.3, where curve A represents the choice in which the economy chooses to better satisfy some present needs while jeopardizing the future growth prospects. Curve B represents the alternative choice in which the economy is ready to sacrifice some of its present consumption in order to gain a higher long run growth rate.

It is, thus, justified that a developing economy should choose to adopt a path of fast industrial growth in early stages of its development. The growth of industry depends upon the assured supplies of steel. The inadequate availability of steel acts as a general drag on the development efforts in almost all sectors of the economy. Planning for production of steel should, therefore, be ahead of planning for rest of the sectors.

It may further be pointed out that planning for steel has to be done on a long-term basis. The installation of new steel capacity is a time taking process. The interval between the decision to set up a steel plant and the time when the unit actually starts production is very long. The ancillary infrastructural facilities such as new mines, washeries and railways have also to be developed accordingly. In the developing countries the problem becomes more acute due to inadequate availability of finances, heavy machinery and required technical skills. Lack of availability of various inputs may act as another bottleneck in the production of steel.

Fig. 1.3 Two Alternatives of Growth for a Developing Economy: Hypothetical Curves

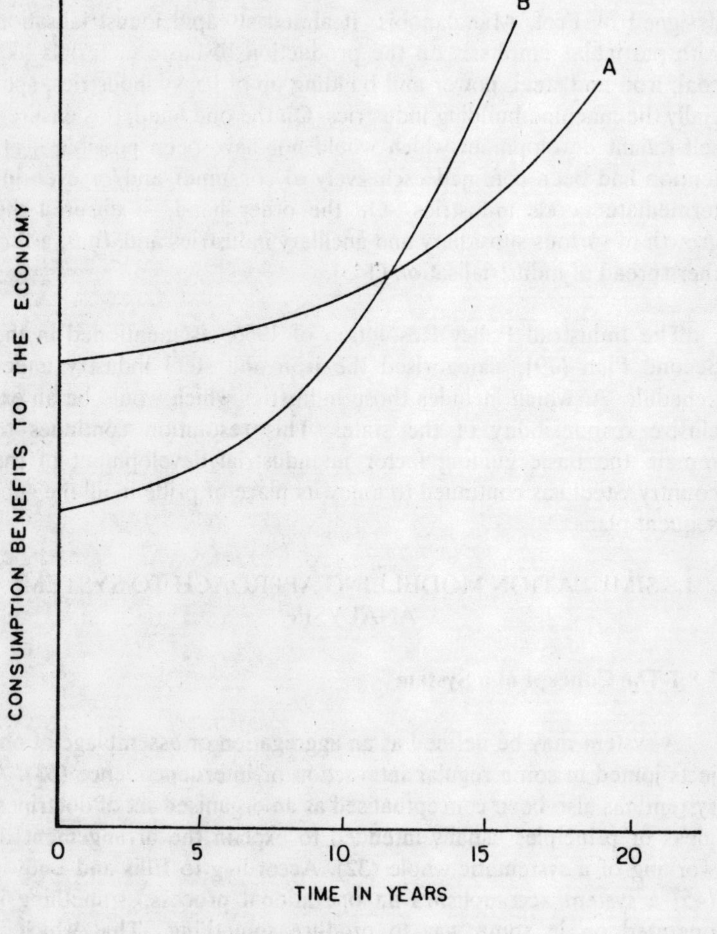

1.7 STEEL IN INDIAN PLANNING

Steel is claimed to be the hard core of India's five year plans. It was realised in the First Five Year Plan (78) that steel should be given the highest priority among all the industries as it is of basic importance to the development of all the sectors of the economy.

The Second Five Year Plan (79) was based on the model designed by Prof. Mahalanobis. It aimed at rapid industrialisation with particular emphasis on the production of basic materials like coal, iron and steel, power and building up of heavy industries, specially the machine building industries. On the one hand, this ensured self-reliant development which would not have been possible if attention had been confined exclusively to consumer and/or even intermediate goods industries. On the other hand, it ensured the growth of various subsidiary and ancillary industries and, thus, a further spread of industrialisation (143).

The Industrial Policy Resolution of 1956, as mentioned in the Second Plan (79), categorised the iron and steel industry under Schedule 'A' which includes those industries which would be an exclusive responsibility of the state. This resolution continues to remain the basic guiding factor in industrial development of the country. Steel has continued to enjoy its place of pride in all the subsequent plans.

1.8 SIMULATION MODELLING APPROACH TO SYSTEMS ANALYSIS

1.8.1 The Concept of a System

A system may be defined as an aggregation or assemblage of objects joined in some regular interaction or interdependence (53). A system has also been conceptualised as an organised set of doctrines, ideas or principles usually intended to explain the arrangement or working of a systematic whole (32). According to Ellis and Ludwig (45) a system accomplishes an operational process; something is operated on in some way to produce something. That which is operated upon is usually called input, that which is produced is called output, and operating entity is called the system. A system may, thus, be defined to be a device, procedure or scheme which behaves according to some description, its function being to operate on information and/or energy and/or matter in a time reference to yield information and/or energy and/or matter (45). This concept of a system is shown in Fig. 1.4.

1.8.2 System Analysis

Deutsch (32) defines system analysis in the spirit of the dictionary definition of 'analysis' mixed with that of a 'system' as given below:

i. separation of a whole into its component parts; and

ii. an examination of a complex, its elements and their relations.

System analysis is, thus, a study of a system. It may be emphasised that a system is not studied as an end in itself. The basic objective of a system study is to analyse a system in order to take some decisions.

1.8.3 Simulation Modelling of a System

The objective of a system study is to analyse the behaviour of the system and to predict its future performance. A system is analysed through the use of a model which represents the relevant aspects of the system.

Computer simulation models have become commonly employed tools for analysing the behaviour of complex economic systems. Simulation may be defined as a numerical technique for conducting experiments with certain types of mathematical and logical models, describing the behaviour of an economic system, on a digital computer over extented periods of time (115). The starting point of any computer simulation experiment with an economic system is to set up an econometric model of the system to be simulated. Under simulation, the experiment is conducted with the model of the system rather than with the actual economic system itself.

Fig. 1.4 The Concept of A System

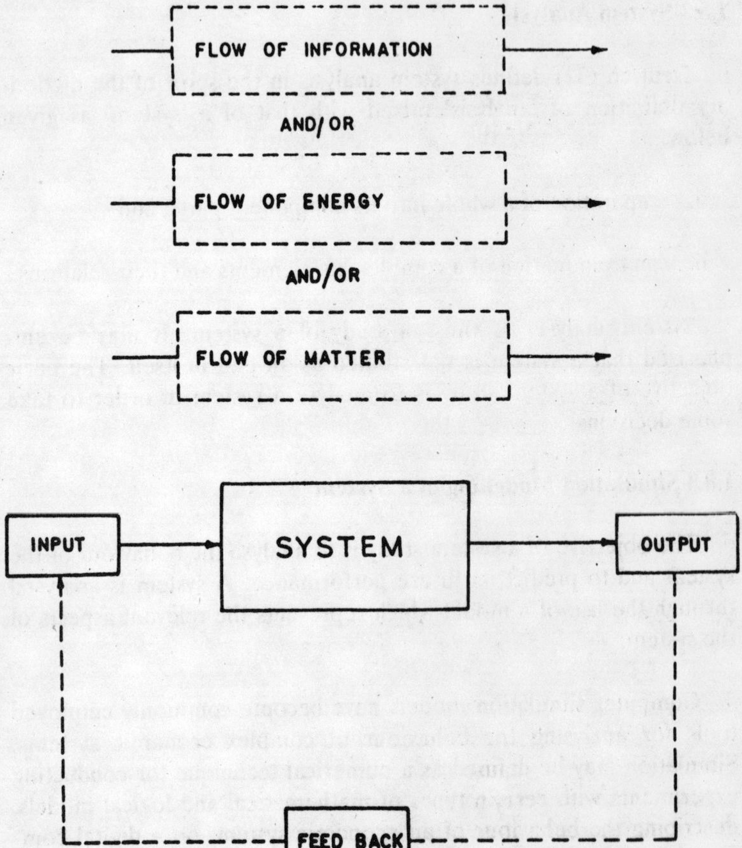

1.9 A SYSTEMS VIEW OF INDIAN STEEL INDUSTRY

The present study views Indian steel industry as a system. This system itself is a sub-system of the wider system of Indian economy. Indian economy, in turn, is a sub-system of the world economy. The present study develops and analyses the system of Indian steel industry through the use of an econometric simulation model.

The interaction of the system of Indian steel industry with the successively wider systems of Indian economy and world economy is shown in Fig. 1.5. The point R_I represents rest of the Indian economy (excluding steel industry) and the point R_W represents rest of the world economy.

The system of Indian steel industry may be analysed in two different ways which are dual to each other, namely the cost function approach and the production function approach. The cost function approach is represented by the solid flow lines between the point R_I, i.e. rest of the Indian economy and the system of Indian steel industry as shown in Fig. 1.5. The corresponding dotted flow lines represent the production function approach to the analysis of Indian steel industry. Indian steel industry also interacts with rest of the world economy through imports and exports of steel.

The state and pattern of growth of the economy determine the economy's steel requirements. The requirements of steel may either be fulfilled through indigenous production and/or through imports. In case of a developing country it is not possible to import huge quantities of steel because of foreign exchange constraints. Further, it is better for a country to be self-sufficient in its steel requirements because of the crucial role it plays in the process of development. The nation should set its future targets of steel production well in advance. Depending upon the existing technology and the prices of various inputs prevailing and likely to prevail in future, the cost function approach specifies the quantities of various inputs required during the period under consideration in order to fulfil the targets of steel production at minimum cost.

Fig. 1.5 Interaction between the System of Indian Steel Industry and the Successively Wider Systems of Indian Economy and World Economy

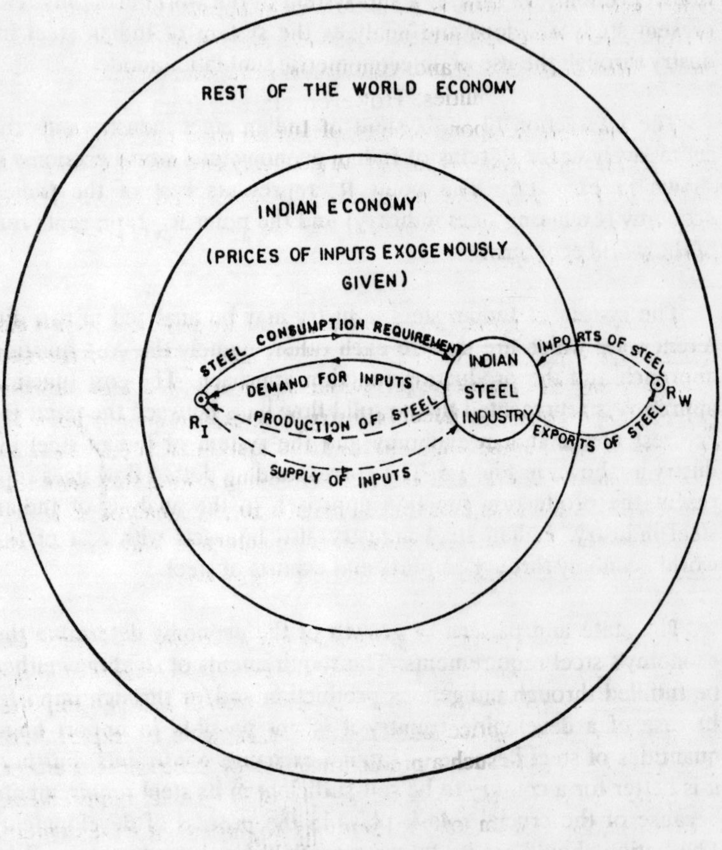

POINT R_I REPRESENTS REST OF THE INDIAN ECONOMY

POINT R_W REPRESENTS REST OF THE WORLD ECONOMY

Conventionally, production function is the primal and cost function its dual. Under production function approach the likely future availabilities of various inputs may be predicted and estimates of resulting steel output made.

The present study attempts to analyse Indian steel industry through cost function approach. The study does not predict the likely future input avalabilities and, thus, does not estimate the likely future production possibilities. However, starting from the estimated cost function, a corresponding production function has been worked back.

1.10 AIMS AND OBJECTIVES OF THE STUDY

The present study takes a systems view of Indian steel industry. The important elements of this system are given below:

i. Steel Consumption Requirements of Indian Economy;
ii. Inputs' Demand in Steel Industry/Cost Function; and
iii. Production Function.

As stated earlier, the last two elements are dual to each other.

The primary aim of the study is to help the planning process by supplying the input information in advance as to what are the likely annual requirements of steel in India upto the year 2005 and how much of each input shall be needed to produce the desired quantity of steel during each year at minimum possible cost. An assumption regarding the future price behaviour of various inputs is a prerequisite while making such a prediction.

Another related aim of the study is to investigate the likely casualities which may occur due to inadequate availability of one or more input(s). The production function can immediately point out the resultant effect on output due to availability-bottlenecks in one or more input(s).

The study also proposes various alternative isoquant packages of inputs as a cure if there is a casuality of the type mentioned above. The packages proposed are such that each is a combination of different quantities of labour, capital, and fuels and yet each results in the same quantity of steel production. However, each inputs package is a cost- minimising one corresponding to a particular assumed future scenario of input prices. The shifting from one package to another in order to achieve the set production targets may adversely affect the costs of production in case the prices of inputs actually prevailing in the market are different from the assumed input price scenario under which the newly chosen package had been worked out to be the cost minimising one. However, such adjustments may not be possible in a short period of time because of the nature of steel making technology.

The study also analyses the interrelationships between inputs for each pair of inputs taken separately using the concept of elasticity of substitution. The elasticities of substitution between different inputs have also been analysed in a dynamic way through the use of a trans-log model given in Appendix (1).

The present study develops a simulation model of Indian steel industry. This model analyses the steel industry for the period 1951-77 and predicts steel requirements of the economy and the corresponding input requirements of the steel industry during the period 1978-2005 A.D.

1.11 PLAN OF THE STUDY

The present book consists of nine chapters. Chapter II critically reviews the existing literature relevant to the present study. Major gaps in the existing literature are identified to substantiate the need for this study.

Chapter III gives the sources of data and identifies the variables used in the system's study.

Chapter IV formulates and estimates the consumption sub-model. A GNP function has also been estimated in this chapter.

Chapter V discusses the formulation and direct estimation of input demand functions for labour, capital and fuels. The demand function for raw materials is also estimated. The chapter also works back a corresponding production function starting from the estimated input demand functions/cost function.

Chapter VI weaves the sub-models developed in the last two chapters into a simulation model of Indian steel industry. The chapter also predicts the behaviour of steel consumption requirements of the economy and the corresponding input demands upto the year 2005 under the assumption of a normal price behaviour scenario of various inputs.

Chapter VII analyses the results obtained in the present study. A sensitivity analysis of the forecasts of input demands has been done with regard to a change in the schedule of future steel production targets and also with respect to tweleve different assumed scenarios of future input prices. Price elasticities of input demands and partial elasticities of substitution between inputs are also analysed. The chapter further analyses the elasticities of steel output with respect to inputs of labour, capital and fuels, respectively.

Chapter VIII outlines the major findings and significant contributions made by the present study.

Chapter IX points out the limitations of the study being reported and suggests the possible extensions for future reasearch efforts in the related area.

TWO

LITERATURE REVIEW

2.1 INTRODUCTION

The seed of the systems theory was sown by Ludwig von Bertalanffy (160), a biologist, in 1950. He postulated the need to study systems and discussed some system properties using calculus and proposed the drawing of a new scientific discipline called 'systems theory'. It was only in 1956 that an analytical framework for the development of a general theory of systems was published by Kenneth Boulding (13). Since then, substantial changes have taken place in the procedures for planning, designing and managing of large scale systems.

Another technique, the development of which has almost been parallel to that of systems theory, is the art of computer simulation. It was with the advent of high speed digital computers in early 1950s that the art of computer simulation started developing. The computer simulation experiments with econometric models have now become commonly employed tools for analysing the behaviour of complex economic systems. The economic analysts have discovered that it is possible to perform controlled laboratory like experiments on an economic system using the technique of computer simulation.

In the past, analysis of Indian steel industry using system simulation approach has not been seriously considered. There has recently been an attempt to analyse the planning system of Rourkela Steel Plant using Systems Dynamics approach (114). This attempt is at a plant level but not at industry level. The present study is an attempt to study steel industry in India at a macro-level.

This chapter briefly reviews the past studies relevant to the study being reported in this book: For the purpose of review, various research papers and books have been grouped under the following heads:

i. Forecasting steel consumption requirements of an economy with special reference to India;
ii. Theory of production functions and its applications to Indian steel·industry; and
iii. Technique of econometric simulation modelling.

The limitations of the existing models/approaches have also been discussed along with role of the present study in filling the existing gaps.

2.2 REVIEW OF THE LITERATURE ON FORECASTING STEEL CONSUMPTION REQUIREMENTS OF AN ECONOMY WITH SPECIAL REFERENCE TO INDIA

2.2.1 Forecasting Steel Consumption Requirements of An Economy

The terms steel consumption requirements and demand for steel in an economy have been used as synonyms in this study. It is assumed that the quantity of steel actually consumed is also the quantity demanded, regardless of the price of steel. Most econometric studies in this field have found prices to be irrelevant or at most of minor importance for the determination of steel demand in an economy (124). The present study treats steel consumption as demand determined.

A number of techniques for forecasting steel demand are available, ranging from a 'sophisticated sector method down to a simple trend extrapolation (70).

In recent years, some macro-econometric models of industrialised economies have been developed in the form of a system of equations. These models facilitate the analysis and determination of steel consumption requirements of the respective economies. Hoglund and Werin (69) have analysed steel consumption in Sweden on the basis of a quantified input-output model of the Swedish economy. The model goes a long way in terms of fragmentation of the economy into various sectors. There are 127 sectors of production and 18 final demand categories.

An alternative to the above approach is to study steel consumption as a function of a small number of variables. The reasons for the search of such an alternative have been discussed by Vinell (157) and are given below :

i. The use of a large number of explanatory variables is undesirable in time-series studies because of problems of statistical estimation; and
ii. The purpose of forecasting makes it imperative that only a small number of explanatory variables be used.

The reduction in the number of variables may be achieved by aggregating the original variables into a smaller number and eliminating the less important ones. A model may then be developed without specifying the more micro-economic details.

In recent years, there has been an increasing interest in models which combine time-series and cross-sectional analysis in forecasting steel demand. Such type of models follow what has come to be known as global method, and are termed as global models. In a global model, steel consumption is expressed as a function of one of the macro-economic variables, such as GNP, industrial production, population, total fixed investment, etc.

The method of relating steel consumption requirements to a macro-economic variable was initiated during the 1930s. Prior to this, many attempts had been made to estimate static demand curves for steel on the basis of simple demand equations with price as the only explanatory variable. It was then experienced that variations in quantity demanded of steel could better be explained by shifts in demand curve rather than by price movements. Whitman (161) gave a shape to the new perspective by considering the demand for steel to be a function of industrial production, price of steel and changes in that price. The later studies have generally eliminated price of steel as a variable determining its demand. It is now felt that demand for steel depends upon total economic activity, specially in the long run.

Shone and Fisher (141) developed a long-term relationship between steel consumption and industrial production in Britain for the period 1954 to 1962. The demand for steel during this period is based on 3 per cent rate of growth in industrial productivity (industrial production per head of indstrial population) in Britain.

Some prominent international organisations such as United Nations Economic Commission for Europe (UNECE) and Organisation for Ecnomic Co-operation and Development (OECD) have substantially contributed towards synthesising and publishing most of the available literature on global models of steel consumption (123, 124, 152).

The global method is also the basis of a study conducted by International Iron and Steel Institute (IISI) on world steel demand (83). The entire world has been divided into 16 geographic regions and separate models are developed for each region. These models relate steel consumption to one of the two macro-economic variables - GNP and population. The projections of steel demand are made for the period 1970-85.

2.2.2 Forecasting Steel Consumption Requirements in India

The method that has been commonly used to forecast steel demand in India is the method of end-uses. Under the end-use approach, the analyst seeks information from a large number of final users regarding the future estimates of their product-output and also their estimated steel consumption requirements per unit of product. This information is then processed in order to get future estimates of steel demand under various categories.

A major work in forecasting steel demand in India has been done by the National Council of Applied Economic Research (NCAER). NCAER published four such studies during the period 1960 to 1971 (109, 110, 111, 112). The basic approach in all these studies is that of end-uses. These studies have generally over-estimated the future demand for steel.

Dastur (28) also preferred the method of end-uses over other methods in forecasting steel demand. His study also grossly over-estimated the future demand for steel.

The method of end-uses has serious limitations, particularly when applied in case of developing countries. There are problems relating to the quality and quantity of available data. The forecast values are reliable only in so far as the right information is available. Reasonsably reliable information of this type is available for industrial requirements of steel while crude methods are generally adopted to estimate steel demand for rest of the economy.

Johnson (84) developed a regression model for predicting steel demand in India. Indents placed with the Iron and Steel Controller were taken to be the indicator of steel demand and were considered to be the dependent variable. The independent variables were industrial production, the ratio of average selling price of steel to general price index and the difference between tonnage indented and actual offtake. Three dummy variables were also used to take into account the changing government controls on steel.

Johnson's model has serious limitations. Firstly, the dependent variable is taken to be a function of itself along with other explanatory variables, as one of the independent variables is the difference between tonnage indented and actual offtake. Secondly, the indents are likely to be a fake index of steel demand because in times of shortage the indents placed are likely to be inflated due to general scare of uncertainty of steel supplies.

The National Productivity Council (NPC) has developed a Systems Dynamics model to forecast the demand for various categories of steel produced by Rourkela Steel Plant (114). The study does not forecast the total steel demand for the economy.

There have been some efforts to analyse steel consumption requirements in India in the spirit of the global method (16, 17). The apparent consumption of crude steel equivalent is considered to be a dependent variable and the GNP has been considered to be the explanatory macro-economic variable. The present study serves to further the cause of global modelling approach by analysing steel consumption requirements of Indian economy.

2.3 REVIEW OF LITERATURE ON THE THEORY OF PRODUCTION FUNCTIONS AND ITS APPLICATIONS TO INDIAN STEEL INDUSTRY

2.3.1 The Concept of a Production Function

Conventionally, a production function specifies the 'maximum' output attainable from any specified set of inputs (134). This function is a single valued mapping from input space into output space, that is, the maximum attainable output has a unique value corresponding to a particular set of inputs. It is assumed that a production function, which may be expressed in a mathematical, graphical or tabular form, exists for each good and service.

Production function is a micro-economic concept which represents the technical opportunities available to a firm. It is purely a technical relationship and is independent of prices of output and of various inputs. It may be expressed in the following form:

$$Q = f(\overline{X}, K) \qquad (2.1)$$

Where Q is the output, $\bar{x}$ is the vector of services of various inputs, and K is the vector of 'knowledge' in the form of technological advancement. If the path, K(t), of technological advancement is assumed to be a function of time, then the production function attains the following form:

$$Q = F(\overline{X}, t) \qquad (2.2)$$

where t denotes time.

2.3.2 Aggregate Production Function

Production function is basically a micro-economic concept representing the technical opportunities open before a productive unit.

Several conceptual problems are encountered when the concept of a production function is applied at an indstry or economy level. Goldar (52) summarises these problems which have already been discussed by Nadiri (106) and Kennedy and Thirlwall (87). It has been pointed out that the aggregate production function differs from the concept of an ideal production function since prices implicitly enter as weights to facilitate aggregation. Secondly, it is very difficult to aggregate various inputs beause of their heterogeneity. Another problem is faced while aggregating a number of different micro-economic production functions since there are technical differences among the corresponding productive units. Strict restrictions have to be imposed on the characteristics of the micro-economic production functions and the nature of technological progress.

In spite of all these theoretical problems, the aggregate production function has been a widely used concept in many of the empirical studies on production and technology.

2.3.3 Evolution of the Theory of Production Functions

Modern production function theory was initiated in late forties with the introduction of the Cobb-Douglas production function (40) which may be expressed as :

$$Q = A L^{\alpha} K^{\beta} e^{\lambda t} \tag{2.3}$$

where Q is the output; L and K are the services of inputs of labour and capital, respectively; A, α, β and λ are the parameters to be estimated. 'α' and 'β' are elasticities of output with respect to inputs of labour and capital, respectively. 't' denotes time and 'λ' is the exponential rate of technological progress.

The above function is a very restrictive representation of production technology as it assumes the elasticity of substitution between L and K to be unity. This implies constant factor shares under competitive equilibrium. Despite its limitations, many of the empirical studies still use this function.

The constant elasticity of substitution (CES) production function was proposed by Arrow et al. (5) in 1961. It assumes the elasticity of substitution between L and K to be constant but not necessarily equal to unity. The CES production function has the following form:

$$Q = Ae^{\lambda t}\left(\delta L^{-\rho} + (1-\delta)K^{-\rho}\right)^{-\frac{\nu}{\rho}} \tag{2.4}$$

where A, t and λ are same as in equation (2.3); δ is the labour intensity parameter; ν is the degree of homogeneity; and, ρ is a constant related to the elasticity of substitution between L and K, such that:

$$\sigma = \frac{1}{1+\rho} \tag{2.5}$$

where σ is the elasticity of substitution between L and K and is a constant.

A serious limitation of the CES function is that it is confined to only two inputs. It has been proved that strict assumptions about partial elasticity of substitution are to be made if more than two inputs are included (100,154).

It may be pointed out that the Cobb-Douglas function is a special case of the CES function with elasticity of substitution (σ) equal to unity.

There have been many attempts to develop production function theory since the introduction of the CES function in 1961 (61). ukerji (104), Dhrymes and Kurz (35) and Gorman (54) have developed n-factor generalised functions which yield constant ratios of partial elasticities of substitution (CRES) among all the inputs. The CRES function allows the elasticities of substitution to deviate from unity and to be different from one another. The latest version, constant ratios of elasticities of substitution, homothetic (CRESH) is due to Hanoch (61).

The prior restrictions on the elasticities of substitution have been gradually relaxed during the evolution of production functions from Cobb-Douglas to CES to CRESH. The requirements of data have steadily gone up during the same time.

The generalisations of production function forms have been made possible because of the following reasons:

i. Larger time series data for different variables are now available. There have also been qualitative improvements in the available data over time. The data are now available regarding the micro aspects of a variable for which only macro-level data were available before;
ii Developments and improvements in the theory of econometrics; and
iii. Availability of high speed digital computers and efficient computing algorithms and packages such as Statistical Analysis System (SAS) (64).

2.3.4 Recent Developments in Production Function Theory

Substantial methodological development has taken place in the theory of production functions since early seventies. Woodland (163) and Fuss and McFadden (51) have extensively discussed these developments. Goldar (52) and Dixon et al. (39) have given excellent summaries of the major advancements in this area. These advancements may be divided into two broad categories :

i. Continuation of the process of generalisation of production function forms; and

ii. Formulation and estimation of new forms using the duality relation between cost and production functions.

A recent step in the generalisation of production function forms is the introduction of flexible torms. In case of a flexible form, no prior restrictions are imposed on the elasticities of substitution except those which arise from the definition or from the assumptions of optimising behaviour. Thirsk (148) has used this type of form in his work. The present study adopts a similar form while analysing the production sub-model of Indian steel industry.

The use of duality theory is the latest step to further develop the art of flexible functional forms. Attempts have recently been made to formulate and estimate new types of aggregate production functions by using the duality relation between cost and production functions.

Duality is a commonly used concept in mathematical programming. Generally, it refers to the relationship between two different theoretical representations of the same problem. The two representations are said to be dual to each other if all the important features of one can also be deduced from the knowledge of the other. In the present context, the concept of duality relates a production function to the corresponding cost function. Under cost minimising assumptions, it is possible to deduce either of the two functions, given the other. The duality relation between production and cost functions was first proved by Shephard (140) and Uzawa (153).

Diewert (36) has empirically shown that production and cost functions are dual to each other. He has developed some flexible functional forms based on the concept of duality. Generalised Leontief (36) and Generalised Cobb-Douglas (37) cost functions are his major contributions.

The most flexible form, using the duality relationship between a cost function and the corresponding production function, has been suggested by Christensen et al. (25) and is known as Transcendental Logarithmic (Translog) form. The translog cost function approach has been used in Appendix (1) of the present book to analyse the dynamic behaviour of partial elasticities of substitution between inputs and price elasticities of input demands.

The cost function approach to the analysis of a producing unit has certain convenient features. It is easier to estimate cost functions than the generalised production functions (120). Algebraically, it is easier to derive input demand functions from a given cost function than from the corresponding production function. According to Shephard's lemma (140), demand for ith input can be derived by differentiating the estimated cost function with respect to the price of ith input.

A constrained minimisation problem has to be solved in order to derive input demand functions from an estimated production function. This may be quite a difficult task except when the production function has some simple form, say Cobb-Douglas or CES. The input demand functions thus derived may have a complex implicit form.

It may, thus, be concluded that whatever be the purpose of investigating a production function, it can be equally served by the knowledge of the corresponding cost function.

2.3.5 Production Function in Indian Steel Industry

Very few attempts have been made to estimate and analyse the production function in Indian steel industry. Whatever scanty literature is avilable, has utilised the old and restrictive forms of production function.

Sarkar (137) used the Cobb-Douglas form in an attempt to study the production function in Indian steel industry. He developed a model with labour, capital and raw-materials (including fuels) as inputs, as given below:

$$Q = A L^{\alpha} K^{\beta} R^{\gamma} \tag{2.6}$$

where R is the input of raw-materials; and γ is the elasticity of output with respect to R. All other symbols are same as explained in case of equation (2.3).

The above model has its obvious theoretical limitations. Further, the coefficient of capital (β) was estimated to be negative for the period 1946 to 1958. Sarkar has given some reasons to justify such an unexpected result. One of the reasons given for negative value of β is that the industry is retaining out-dated machineries and technology. Secondly, high values of α and γ act as disincentives for further investments in the industry. The excess capacity in the industry is given as the third reason for low or negative value of β. The reasons given are, however, not quite convincing.

Dholakia (34) reported another study on production function in Indian steel industry. His basic aim was to demonstrate the fact that the estimates of time series production functions are highly elastic with respect to the way capital input is measured.

Dholakia points out that there have been several studies (58, 59, 60, 102, 138) examining the relative contributions of various factors of production and technical change to the growth of output in some large-scale Indian industries. Most of these studies have reported paradoxical results. Dholakia did not point out the common weakness of all these studies, that is the use of very restrictive forms of production function. Instead, he blamed the conceptual and statistical differences in the specification and measurement of the major variables involved, which, no doubt, is another major weakness of these models.

Dholakia also used the Cobb-Douglas form to estimate the production function in Indian steel industry for the period 1946 to 1966. He pointed out that most of the studies on time series production functions for Indian industries had used either depreciated book value of capital assets or depreciated value of capital assets at some constant base-period prices as the measure of capital input. Dholakia found that the use of gross stock of capital assets at some constant base-period prices led to a remarkable improvement in the precision of the estimated coefficients and also in the overall explanatory power of the estimated production function.

While the study by Sarkar (137) included raw-materials input, along with labour and capital inputs, for estimating the production fuction in Indian steel industry, the results obtained by him appear somewhat contradictory and unacceptable. On the other hand, Dholakia obtained meaningful estimates for the parameters but his model did not take into account the inputs of fuels and raw-materials.

2.4 REVIEW OF LITERATURE ON THE TECHNIQUE OF ECONOMETRIC SIMULATION MODELLING

2.4.1. The Concept of Simulation

During the past three decades, computer simulation experiments with econometric models have become commonly employed tools for analysing the behaviour of complex economic systems. Simulation may be defined as a numerical technique for conducting experiments with certain types of mathematical and logical models describing the behaviour of an economic system on a digital computer over extended periods of time (115). The formulation of an econometric model of the economic system to be simulated is the starting point of any computer simulation experiment. It is, thus, assumed that an econometric model has already been formulated and its parameters specified before the simulation experiment is conducted. Given the econometric model of the system to be simulated, simulation is simply the mathematical solution of the model (126).

The principal difference between a simulation experiment and a 'real-world' experiment is that, while the former is conducted with a model of the economic system under consideration, the latter with the actual system itself.

Given a model of an economic system, the following steps are important for designing a computer simulation experiment with the model (116) :

i. Formulation of a computer programme;

ii. Validation of the simulated results;

iii. Experimental design; and

iv. Analysis of the simulated results.

2.4.2 Empirical Studies Using Econometric Simulation Modelling Technique

The technique of simulation may be used for a variety of reasons, including model testing and evaluation, historical policy analysis and forecasting. There are published instances to show that simulation technique has been used to analyse and predict systems behaviour in various industries.

Cohen (26) analysed the aggregate behaviour of the shoe retailers, shoe manufacturers and cattlehide leather tanners for the period 1930 to 1940. The industry has been divided vertically into five segments - consumers, shoe-retailers, shoe-manufacturers, cattlehide tanners and hide dealers. The principal exogenous variables are the consumers' price index, disposable personal income and the stocks of hides held by hide dealers. The major classes of endogenous variables are price and physical flows between the vertically linked segments.

Cohen formulated and experimented with two mathematical models, a one-period-change model (econometric model) and a process-model (computer simulation model). In the one-period-change model, lagged endogenous variables refer to their actually observed values, while in the process model, the same refer to the values generated by the model.

The time paths for the endogenous variables were generated with the help of a computer and compared with the observed time paths of these variables during the period 1930 to 1940. A close correspondence was observed between the two series.

Naylor, Wallace and Sasser (117) developed a computer simulation model of the U.S. textile industry for the period 1953 to 1962. It is a nine equation econometric model. The endogenous variables include apparel output and demand, employment, wages, profit and investment. The time paths of these variables were generated with the help of computer simulation technique. As the model is completely recursive, simple ordinary least squares (OLS) method yields unbiased estimates of the parameters.

A number of experiments were conducted with the model to evaluate the impact of certain government policies on the U.S. textile industry. Three different techniques have been used to compare the simulated data generated through the model with the observed data, namely graphical analysis, spectral analysis and total variance analysis.

Vernon, Rives and Naylor (156) developed a model of the U.S. tobacco industry. The model attempts to explain the behaviour of the tobacco industry over the period 1949 to 1966, on an annual basis. The model determines the annual production (supply) of flue-cured tobacco leaf, the annual production of cigarettes (and, thus, demand for tobacco leaf), and by equating demand and supply, the price of tobacco leaf. All these variables were assumed to be at least partly dependent on certain government controls. This model can, thus, be a tool to forecast tobacco prices and measure the impact of government controls on these prices.

A historical simulation of this model was performed to test its validity. The results indicate that the model is only of a limited use in forecasting. This is as expected, since the model employed was rather simple.

2.4.3 Econometric Simulation Models Versus Industrial Dynamics Models

The 'industrial dynamics' of Forrester (47) seems to be somewhat controversial technique in developing simulation models of the firm and industry. Naylor and Vernon (118) observe that industrial dynamics is a methodology for studying business and economic systems utilising computer simulation as a tool of analysis, but, it is not a simulation model in itself. Industrial dynamics has led to development of a broader concept of systems dynamics.

The industrial dynamics approach to simulation is similar to the one adopted by an econometric simulation model, in the sense that a firm, an industry or an economy is represented in the form of a set of lagged difference equations. However, in case of industrial dynamics, a special computer language, DYNAMO, is used to trace the time paths of the endogenous variables of the model.

The proponents of industrial dynamics approach claim to follow a 'data-less' approach. The model is not built on the basis of the past data. To begin with, a set of hypothetical relationships is specified. The parameters of these relationships are assigned values on the basis of 'intuition' or else on estimates produced by examining averages, sporadic data points or, perhaps, just the opinion of the experts. In case of an econometric model, these relationships are estimated and tested by fitting them to available data. It may be pointed out that even the systems dynamics models are validated when the simulated values of endogenous variables match well with the available, even though limited, historical data. Further, the 'intuition' or the 'opinion' of the experts in evaluating different parameters is also guided by the past experience. Thus, historical experience still remains a guiding factor in constructing a systems dynamics model, albeit implicitly.

Forrester's work has been criticised because many relationships used in his models have not been sustained or validated (126). A problem with this technique is that it provides no safety check on the reasonableness of the individual relationships that make up the model. In case of developing an econometric model, the model-builder tests many hypothetical relationships against data in search of a statistically acceptable form. This is an important check on the model-builder. As this check is missing in the so-called 'data-less' approach to modelling, this approach must be used only with great caution (126).

Forrester's approach has not been very widely accepted by many economists and some management scientists even though some economists consider industrial dynamics to be an interesting approach to the analysis of the behaviour of firms and industries. It is not possible to replace economic theory, which has very strong and proven merits, by industrial dynamics (118). These were some of the considerations that led to adopt econometric simulation modelling approach rather than systems dynamics approach in the research study being reported in this book.

2.5 LIMITATIONS OF THE EXISTING MODELS AND RELEVANCE OF THE PRESENT STUDY

The basic limitation of the available literature on Indian steel industry is that it does not treat this industry as a system. None of the available papers analyses this industry in its totality. The studies by the National Council of Applied Economic Research (109, 110, 111. 112), Dastur (28) and Johnson (84) have analysed only the demand aspects of steel, but have not considered the production sub-system. On the other hand, Sarkar (137) and Dholakia (34) have attempted to formulate and estimate the production function in Indian steel industry. The National Productivity Council has recently attempted a systems dynamics study of Rourkela Steel Plant (114) but not of steel industry as a whole. The present study is an attempt to look into the totality of this industry. The study estimates the consumption requirements of the economy on the basis of the level of GNP and its behaviour over time, and translates these requirements into production targets. Depending upon a particular assumed future scenario of input prices, the study works out the quantitative requirements of various inputs in future in order to achieve the production targets at the minimum cost. The present study, thus, attempts to analyse Indian steel industry by analysing the interrelationships among the various constituent elements of this industry.

The second limitation of the available literature is that serious attention has not been paid to exploring the possibility of applying global method to forecast steel consumption requirements in India. This method has been criticised by the proponents of the end-use method who have, themselves, invariably overestimated the demand for steel in India. The end-use method has its serious limitations. Its success depends upon the availability of correct and reliable information. It is very difficult to seek information from thousands of manufacturers who use steel as raw-material in their production processes. Further, this method is applicable only to industrial sector. The present study extensively explores the possibility of estimating a global model that can best explain the behaviour of steel consumption requirements in India based on the level and behaviour of the GNP. The global method, generally used in context of developed countries, has been improved upon to adapt it to Indian conditions.

The third limitation is that only two models of production function in Indian steel industry have been developed so far (34, 137). Both the models are crude and put strict a priori restrictions on the elasticities of substitution between inputs. These models use Cobb-Douglas form which is the earliest approach to study production technology of a firm or an industry. Many developments have taken place in production function theory since the introduction of Cobb-Douglas form in 1948. Further, both Sarkar and Dholakia begin with an assumption of constant returns to scale which may not be true in practice. The present study employs one of the most recent techniques, based on the concept of duality, to analyse the technology of Indian steel industry. This is a flexible functional form which puts no a priori restrictions on the elasticities of substitution between inputs except those which arise from the definition or from the assumption of optimising behaviour. Further, the real behaviour of production function in Indian steel industry has not been camouflaged by the assumption of homogeneity which is generally made for the sake of convenience. The present study has even analysed the dynamic behaviour of elasticities of substitution and price elasticities of input demands over the period of study.

The fourth and the last major limitation of the available literature is that there seems to be no serious attempt to apply simulation modelling approach to analyse Indian steel industry, or any other Indian industry. Simulation modelling approach is a fast developing technique that can be helpful in the analysis of complex economic systems. The present study is a modest attempt in this direction.

2.6 CONCLUDING REMARKS

It is observed that in spite of the gradual evolution of a more realistic and sophisticated framework to analyse a firm or an industry in its totality, its application to Indian steel industry has ben lacking. Only cruder forms of analysis have been employed so far in context of Indian steel industry; and the same seems to be true for other Indian industries as well. The present study is a modest attempt to overcome these weaknesses and open a new methodology of research on Indian industries.

THREE

IDENTIFICATION OF SYSTEM VARIABLES

3.1 INTRODUCTION

It is important to specify and identify the variables that are used in a system's study. The present study is based on the time-series data of various relevant variables. The form in which the required data are available may not suit the needs or fit into the objectives of the system's study under consideration. For example, the data on fixed capital in Indian iron and steel industry are available in the form of a series of depreciated book value of fixed capital at purchase prices, on an annual basis (72, 73), while the present study requires the series in terms of gross value of fixed capital at some constant base-year prices. The available data may, thus, have to be modified into a suitable form before the analysis of the system is undertaken. It is, therefore, an important ground-work to identify the data on each variable in the light of the requirements of the system's study.

The present chapter specifies various sources from which the data have been taken in context of the study being reported in this book. The data on some of the variables are explicitly available from the relevant sources while the data on other variables are only implicitly available. Even the explicitly available data on various variables, except on production and consumptin of steel, are required to be modified into suitable forms.

3.2 SOURCES OF DATA

3.2.1 The Sources

The annual data on production and consumption of steel in terms of crude steel equivalent have been taken from the series of the United Nations Statistical Year Book (150). The annual data on Gross National Product (GNP) of India, at factor cost, have been taken from the series of Economic Survey (75). The annual data on the inputs of labour, capital, fuels and raw-materials used in the production process of steel are explicitly available from the series of Census of Indian Manufactures (CMI) (72) and Annual Survey of Industries (ASI) (73). Each of these inputs consists of various heterogenous elements. These elements have been reduced into a homogeneous measure in the form of annual time series in case of each input variable. The data on price series corresponding to the series of homogeneous measure of each input are not explicitly available. Such price series are computed with the help of time series data on expenditure incurred on each of the four inputs and the services thereof. Such data are available from the series of CMI (72) and ASI (73). The detailed versions of ASI were available only upto the year 1971 at the time of carrying out the analysis relevant to the present study. The data on four inputs, namely labour, capital, fuels and raw-materials were available in aggregate form in the post-1971 period, upto 1977. The price series corresponding to each of the inputs was extrapolated during the period 1971 to 1977 with the help of the data on price series compiled by Chandhok (21).

3.2.2 CMI and ASI Data on Inputs

The CMI series are available from 1946 to 1958 (72). The period covered for each annual census refers to a calendar year. The primary unit of enumeration is the factory. The CMI data cover only those factories (i) which are registered as such under Indian Factories Act, 1948, (ii) which employ more than 20 persons on any day, and (iii) which use power.

From 1959 onwards, the relevant data are available in ASI (73). It covers the entire factory sector except factories under the control of Ministry of Defence, oil storage depots and technical training institutes. A factory is defined as a unit (i) which employs 10 or more workers with the aid of power, or (ii) which employs 20 or more workers without the aid of power.

The factories which employ 50 or more workers with the aid of power, or 100 or more workers without the aid of power are completely enumerated and form the Census Sector of ASI. The remaining factories are covered on the sampling basis and form the Sample Sector of ASI. The present study utilises the data on Census Sector as the detailed ASI data are available only in this form.

The definitions of variables relevant to this study have remained almost unchanged over the years and are similar under both CMI and ASI. The way capital, labour, fuels and raw-materials have been defined is quite consistent over the period 1951 to 1977. The definition of gross emoluments to the workers, the amount spent on fuels and raw-materials, gross and net value added have virtually remained consistent under both CMI and ASI.

Johri and Agarwal (85) have listed those ASI industries which may be treated as comparable to CMI industries. Indian steel industry is also included in this list.

There has been some change in the reference period, over time. The reference period in CMI is calendar year. Calendar year remained to be the reference period in ASI during 1959 to 1965. During the post 1965 period, the reference period is taken as the accounting year of a factory.

It has been assumed in the present study that the data on all the variables are available in terms of calendar years. This assumption is necessary to facilitate the analysis of the system since data on some of the variables are available with calendar year as the reference period and for other variables accounting year is the period of reference. Moreover, for some variables, calendar year was the period of reference upto 1965, and the accounting year during the post-1965 period.

The details on input data are not available for the years 1967 and 1972. The method adopted to fill-up this data gap for each variable is based on taking simple average of the preceding and the succeeding years.

The data on various inputs, as taken from the series of CMI and ASI, are reported in Appendix Tables A1, A2 and A3.

3.3 GROSS NATIONAL PRODUCT

The national income or product of a country generally refers to the final figure arrived at when the measuring rod of money is applied to the diverse goods and services that the nation produces with its land, labour and capital resources (135).

There are three commonly known concepts and measures of national income or output, namely Gross National Product (GNP), Net National Product (NNP) and National Income (NI).

The GNP can be measured in two different ways :

a. As the value of output
b. As the sum of gross income shares.

The GNP measured in terms of market value of the output of goods and services produced by a nation's economy during a stated period of time is equal to the sum of personal consumption, gross private investment (domestic and foreign), and government purchases of goods and services.

The GNP may also be measured as the sum of shares of gross national income accruing to different members of the community. Viewed in this sense, the GNP includes compensation of employees, rental and interest incomes of persons, profits of un-incorporated business, corporate profits, indirect business taxes and capital depreciation allowance.

The Net National Product (NNP) is the figure arrived at when the value of capital goods produced for replacement purposes is subtracted from the GNP. The NNP during any period is, therefore, simply GNP minus capital depreciation during the period.

The measure National Income (NI) is also known as NNP at factor cost. It is arrived at when indirect business taxes are subtracted from and subsidies added to the NNP at market prices.

The present study has utilised the GNP of India as a measure of nation's income to analyse steel consumption requirements of the economy. The GNP is considered to be a good indicator of economic growth of a nation. Some important studies analysing the consumption behaviour of steel in different countries have used the GNP as an explanatory variable (83, 124).

TABLE 3.1
Series of GNP, Consumption, Production and Net Imports of Steel in India (1951-1977)

Year	GNP at Factor Cost (Rs. crores at constant (1970-71) prices)	Consumption (thousand tonnes of crude steel equivalent)	Production (thousand tonnes of crude steel equivalent)	Net Imports (Consumption-production)
1951	17841	1724	1524	200
1952	18483	1849	1603	246
1953	19660	1874	1531	343
1954	20190	2244	1712	532
1955	20854	2800	1732	1068
1956	21988	3591	1766	1825
1957	21593	3619	1742	1877
1958	23413	3637	1842	1795
1959	23802	3525	2473	1052
1960	25424	4643	3286	1357
1961	26293	5385	4084	1301
1962	26834	6437	5149	1288
1963	28210	7280	5885	1395
1964	30399	7442	6033	1409
1965	28791	7422	6470	952
1966	29081	6784	6660	124
1967	31590	6442	6440	2
1968	32460	5819	6495	-676
1969	34518	6059	6514	-455
1970	36452	6432	6286	146
1971	37000	7710	6376	1334
1972	36599	9227	6907	2320
1973	38410	8232	7354	878
1974	38857	8449	6740	1709
1975	42571	8500	7925	575
1976	43124	8202	9310	-1108
1977	46854	10185	9912	273

Sources : 1. Economic Survey (75).
2. UN Statistical Year Book (150).

The annual GNP figures at factor cost (at constant (1970-71) prices) for the period 1951 to 1977, in case of India, are given in Table 3.1.

3.4 PRODUCTION AND CONSUMPTION OF STEEL

The present study uses the data on production and consumption of steel in India in the form of crude steel equivalent. The main reason for using crude steel and not the finished steel is that the crude steel is a homogeneous measure whereas finished steel is not. Secondly, it is the crude steel which is generally the bottleneck in the production process of steel industry.

The consumption of steel may be measured in various ways (158), namely, apparent steel consumption, total deliveries to consumers and actual steel consumption, such that :

$$APC = Q + IM - EX \tag{3.1}$$

$$TDC = APC - dI_p - dI_w \tag{3.2}$$

$$ACC = TDC - dI_C \tag{3.3}$$

where

APC = apparent steel consumption;
TDC = total deliveries to consumers;
ACC = actual steel consumption;
Q = production of steel;
IM = imports of steel;
EX = exports of steel;
dI_P = inventory increases by producers;
dI_W = inventory increases by wholesalers; and
dI_C = inventory increases by consumers.

It is because of the lack of inventory data that most of the international studies have considered APC and not ACC in the analysis of steel consumption. The present study has also used the concept of APC in the analysis and denotes it as 'S'. It may, however, be mentioned that apparent steel consumption has been measured in terms of crude steel equivalent. It may be written as follows :

$$S = APC_{cr} = Q_{cr} + \sum_{i=1}^{n} k_i \left(IM_i - EX_i \right) \tag{3.4}$$

where,

S = APC_{cr} = apparent steel consumption in terms of crude steel equivalent;

Q_{cr} = production measured at crude steel stage;

n = number of forms of steel imported and/or exported; and

k_i = the conversion factor used to convert net imports of ith form of steel into its crude steel equivalent.

The conversion factor, k_i, is the inverted value of the yield in the production of the ith form of steel. Some losses are incurred as a result of rolling. The yield is expressed as the ratio of finished steel to the input of crude steel. The conversion factor, k_i, differs from one form of finished steel to the other. It has been observed that for a particular finished steel form, the conversion factor is similar in different countries.

The annual values of production, consumption and net imports of steel for the period 1951 to 1977, in case of India, are given in Table 3.1, in terms of crude steel equivalent.

3.5 MEASUREMENT OF CAPITAL INPUT AND ITS PRICE

3.5.1 Theoretical Issues in Measuring Capital Input

Of all the system variables, the most difficult to define conceptually, as well as to measure, is the capital input (138). The set-up of capital equipment differs from one steel plant to the other. Further, the components of a particular set-up of capital equipment are not homogeneous. It is, thus, difficult to find a homogeneous measure of capital in an industry. Sastry (138) points out that the relative conversion units of different types of equipments depend upon their relative productivities. The problem may be solved by making the following assumptions :

i. The basic structure of equipments by type is same over time; and
ii. Their market prices reflect their relative productivities.

The capital input may, then, be measured as the aggregate monetary value of the existing equipments at some base-year constant prices.

The capital input measured in the above mentioned manner is a 'stock' concept. Strictly speaking, the capital input should be a 'flow' concept in the form of services that the existing stock of capital renders in the production process. This, however, poses a problem since the reliable data regarding capital consumed in the production process are not available. An assumption is, therefore, made that the flow of capital services is proportional to the stock of capital. The series of real stock of capital may be taken as an index of the capital input.

Dholakia (34) has pointed out that capacity utilisation should also be considered while measuring capital input since, in case of a production function, it is more important to know capital in use rather than the real stock of capital in existence. However, on account of non-availability of data on year to year fluctuations in the degree of utilisation of capital, the real stock of capital serves as an indicator of capital input.

Another important issue that has to be considered while measuring the capital input is regarding depreciation and obsolescence. Kendrick (86) is of the opinion that the capital embodied in a specific asset goes on declining over time due to depreciation and obsolescence. Denison (29) agrees with Kendrick regarding the treatment of depreciation but argues that obsolescence should be charged at the time when a particular capital asset is discarded and should be subtracted from gross capital formation instead of being added to capital consumption.

Goldar (52) has discussed in detail various theoretical and empirical issues regarding measurement of capital input. A detailed discussion on Denison's methodology of measuring capital input (29) has also been given by Goldar.

3.5.2 A Good Measure of Capital Input

Goldar (52) finds that the measures of capital input that have been used in most of the earlier studies on Indian manufacturing industries are quite unsatisfactory. Dholakia (34) points out the considerable differences that exist in estimating the capital input series among various studies.

Both Dholakia and Goldar have pointed out the weaknesses of directly using the published data (series of CMI and ASI) on capital stock. The published series of fixed capital refers to the depreciated book value of fixed capital at purchase prices and, thus, does not correspond to the appropriate concept of capital, discussed in subsection 3.5.1. Modifications have, therefore, to be done so as to make the data suitable for the analysis of production function.

The studies of Gujarati (58), Narsimhan and Febrycy (108), Sarkar (137) and Gupta (59) have used the published data without any modifications. Reddy and Rao (129), Raj Krishna and Mehta (94) and Mehta (101) have deflated the series of depreciated book value of capital stock by different price indices of capital goods. The main weakness of this procedure is that it ignores the fact that the capital assets are of different vintages, bought at different points of time.

Some of the earlier studies have, however, deflated the annual additions to capital stock (perpetual inventory method) and not the capital stock itself. Sankar (136), Sastry (138), Mehta (102) and Gupta and Patel (60) have used perpetual inventory method. The weakness of these studies is that the estimated capital series excludes depreciation. In fact, the reported depreciation grossly overestimates the true capital consumption.

Many of the recent studies favour gross stock measure of capital over the net stock measure for the purpose of estimating production function and other related analysis. Banerji (7), Barna (8), Dholakia (34), Goldar (52) and Hashim and Dadi (62) hold this opinion.

3.5.3 Capital Input Series in Indian Steel Industry as Used in the Present Study

The present study follows the 'perpetual inventory method' to construct the series for gross fixed capital at constant (1960-61) prices. This series is similar to the one developed by Dholakia (34) for Indian iron and steel industry for the period 1946 to 1966. The present study considers the period 1951 to 1977. The definition of fixed capital also includes land. The working capital has not been included in the series of capital input. Banerji (7) puts forward the following reasons for excluding working capital:

i. Technological factors have a greater influence on the relationship between fixed capital and output than on that between working capital and output; and
ii. The composition of working capital is such that it is difficult to arrive at a suitable price index for applying price corrections.

The series of fixed capital has been divided into two components, as done by Dholakia (34) :

a. Buildings and Construction (including land improvement); and
b. Plant, Machinery and Equipment.

It has been assumed on the basis of the study reported by Hashim and Dadi (62) that the assets acquired before 1946 (valued at constant 1960 prices) are scrapped at a linear rate of 4.47 per cent per annum so that during 23 years period (after 1945) all the assets that were acquired before 1946 are scrapped. This means that 98.34 per cent of such assets were discarded by 1967 (4.47x22 = 98.34) and the rest 1.66 per cent were discarded during the twenty third year, i.e., 1968.

It is assumed in the present study that there is no scrapping of the assets purchased after 1945.

The ratios of the gross value to the net value of fixed capital assets at purchase prices for the two components of the fixed capital for the year 1960 are obtained from the study reported by Hashim and Dadi (62). The gross-net ratios for the iron and steel industry have been computed to be 1.3297 for buildings and construction and 1.5777 for plant, equipment and machinery. The gross stock of fixed capital in iron and steel industry in 1960, valued at purchase price, is worked out using these gross-net ratios.

The value of the gross fixed capital acquired before 1946 (i.e., upto the end of 1945) is Rs. 177.4 crores at constant (1960-61) prices. It includes Rs. 8.5 crores for structures and construction, and Rs. 168.9 crores for plant, machinery and other equipment (34).

The value of the gross fixed capital for the year 1951 is Rs. 153.9 crores at constant (1960-61) prices (34). The value of structures and construction is Rs. 11.84 crores and that of plant, machinery and other equipment Rs. 142.06 crores.

On the basis of the available information it is assumed that the average rate of accounting depreciation charged on buildings and construction is 7 per cent of the net value of the stock in each year. The remaining part of the total reported depreciation represents the accounting depreciation charged on plant, machinery and other equipment.

The present study requires a series of gross stock of fixed capital at constant (1960-61) prices for the period 1951 to 1977. Separate series are constructed for each of the two components of fixed capital and, later, the two series are added together to compute the aggregate capital series.

The required time series for a particular component of fixed capital is derived using the following identity :

$$GK_i(t) = GK_i(t-1) + GA_i(t) - AD_i(t) \tag{3.5}$$

where 'i' may either represent the buildings and construction component or the plant, machinery and other equipment component of the fixed capital; $GK_i(t)$ and $GK_i(t\text{-}1)$ indicate the gross stock of the ith component at the end of the years t and (t-1), respectively; $GA_i(t)$ represents the value of gross addition to the ith component at (1960-61) prices during the year t; and $AD_i(t)$ represents the assumed value of assets scrapped during the year t, valued at constant (1960-61) prices.

The series of $GA_i(t)$ during the period 1951 to 1977 is derived by deflating the annual gross addition to ith component (at current prices) by its corresponding price index. The annual gross addition (at current prices) during the year t is computed by adding the increment in depreciated book value of the ith component between years (t-1) and t, to the estimate of reported depreciation in the ith component during the year t.

The methodology used in constructing the series of gross stock of fixed capital, at constant (1960-61) prices, is similar to the one used by Dholakia (34).

The price indices for construction, and for machinery and equipment are taken from Dholakia (33) upto the year 1966. From 1967 onwards, the price index series for machinery and equipment is taken from the work compiled by Chandhok (21). The price index series for construction is extended forward in the post-1966 period with the help of data from National Accounts Statistics (74) which gives the annual values of construction at current and at constant prices. The price series for these components for the period 1951 to 1977 are given in Appendix Table A2.

The relevant data for the years 1967 and 1972 are not available from the series of ASI. The 1967 value of the gross fixed capital at constant (1960-61) prices is taken as a simple average of those for the years 1966 and 1968. This value is divided into two components by assuming that the ratio between the values of structures and construction, and plant machinery and other equipment for the year 1967, is a simple average of the similar ratios corresponding to the years 1966 and 1968.

In 1972, the depreciated book value of capital, for each component, is taken to be a simple average of the values corresponding to the years 1971 and 1973.

The identified annual values of gross fixed capital series at constant (1960-61) prices are given in Table 3.2, for the period 1951 to 1977. For the sake of convenience, these values shall be written in terms of constant 1960 prices instead of constant (1960-61) prices.

TABLE 3.2
Identified Input Values in Indian Steel Industry
(1951-1977)

Year	Capital (Gross fixed capital in Rs. lakhs at constant 1960 prices)	Labour (Lakh man-hours : all employees)	Fuels (Lakh tonnes of coal replacement equivalent)	Raw-materials (Rs. lakhs at constant 1960 prices)
1951	15390	2069	44.28	5644
1952	14718	1982	43.16	6144
1953	14590	1989	38.27	5714
1954	14979	2227	34.16	5381
1955	15168	2323	33.93	5628
1956	16261	2367	32.36	5682
1957	19359	2354	36.04	5186
1958	25161	2373	38.69	5381
1959	30473	2119	44.85	7372
1960	31246	2378	46.81	8537
1961	32307	2436	48.63	8897
1962	83997	4547	86.10	15997
1963	89942	4335	88.31	16844
1964	94991	4731	73.07	17706
1965	100375	4712	82.91	15788
1966	113823	4852	77.71	18146
1967	119667	4939	78.49	18730
1968	126430	5025	79.26	19203
1969	129862	5070	87.70	20859
1970	132365	4985	92.31	20060
1971	135075	5488	83.11	23048
1972	141165	5400	82.58	24195
1973	146446	5312	82.05	22816
1974	146554	4933	71.59	21831
1975	181236	6200	93.51	25137
1976	191505	6248	96.50	24607
1977	202022	6728	82.33	29476

3.5.4 Price of Capital Input

It is assumed in the present study that the returns to labour and capital exhaust value added. Humphrey and Moroney (71) have computed the cost of capital as gross-quasi rent (value added minus wage-bill) divided by the gross book value of the capital stock. A better measure of the price of capital is given by Moroney and Trapani (103), i.e., the cost of constant-rupee capital is computed as the ratio of gross-quasi rent to the capital stock at some constant base period price. The cost (or price) of capital measured in this way is the average rate of return (inclusive of indirect business taxes) on the real capital stock. Indirect business taxes could not be subtracted as the data regarding the same are not available for the Indian steel industry as a whole. It is, therefore, assumed that these taxes remain approximately proportional to the gross-quasi rent throughout the period under study. This method, no doubt, over-estimates the true cost of capital, but the trend in true series is not disturbed.

The values of gross-quasi rent for the years 1967 and 1972, for which the ASI data were not available, are taken to be the simple averages of their values in corresponding preceding and succeeding years.

The present study adopts the concept given by Moroney and Trapani (103) in computing the price (or cost) of capital series. The price of capital during a particular year is the ratio between gross-quasi rent to the value of gross fixed capital at constant (1960-61) prices. The identified time-series of price of capital is given in Table 3.3.

3.6 MEASUREMENT OF LABOUR INPUT AND ITS PRICE

3.6.1 Labour Input

There has been some controversy with regard to the definition of labour input in the production process of an industry. Different studies have used different measures of labour input. Various alternative concepts are available to measure labour input, such as, 'workers', 'employees', 'man-hours of workers', 'man-hours of employees', etc. The present study uses 'man-hours worked by employees' as the measure of labour input in Indian iron and steel industry.

Denison (30) has favoured the use of taking 'workers' as labour input. He argues that the efficiency of a typical worker does not remain the same in all his working hours on a particular day. He points out that a reduction in man-hours per week results in an increase in labour input per hour.

TABLE 3.3
Identified Input Prices for Indian Steel Industry
(1951-1977)

Year	Capital Price Series in Percentage Terms (Rs. per rupee of capital input)	Labour Price Series (Rs. per man-hour)	Fuels Price Series (Rs. per tonne of coal replacement equivalent)	Raw-materials Price Series (Price index: 1960 = 1.0000)
1951	0.0840	0.7651	20.69	0.4079
1952	0.1074	0.8537	21.35	0.4653
1953	0.1420	0.8291	22.66	0.4685
1954	0.1829	0.8141	25.81	0.5728
1955	0.1919	0.8218	26.41	0.6260
1956	0.2423	0.8606	29.69	0.7802
1957	0.1931	0.9053	33.25	0.8917
1958	0.1515	0.9595	37.50	0.9890
1959	0.1224	1.2067	34.34	0.9944
1960	0.0993	1.1312	38.85	1.0000
1961	0.1168	1.1552	44.65	1.0277
1962	0.0775	0.9826	43.79	0.8975
1963	0.0925	1.1571	56.23	1.0019
1964	0.1092	1.2663	60.63	1.1175
1965	0.1077	1.4151	59.67	1.2431
1966	0.0845	1.5754	68.05	1.2578
1967	0.0840	1.7526	77.45	1.4047
1968	0.0830	1.9240	86.84	1.5516
1969	0.0740	2.0270	84.80	1.5450
1970	0.0785	2.3779	86.45	1.7067
1971	0.0604	2.4105	103.17	1.8756
1972	0.0808	2.8063	106.10	1.9604
1973	0.1001	3.2125	134.05	2.2631
1974	0.1669	3.7762	226.36	2.7229
1975	0.1452	3.9144	254.86	3.0784
1976	0.1451	3.9216	270.67	3.3273
1977	0.1064	4.2249	275.31	3.3908

Sinha and Sawhney (145) have argued that man-hour series, as available in ASI, considers only workers and leaves out persons other than workers. The reason that they put forward for taking employees as labour input is that persons other than operating workers, such as those working in administration, marketing, finance, and research and development are equally important in getting the work done as the operating workers. Goldar (52) has also preferred to use 'employees' as the labour input.

In spite of the above criticism, many studies have preferred to use 'man-hours' as the measure of labour input. Humphrey and Moroney (71), Moroney and Trapani (103), Sarkar (137) and Dholakia (34) have used 'man-hours worked by employees' as the measure of labour input. The same measure is used in the present study.

A problem faced in case of Indian iron and steel industry is that the data on man-hours worked by employees are not directly available except for the years 1976 and 1977. For the period 1951 to 1958, the series available is in terms of man-hours of directly employed workers, whereas the one available for the period 1959 to 1975 is in terms of man-hours of all workers. In order to construct a series for man-hours of all employees the following assumptions are made :

i. For the period 1951 to 1958, the average number of hours worked by employees is equal to those worked by directly employed workers; and
ii. For the period 1959 to 1975, the average number of hours worked by employees is equal to those worked by all workers (direct and contractual).

The series of man-hours worked by employees may, thus, be written as :

a. For the period 1951 to 1958

$$H_E = \frac{H_{DW}}{DW} x E \tag{3.6}$$

where,

H_E = man-hours worked by employees;

H_{DW} = man-hours worked by direct workers;

DW = number of direct workers; and

E = number of employees.

b. For the period 1959 to 1975

$$H_E = \frac{H_{AW}}{AW} x E \qquad (3.7)$$

where,

H_{AW} = man-hours worked by all workers (direct and contractual);

AW = number of all workers; and

HE and E are same as in equation (3.6).

For the years 1976 and 1977, the data are available in the form of employee man-days. It is assumed that each man-day consists of eight working hours. The data on employee man-days are multiplied by eight to convert the series into the figures of man-hours worked by employees.

The ASI data are not available for the years 1967 and 1972. Employee man-hours in each of these two years are estimated by taking a simple average of the employee man-hours of the preceding and succeeding years corresponding to the year under consideration.

The identified series of labour input in terms of man-hours worked by employees, for the period 1951 to 1977, is given in Table 3.2.

3.6.2 Price of Labour Input

The price of labour input is computed in terms of the average hourly wage rate of the employees. The hourly wage rate during a particular year is calculated through dividing total payments to labour by total number of employee man-hours worked during that year. The total payments to labour include wages, salaries, benefits and contributions paid to all the employees. The benefits include subsidised housing, foodgrains at concessional rates, medical aids. etc.

Sastri (138) and Williams and Laumas (162) have used a similar concept to compute the wage rate or the price of labour input.

The time-series of price of labour input (wage-rate) for the period 1951 to 1977 is given in Table 3.3.

3.7 MEASUREMENT OF FUELS INPUT AND ITS PRICE

3.7.1 Fuels Input

The energy required in the steel making process is supplied through various forms of fuels, such as, coal, coke, coal gas, firewood, charcoal, motor spirit, diesel oil, other fuel oils, electricity, etc.

The annual time-series of quantities of different categories of .uels used in Indian iron and steel industry are available from the series of CMI (72) and ASI (73) and are given in Appendix Table A3. Each category of fuels is converted into its 'coal replacement' measure[1] with the help of a conversion table taken from Fuels Policy Committee Report (76), as given in Appendix Table A4. Whereas the 'coal-equivalent' measure of a particular category of fuels expresses the heat content of that category in terms of heat content of the average category of indigenous coal, the 'coal-replacement' measure takes into account the efficiency of fuel use in India (31). For the conversion of liquid fuels into 'coal replacement' measure, the knowledge of specific gravity of different fuels is also required. Appendix Table A5 gives the specific gravities of motor-spirit, diesel oil and other fuel oils.

The amount spent on the category 'other fuels' as given in Appendix Table A3, is converted into its 'coal replacement' measure through dividing it by the current price of an average unit of coal. The current price of an average unit of coal is computed by dividing the expenditure incurred on coal in Indian steel industry by its total tonnage used. The data on time-series of expenditure incurred and tonnage of coal used in Indian steel industry, as available from the

---

1. It may also be written as coal replacement equivalent

series of CMI and ASI, are reported in Appendix Table A3.

A time-series of the homogeneous measure of fuels is constructed for the period 1951 to 1971, by adding up 'coal replacement' measures of various categories of fuels for each year. The measure for the year 1967, for which the data were not available, has been estimated by taking a simple average of the computed homogeneous measures for the years 1966 and 1968.

One faces a problem in extending the series of 'coal replacement' measure during the post-1971 period. The detailed data on various categories of fuels consumed during the years 1972 to 1977 were not available from the available summaries of ASI. The only available information is regarding the total fuels-bill (in current rupee terms) incurred during the years 1973 through 1977. These figures are given in Appendix Table A9. The figure for 1972 was not available. This series of fuels-bill is converted into a corresponding series of 'coal replacement' measure through deflating it by the price index series of the homogeneous 'coal replacement' measure, as extended upto 1977 in the following sub-section. The figure of the homogeneous measures of 'coal replacement' for the year 1972 is taken to be the simple average of the measures corresponding to the years 1971 and 1973.

The identified series of 'coal replacement' measure of various fuels used in Indian iron and steel industry, during 1951 to 1977, is given in Table 3.2.

3.7.2 Price of Fuels Input

The price of the homogeneous measure of energy consumed in Indian iron and steel industry (as computed in the preceding subsection) during a particular year is computed by dividing the total rupee-bill of the fuels consumed by the tonnage of their homogeneous measure. The price series of the 'coal replacement' measure of various fuels is, thus, obtained for the period 1951 to 1971 (except for 1967).

The next problem is to extend this price series upto the year 1977. The price series of the homogeneous 'coal replacement' measure obtained in the above mentioned manner is regressed on the price-series of fuel, power, light and lubricants, as reported by Chandhok (21). The regression equation thus obtained is as follows :

$$HP_t = -113.34 + 2.15CP_t \qquad (3.8)$$

where,

HP_t = current price of one tonne of the homogeneous 'coal-replacement' measure during the year t;

CP_t = price index of fuel, power, light and lubricants as reported by Chandhok (21) converted into a series with base year 1960; and

t = 1951 to 1971.

Chandhok's price series, CP_t, for the years 1951 to 1971 is given in Appendix Table A7; and, for the years 1972 to 1977, it is given in Appendix Table A8.

The series HP_t can now be extrapolated during the period 1972 to 1977 by substituting the known values of CP_t in equation (3.8).

The identified time-series of 'coal-replacement' measure is given in Table 3.3.

3.8 MEASUREMENT OF RAW MATERIALS INPUT AND ITS PRICE

3.8.1 Raw-Materials Input

The current rupee values of total raw-materials consumed in Indian iron and steel industry during the period 1951 to 1977 (except for 1967 and 1972) are available from the series of CMI (72) and ASI (73) and are given in Appendix Table A10. For each of the two years, 1967 and 1972, the rupee value of total raw materials consumed is taken to be the simple average of the values of the preceding and succeeding years. This series has to be converted into a corresponding series at some constant base-period price before being used as a measure of raw-materials input in the production function analysis. This is done through deflating the available series by the series of price-index of raw-materials used in Indian iron and steel industry. The required price index series of raw-materials is estimated in the following sub-section.

The identified series of raw-materials used (in real terms) in Indian iron and steel industry is given in Table 3.2.

3.8.2 Price of Raw-Materials Input

There are many different types of raw-materials used in the steel making process. A different price-index series corresponds to each category of raw-materials. However, nine major categories of raw-materials have been identified as a representative-block for the purpose of constructing a weighted price-index series for the raw-materials used. These categories are chosen in such a way that the share of their rupee-value in the total rupee-value of all the raw-materials varies between 65 to 81 per cent during the period 1951 to 1971. The following are the major raw-materials used in Indian iron and steel industry :

i. Iron Ore;
ii. Lime Stone;
iii. Scrap Steel, Pig Iron, Steel;
iv. Aluminium;
v. Tin;
vi. Spelter (Zinc);
vii. Chemicals;
viii. Magnesite; and
ix. Coal (reported 1960 onwards).

The time-series data of the tonnage and current rupee-value of each of the above categories are available from the series of CMI and ASI for the period 1951 to 1971 (except for 1967) and are reported in Appendix Table A6. One of the exceptions is for chemicals, for which the data are available only for their current rupee-value and not for quantity.

The time-series of price-index for each major category of raw-materials is computed with the help of the knowledge of its tonnage and current rupee-value during the period 1951 to 1971. In case of chemicals, the price-index series has been taken from Chandhok (21) and is reported in Appendix Table A7 (1951 to 1971) and A8 (1971 to 1977). The price series for each category is computed with 1951 as the base year.

In the post-1971 period, the time-series of price-index of each major category of raw-materials is computed with the help of the corresponding time-series as reported by Chandhok (21) and given in Appendix Table A8. It is assumed that the prices of major categories of raw-materials used in Indian iron and steel industry behave in the same way as reported by Chandhok, during the period 1972 to 1977. The price-series already computed for each major category for the period 1951 to 1971 is extrapolated for the period 1972 to 1977.

To compute an overall weighted price-index series of the raw-materials, weights are attached to each major category for each year from 1951 to 1971. There are eight major categories during the period 1951 to 1959, and nine during 1960 to 1971. The weight attached to a particular category during a particular year is the proportion of its rupee-value in the total rupee-value of all the major categories of raw-materials. The weights, thus attached, are such that these add up to unity in any particular year.

Since the detailed category-wise data are not available during the post-1971 period, it is assumed, for the sake of convenience, that the weights attached to various major categories remain constant and are equal to the average value of the weights attached to the respective categories during the four year period, 1968 to 1971.

The weighted price-index of the major categories of raw-materials is computed in the following manner :

$$WPI_t = \sum_{i=1}^{8} W_{it} P_{it} \qquad (3.9)$$

for t = 1951 to 1958

where,

WPI_t = weighted price index during the t-th year;

W_{it} = weight attached to the ith category during the t-th year; and

P_{it} = price-index of the ith category during the t-th year.

The detailed category-wise data are not available for the year 1959

From 1960 onwards, the weighted price-index is given as follows :

$$WPI_t = \sum_{i=1}^{9} W_{it} P_{it} \tag{3.10}$$

for t = 1960 to 1977.

This is so because there are nine major categories of raw-materials reported from 1960 onwards.

The weighted price-indices could not be computed for the years 1959 and 1967. For each of these two years, the weighted price index is taken to be the simple average of the weighted price-indices of the preceding and the succeeding years.

The weighted price-index series so formed is then normalised so that the value of weighted price index is equal to unity during the year 1960, such that :

$$WPI_{1960} = 1.00 \tag{3.11}$$

The weighted price-series so computed is assumed to be the representative price-index series of all the raw-materials consumed in Indian iron and steel industry during the period 1951 to 1977. The series so computed is given in Table 3.3.

3.9 THE PERIOD OF ANALYSIS

Due to the problems of availability of data on various relevant variables, the period of analysis has been fixed to be 1951 to 1977. The starting year has been taken as 1951 which is a landmark year because the planning process in independent India was started in this year. Moreover, it is a judgemental decision that the data prior to 1951 is not of much relevance now. The last year of analysis has been taken as 1977 since the data on steel consumption (in terms of crude steel equivalent) and various inputs used in Indian steel industry were not available for the post-1977 period at the time of estimation of the steel consumption and input demand functions.

3.10 CONCLUDING REMARKS

The relevant system variables have been clearly identified in the present chapter. The time-series of the GNP, production and consumption of steel, homogeneous measures of various inputs used in the steel production process, namely labour, capital, fuels and raw-materials, and their corresponding prices have been computed with the help of information available from the current relevant literature and various sources of data, referred to at relevant places. The stage is now set to proceed to analyse the system of Indian steel industry. The following chapters attempt to develop the models of sub-systems and eventually a simulation model of Indian steel industry as a system with a view to develop future scenarios which can provide useful insight into the steel planning process at a national level on a long-term basis.

FOUR

THE STEEL CONSUMPTION SUB-MODEL[1]

4.1 INTRODUCTION

The basic purpose of this chapter is to analyse the past behaviour of steel consumption in Indian economy in order to estimate a steel consumption function which relates the behaviour of steel consumption in India to its Gross National Product (GNP). In the present study, this consumption function has been used to forecast the future steel requirements in Indian economy upto the year 2005.

The finished steel products enter as raw-materials to many other industries of the economy because of a very high combined linkage score of this industry vis-a-vis other industries (68). Thus, the demand for steel may be derived from the overall level of demand in the economy. The changes in consumption of steel may, thus, be explained in terms of changes in one of the macro-economic variables, such as, GNP, industrial production, population, total fixed investment, etc. Such types of models follow the technique of global modelling, already discussed in Chapter Two.

Whatever may be the variable chosen to be the explanatory vari-

---

1. Part of this chapter has been published in

   i. *24th National Convention of IIIE,* New Delhi, February, 1982.
   ii. *14th Annual Convention of ORSI,* Bombay, March, 1982.
   iii. *OPSEARCH,* vol. 19 (No. 2), 1982.
   iv. *Journal of Engineering Production,* Vol. 5 (No. 3), 1982.

able, a forecast of steel consumption requires a forecast of the explanatory variables as well. The present study considers GNP to be the explanatory variable and, therefore, a GNP function has also been estimated to forecast the future GNP of India upto the year 2005.

The consumption sub-model, thus, consists of two functions :

i. Consumption Function;
ii. GNP Function.

4.2 ECONOMIC INTERDEPENDENCE BETWEEN STEEL CONSUMPTION AND GROSS NATIONAL PRODUCT

Steel consumption in an economy is influenced by the level and behaviour of GNP which is an overall economic indicator. GNP, in turn, is influenced by the changes in steel consumption in the economy because of the very high combined linkage score of steel industry vis-a-vis other industries. However, if the GNP forecasts are made under the assumption of balanced growth, such an influence is already implied in these forecasts (124). The development of steel consumption may, then, be predicted as being consistent with GNP development. GNP may be treated as a purely exogenous variable under these circumstances.

The strategy accepted and adopted for the planned development of the Indian economy is that of balanced growth and comprehensive planning (78, 79). Further, the GNP function is estimated on the basis of its past behaviour. The forecast of GNP series may, therefore, be treated to be purely exogeneous for the purpose of forecasting steel demand or steel consumption requirements in India.

4.3 CONSUMPTION VERSUS DEMAND OF STEEL IN INDIA

The concept of steel consumption in an economy is usually interpreted as the quantity of steel demanded by the economy. In case of economically advanced countries, the observed steel consumption is determined in the market by an interplay of supply and demand forces (124). It may be assumed that steel demand in the short term is quite inelastic with respect to price changes, while supply (including net imports) is highly elastic in such countries. Thus, the quantity actually consumed is also the quantity demanded, regardless of its price. This may be only partially true in case of the Indian economy.

A concept of 'steel consumption requirement' in place of 'steel consumption' has been introduced in the present study. It is admitted that in case of India, there may be a difference between steel consumption and quantity of steel demanded. In spite of this, 'steel consumption requirement' is always equal to the actual demand for steel.

It has been a common experience in Indian planning that the realised level of economic growth in many years (since 1951) has been lower than the desired level. Correspondingly, there are two concepts of steel demand :

i. Steel demand corresponding to the desired level of economic development; and
ii. Steel demand corresponding to the realised level of economic development.

It has been depicted in Fig. 4.1 that the desired steel demand has generally been higher than the actual steel requirement in many years since 1951.

Thus, the commonly quoted statement that Indian economy is not able to fulfil its steel demand is only apparently true. Implicitly, this statement implies that the desired steel demand is greater than the quantity of steel actually consumed in India. It should, therefore, be noted that the demand for steel during a particular year should be visualised corresponding to the realised level of economic development. This is the concept of actual steel demand and is equal to the 'steel consumption requirement' of the economy.

Henceforth, the concepts of steel demand and steel consumption requirement (or even steel consumption) shall be used as synonyms. It has, thus, been assumed that steel consumption is determined by its actual demand.

Fig. 4.1 Desired Versus Actual Steel Demand During the Year 't'

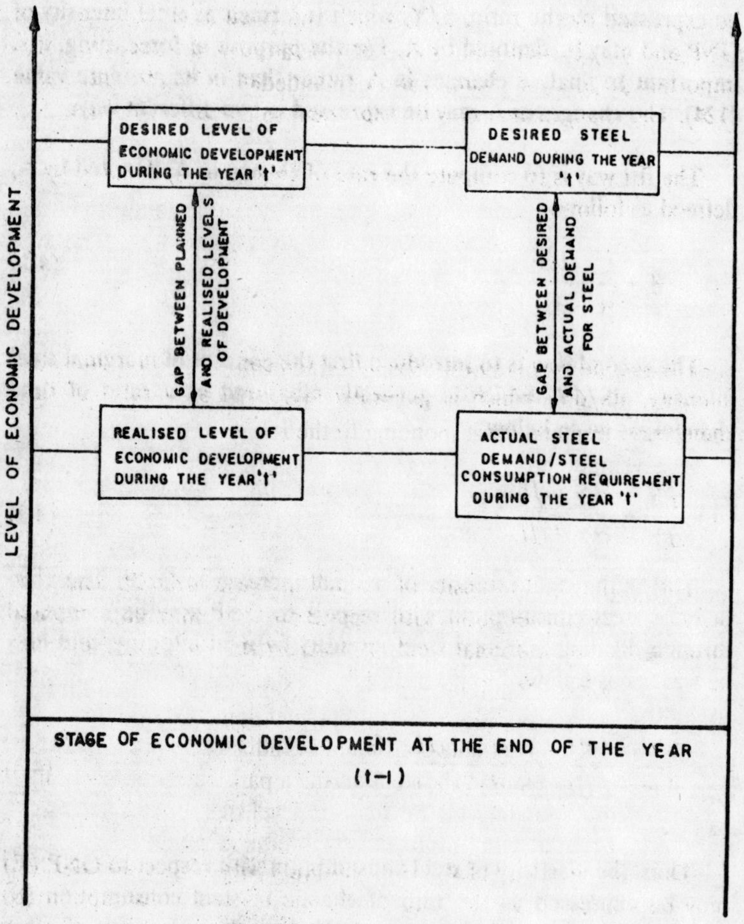

4.4 BASIC CONSIDERATIONS IN ESTIMATING A GLOBAL MODEL OF STEEL CONSUMPTION FUNCTION

4.4.1 Some Basic Concepts

The relation between steel consumption (S) and GNP (Y) may be expressed by the ratio, S/Y, which is termed as steel intensity of GNP and may be denoted by A. For the purpose of forecasting, it is important to analyse changes in A rather than in its absolute value (124). The changes in A may be expressed in two different ways.

The fist way is to compute the rate of change in A, denoted by A, defined as follows :

$$\dot{A} = \frac{1}{A}\frac{dA}{dt} \tag{4.1}$$

The second way is to introduce first the concept of marginal steel intensity, dS/dY, which is generally measured as a ratio of time changes, as given below :

$$\frac{dS}{dY} = \frac{dS/dt}{dY/dt} \tag{4.2}$$

This is the steel intensity of a small increase in GNP. The elasticity of steel consumption with respect to GNP may be computed through dividing marginal steel intensity by steel intensity, and may be written as follows :

$$E = \frac{1}{A}\frac{dS/dt}{dY/dt} = \frac{Y}{S}\frac{dS/dt}{dY/dt} = \frac{\dot{S}}{\dot{Y}} \tag{4.3}$$

Thus, the elasticity of steel consumption with respect to GNP (E) may be expressed as the rate of change in steel consumption ($\dot{S}$) divided by the rate of change in GNP ($\dot{Y}$). The elasticity, E, is a dimensionless measure.

A relationship between $\dot{A}$ and E can be deduced as follows :

$$\dot{A} = \frac{1}{A}\frac{dA}{dt} = \frac{Y}{S}\frac{d}{dt}\frac{S}{Y} = \frac{Y}{S}\frac{Y\frac{dS}{dt} - S\frac{dY}{dt}}{Y^2}$$

$$= \frac{1}{S}\frac{dS}{dt} - \frac{1}{Y}\frac{dY}{dt}$$

$$= \dot{S} - \dot{Y} = \dot{Y}\left(\frac{\dot{S}}{\dot{Y}} - 1\right)$$

$$= \dot{Y}(E - 1) \qquad (4.4)$$

Hence, the rate of change of steel intensity is equal to the difference between the rates of change in steel consumption and GNP. If GNP increases, i.e. $\dot{Y} > 0$, then A has the same sign as (E-1). Thus, an increase in A corresponds to elasticity greater than unity.

4.4.2 Aggregate Steel Intensity and Stage of Economic Development

It is quite likely that the sectoral composition of production is subject to changes as an economy undergoes different stages of development. Maizel (97) finds that steel intensity of an economy depends upon its stage of industrial development. Based on Maizel's study, Vinell (158) makes the following observations about economic growth and structural changes :

i. In initial stages of development, production is mostly confined to necessary commodities such as food and clothing;
ii. During the industrialisation process, the building sector and heavy industry undergo a rapid process of expansion;
iii. Engineering industries increase their share of total production mostly at the expense of foodstuff and textile sectors; and
iv. The output of engineering firms goes towards lighter products in advanced economies.

Thus, steel intensity is low in the early stages of industrial development but rises at a rapid rate during the process of industrialisation. In a highly industrialised economy, steel intensity exhibits a phase of stagnation or even a slow decline

Per capita GNP may be used to measure the stage of industrial development. Fig. 4.2 shows a hypothetical curve showing steel intensity as a function of stage of industrial development.

Fig. 4.2 Steel Intensity of GNP and the State of Economic Development : A Hypothetical Curve

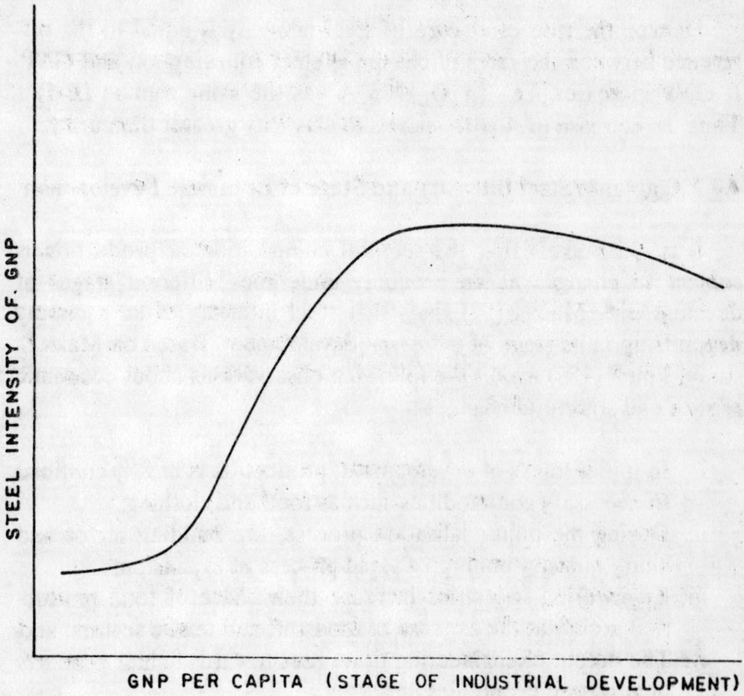

A study conducted by International Iron and Steel Institute also reports a similar theoretical curve as given in Fig. 4.2. The curve was developed on the basis of a study conducted on twenty different countries (83).

4.4.3 Basic Hypotheses for the Model

Steel consumption during any period is determined by two types of forces (159), as given below :

i. Short term forces; and
ii. Long term forces.

In short term, business cycle affects the apparent steel consumption in two ways :

a. Directly, by changes in the levels of inventory; and
b. Indirectly, by way of changes in the composition of GNP and production structure.

It has been observed that it is the growth rate of GNP tht causes fluctuations in steel consumption or rather in steel intensity in short term.

The long term development in steel consumption is dominated to a large extent by the proportionality between steel consumption and the GNP. Vlemmings (159) makes the following assumptions to allow for changes in economic structure :

i. A part of the additional GNP has no steel consumption at all, or in the opposite case, a part of the steel consumption has an autonomous character and is not influenced by the growth rate of GNP. This type of a model can be written in a linear form as :

$$S = \alpha + \beta Y \tag{4.5}$$

ii. The additional amount of GNP has a steel intensity that is a constant proportion of the original steel intensity such that :

$$\frac{\Delta S}{\Delta Y} = k\,A = k\,\frac{S}{Y} \qquad (4.6)$$

where K is a constant.

Equation (4.6) can be written in the following form :

$$\frac{\Delta S}{S} = k\,\frac{\Delta Y}{Y}\,,\ \text{or}\ \dot{S} = k\,\dot{Y} \qquad (4.7)$$

Thus, the second assumption implies a constant elasticity, E=K, where E may be higher or lower than unity.

It is clear from the above analysis that a global model of steel consumption should take care of both short term and long term forces. Such a model may be expressed in the following general form:

$$S = f(Y\,,\dot{Y}\,,t) \qquad (4.8)$$

4.5 BEHAVIOUR OF STEEL CONSUMPTION IN INDIA DURING 1951 TO 1977

Before attempting model-building, it is relevant to observe and analyse the behaviour of steel consumption in India during the period 1951 to 1977. This analysis also reflects the demand behaviour of steel in India. In fact, it is the past behaviour of steel consumption that has been used to forecast future steel demand, under certain assumptions.

The apparent consumption (S) in terms of crude steel equivalent has grown with a linear trend over time during the period 1951 to 1977, as shown in Fig. 4.3. There have been marked cyclical fluctuations around the linear trend. The trend in S, over the period 1951 to 1977, is estimated in the following regression equation:[2]

---

2. The equations estimated in this chapter use the data in the form specified in Table 3.1.

Fig. 4.3 Behaviour of Steel Consumption in India During 1951 to 1977

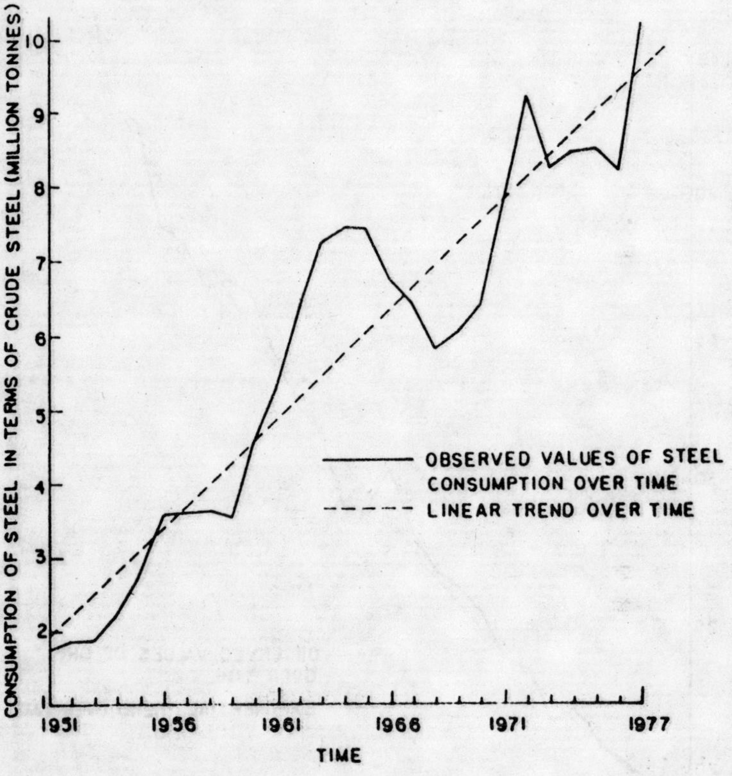

Fig. 4.4 Behaviour of GNP of India During 1951 to 1977

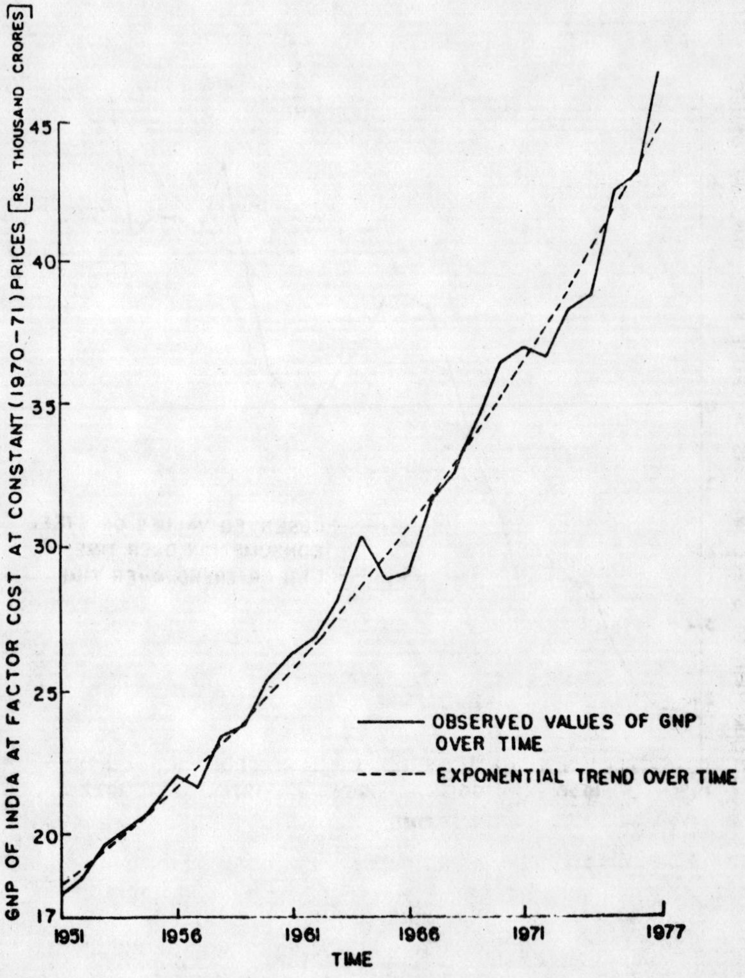

$$S_t = 1640.7 + 294.2t$$

$$\bar{R}^2 = 0.88 \qquad (4.9)$$

where,

t = 1 to 27 (i.e. 1951 to 1977)

S_t = apparent steel consumption in terms of crude steel equivalent ('000 tonnes) during the year.

An interesting feature of the steel consumption during the twenty seven years period has been that every period of four to five years of imporvement has been followed by a roughly equal period of fall in steel consumption.

The GNP of India has grown exponentially over time as shown in Fig. 4.4. The exponential trend in GNP, over the period 1951 to 1977 is estimated in the following equation :

$$\ln Y_t = 9.771 + 0.035t$$

$$\bar{R}^2 = 0.99 \qquad (4.10)$$

where,

Y_t = GNP at factor cost at constant (1970-71) prices (Rs. crores) during the year t; and

ln Y_t denotes the natural logarithm of Y_t.

The steel intensity of GNP (S/Y) has increased from approximately 100 tonnes of steel per crore rupees of GNP in 1951, to more than 200 tonnes in 1977, with marked cyclical fluctuations. The annual steel intensity behaviour is shown in Fig. 4.5.

The elasticity of steel consumption with respect to GNP (E) has already been defined in equation (4.3). The behaviour of five-yearly moving period elasticity is shown in Fig. 4.6. The elasticity value seems to be declining and tapering off around unity.

Fig. 4.5 Behaviour of Steel Intensity of India's GNP During 1951 to 1977

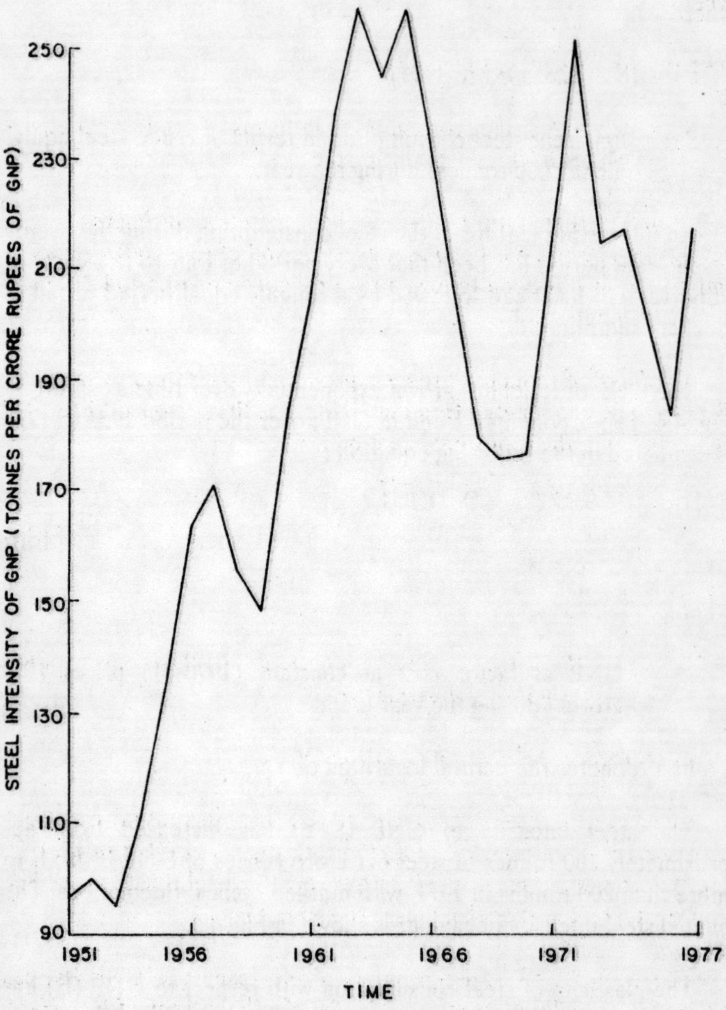

Fig. 4.6 Behaviour of Five-Yearly Moving Period Elasticity of Steel Consumption With Respect to GNP During 1951 to 1977

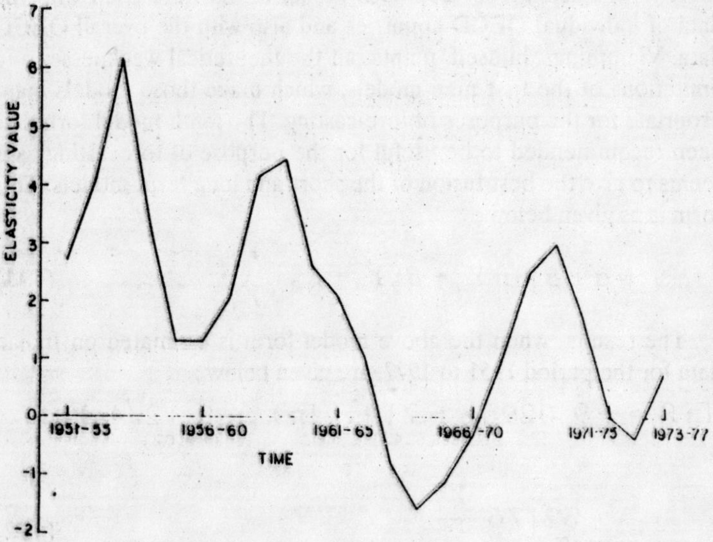

4.6 ESTIMATING A MODEL OF THE STEEL CONSUMPTION FUNCTION IN INDIA

4.6.1 Relevance of OECD Models in Indian Context

Based on the general model-form expressed in equation (4.8), Vlemmings (159) experimented with various possible combinations of such models, starting from the simple linear model (as given in equation (4.5)) without provisions for technological change and short term fluctuations. Ten such model forms were tried with the data of individual OECD countries and also with the overall OECD data. Vlemmings, himself, points out the theoretical weaknesses and limitations of the first nine models, which make those models inappropriate for the purposes of fore-casting. The tenth model form has been recommended to be useful for the purpose of forecasting as it seems to give the best fusion of the short and long term models. This form is as given below :

$$\ln S_t = \alpha + \beta_1 \ln Y_t + \beta_2 \dot{Y}_t + \beta_3 \frac{\dot{Y}_t}{Y_t} \tag{4.11}$$

The results, when the above model form is estimated on Indian data for the period 1951 to 1977, are given below :

$$\ln S_t = -9.0295 + \underset{(6.45)^*}{1.7194} \ln Y_t - \underset{(-0.02)}{0.1274} \dot{Y}_t - \underset{(-0.33)}{52176} \frac{\dot{Y}_t}{Y_t} \quad \ldots . (4.12)$$

$$\bar{R}^2 = 0.84 ; DW = 0.43 ; \quad Corr.(\dot{Y}_t, \dot{Y}_t / Y_t) = 0.92 .$$

The growth rate of GNP of period t over GNP of period (t-1) has been defined as ($\ln Y_t - \ln Y_{t-1}$) in equation (4.13) and in all estimated equations which follow in this chapter.

The model form given in equation (4.12) is inappropriate under Indian conditions because the results obtained through this form (as given in equation (4.13)) have the following serious weaknesses :

3. * The value given in parentheses below an estimated parameter is the 't-ratio' statistic of that parameter.

i. Very low t-ratio values corresponding to the estimated coefficients of $\dot{Y}_t$ and $\dot{Y}_t / Y_t$;
ii. High correlation between $\dot{Y}_t$ and $\dot{Y}_t / Y_t$; and
iii. Low DW value.

Thus, the estimated coefficients of $\dot{Y}_t$ and $\dot{Y}_t / Y_t$ are statistically insignificant, there is a problem of multicollinearity between $\dot{Y}_t$ and $\dot{Y}_t / Y_t$, and the error terms are serially correlated.

It may, thus, be pointed out that the model that was found to be appropriate in explaining and forecasting steel consumption in OECD countries is inappropriate when tried on Indian data. There seems to be a need for adding a new dimension to the existing approach in order to analyse and forecast steel consumption requirement of Indian economy.

4.6.2 Developing a Model of Steel Consumption Function in India

4.6.2.1 Theoretical Considerations

This section attempts to formulate and estimate a steel consumption function specific to Indian economy. The need to develop such a model has already been justified in sub-section 4.6.1.

It has been observed in section 4.5 that the steel consumption has grown with a linear trend over time. There have been marked cyclical fluctuations around this trend. It was intuitively visualised that the fluctuations around the trend may have some relationship with the growth rates of GNP in the past few years. A high growth rate of GNP in the recent past has a boosting effect on current year's demand for steel. A period of boom in the economy indicates an upward trend in overall economic activity and a higher general level of demand. Steel demand being a derived demand, also gets boosted up. This period of overall prosperity may have a positive effect on future steel demand in two ways :

i. By encouraging higher overall investments and thereby implying greater production of capital goods and an increase in construction activity; and
ii. Some of the new projects which are taken up during the boom period shall start consuming steel, as a raw-

material, when completed. These projects consume steel, as input, even during the period of their coming up.

The above discussion partially explains as to why the growth rate in GNP has a lagged effect on steel consumption. It is, therefore, visualised that a model of the steel consumption function should be of the following form :

$$S_t = F\left(S_{t-1}, Y_t, \dot{Y}_t, \dot{Y}_{t-1}, \dot{Y}_{t-2}, \ldots, \dot{Y}_{t-n}\right) \tag{4.13}$$

where,

S_t = steel consumption during the period t;
Y_t = GNP during the period t;
$\dot{Y}_t$ = growth rate of GNP during the period t; and
$\dot{Y}_{t-i}$ = growth rate of GNP during the period (t-i), such that, i = 1, 2, ..., n.

The next step is to estimate the value of n, such that the growth rate of GNP during the (t-n)th year has a significant effect on current year's demand of steel but, the growth rates of GNP corresponding to the years which are further past beyond (t-n)th have no significant effect on the current year's steel demand. It is assumed that the GNP growth rates corresponding to the years (t-1), (t-2), ... and (t-n + 1) significantly affect the current year's steel demand. In order to carry out such an exercise, it is not feasible to use the data corresponding to the entire period (1951 to 1977), since lagged GNP values are required as independent variables. The available GNP series starts from 1950. The figures of GNP corresponding to the years 1948 and 1949 have been estimated with the help of the available figures of Net National Product (NNP) corresponding to these two years. These NNP figures have been transformed into the corresponding GNP figures (estimated) through the knowledge of the ratio between GNP and NNP during the following three years, 1950 to 1952, which remained almost stable. The same ratio has been assumed for the years 1948 and 1949.[4]

Based on the general model-form expressed in equation (4.14), various combinations of such models have been tried on Indian data

---

4. * Some GNP figures relevant to this chapter, which were not included in Table 3.1, are given in Table 4.1.

for the 19 years, 1959 to 1977. This is a judgemental decision that the GNP growth rate of the year which is more than a decade back may not have any meaningful effect on the current year's steel demand. The models successively continue to search the effect of past GNP behaviour in an attempt to estimate the best fit model.

TABLE 4.1

Some More Relevant GNP Figures (Years : 1948 to 1950, 1978 and 1979)

Year	GNP at Factor Cost (Rs. crores at constant (1970-71) prices)
1948	17073
1949	17481
1950	17469
1978	49343
1979	46966

Sources: 1. National Accounts Statistics, 1981 (74).
2. Economic Survey, 1981 (75).

It may be observed that the general model-form expressed in equation (4.14) incorporates another major change over the one expressed in equation (4.8). The lagged value of steel consumption (with one year lag) has been included as an independent variable. Koutsoyiannis (93) points out that recent versions of the consumption function depends on past values, due to 'habit persistence', on current income and past levels of income, and other factors.

Thus, the general model-form expressed in equation (4.14) incorporates two basic changes as compared to the one expressed in equation (4.8), as given below :

i. Last year's level of steel consumption has been added to the list of independent variables; and
ii. Growth rates of GNP corresponding to the past years have been added to the list of independent variables.

Initially, a model of the following type has been attempted :

$$\ln S_t = \alpha + \beta_1 \ln Y_t + \beta_2 \ln S_{t-1} \qquad (4.14)$$

This model does not take into account the effect of growth rates of GNP in the current and in the past years. The estimated results are not satisfactory, so another model of the following type is estimated :

$$\ln S_t = \alpha + \beta_1 \ln Y_t + \beta_2 \ln S_{t-i} + \beta_3 \dot{Y}_t \qquad (4.15)$$

As the results are still not quite satisfactory, independent variables of the type $\dot{Y}_{t-i}$ (i = 1, 2, ..., n) are successively added to the model form expressed in equation (4.16). Various models have then been estimated in search of the most appropriate model, which can explain steel consumption behaviour of Indian economy vis-a-vis its GNP. These models may be expressed in the following general form:

$$\ln S_t = \alpha + \beta_1 \ln Y_t + \beta_2 \ln S_{t-1} + \sum_{i=0}^{n} \beta_{i+3} \dot{Y}_{t-i} \qquad (4.16)$$

where n takes successive values, such as, 0, 1, 2, ..., 6. In fact, the search ends at n=5 as this model is found to be the most appropriate one.

A very important check on the appropriateness of an estimated steel consumption function of the form expressed in equation (4.17) is the estimated value of the elasticity of steel consumption with respect to GNP (E), as explaind under section 4.4 and defined in equation (4.3). It has been pointed out under sub-section 4.4.2 that during the industrialisation process, the heavy industry and building sector undergo a rapid process of expansion. This implies a rapidly rising steel intensity during the process of industrialisation. As Indian economy has still a long way to go on the path of industrial development, the steel intensity of its GNP is expected to rise. It is clear from equation (4.4) that an increase in steel intensity (A) corresponds to elasticity (E) greater than unity. Thus, for an estimated steel consumption function (of the form expressed in equation (4.17)) to be appropriate under Indian conditions, it is necessary that the value of the long-run elasticity (E) computed from the estimated function should be greater than unity.

In order to compute the long-run elasticity of steel consumption with respect to GNP, one must look at the steady state solution of the equation (4.17), where S_t is assumed to be equal to S_{t-1} (128). Further, Vlemmings (159) points out that $\dot{Y}$ is considered to be constant in the long run so that :

$$\dot{Y}_t = \dot{Y}_{t-1} = \dot{Y}_{t-2} = \ldots = \dot{Y}_{t-6} = \dot{Y} \tag{4.17}$$

in the long-run, where $\dot{Y}$ is a constant.

The equation (4.17) may now be written as follows:

$$\ln S_t = \alpha + \beta_1 \ln Y_t + \beta_2 \ln S_t + \beta_{sum} \dot{Y} \tag{4.18}$$

where, S_t has been assumed to be equal to S_{t-1}, and

$$\beta_{sum} = \sum_{i=0}^{n} \beta_{i+3} \cdot$$

Equation (4.19) may also be written in the following form :

$$\ln S_t = \frac{\alpha}{1-\beta_2} + \frac{\beta_1}{1-\beta_2} \ln Y_t + \frac{\beta_{sum}}{1-\beta_2} \dot{Y} \tag{4.19}$$

Differentiating equation (4.20) with respect to time it follows that:

$$\frac{d}{dt}(\ln S_t) = \frac{\beta_1}{1-\beta_2} \frac{d}{dt}(\ln Y_t) \tag{4.20}$$

It may be pointed out that the first and the third terms on R.H.S. of equation (4.20) are constants.

Equation (4.21) may be further solved as given below :

$$\frac{1}{S_t}\frac{dS_t}{dt} = \frac{\beta_1}{1-\beta_2} \frac{1}{Y_t}\frac{dY_t}{dt}$$

or

$$\dot{S}_t = \frac{\beta_1}{1-\beta_2} \dot{Y}_t, \text{ or } \frac{\dot{S}_t}{\dot{Y}_t} = \frac{\beta_1}{1-\beta_2} \tag{4.21}$$

The elasticity (E) has been defined as S/Y in equation (4.3). Therefore, it follows that :

$$E = \frac{\dot{S}_t}{\dot{Y}_t} = \frac{\beta_1}{1-\beta_2} \tag{4.22}$$

Here, E is the long run elasticity of steel consumption with respect to GNP.

4.6.2.2 Model Estimation

The following are the estimated steel consumption functions based on the model form given in equation (4.15) and the general model form expressed in equation (4.17). The relevant statistical test values and the value of the estimated long run elasticity are given along with each estimated function. These models are estimated on 19 years data (1959 to 1977) and are given below.

Model 1 :

$$\ln S_t = -0.2594 + \underset{(1.56)}{0.3166} \ln Y_t + \underset{(4.55)}{0.6607} \ln S_{t-1} \quad ...(4.23)$$

$\bar{R}^2 = 0.82$; $DW = 1.42$; $h = 1.633$;

ESS $= 0.1804$; V(e) $= 0.0113$;

$E = 0.93$.

ESS denotes the sum of error squares (residual squares).

This model is not acceptable in case of India as the long-run elasticity (E) is less than unity.

Model 2 :

$$\ln S_t = -0.3527 + \underset{(1.48)}{0.3358} \ln Y_t + \underset{(4.09)}{0.6492} \ln S_{t-1} - 0.1628 \dot{Y}_t \quad ...(4.24)$$

$\bar{R}^2 = 0.81$; $DW = 1.42$; $h = 1.753$;

$ESS = 0.1799$; $V(e) = 0.012$;

$E = 0.96$.

This model is not acceptable because :

i. E is less than unity;
ii. Unexpected sign of the coefficient of Y ; and
iii. h-statistic has a value higher than the critical value at 95 per cent level of confidence, which is ± 1.645.

Model 3 :

$$\ln S_t = -0.5383 + \underset{(1.74)}{0.4251}\ln Y_t + \underset{(3.21)}{0.5696}\ln S_{t-1}$$

$$-\underset{(-0.64)}{0.5498}\dot{Y}_t - \underset{(-1.00)}{0.8292}\dot{}_{t-1} \tag{4.25}$$

$\bar{R}^2 = 0.81; DW = 1.25; h = 2.570;$

$ESS = 0.1679; V(e) = 0.012;$

$E = 0.9572.$

This model is not acceptable because :

i. E is less than unity;

ii. Unexcepted signs of the coefficients of $\dot{Y}_t$ and $\dot{Y}_{t-1}$; and

iii. h-statistic value is above the critical limit.

Model 4 :

$$\ln S_t = 0.2414 + \underset{(0.81)}{0.1956}\ln Y_t + \underset{(4.21)}{0.7394}\ln S_{t-1}$$

$$+\underset{(0.15)}{0.1215}\dot{Y}_t + \underset{(0.22)}{0.1877}\dot{Y}_{t-1} + \underset{(2.19)}{1.5817}\dot{Y}_{t-2} \tag{4.26}$$

$\bar{R}^2 = .85; DW = 1.74; h = 0.881;$

$ESS = 0.1226; V(e) = 0.0094;$

$E = 0.75$

This model is not acceptable because :

i. E is less than unity; and

ii. Estimated coefficient of ln Y_t is statistically insignificant, which is an unexpected result.

Model 5 :

$$\ln S_t = 0.1499 + \underset{(0.78)}{0.1862} \ln Y_t + \underset{(4.34)}{0.7543} \ln S_{t-1}$$

$$\underset{(0.37)}{0.3019} \dot{Y}_t + \underset{(0.55)}{0.4916} \dot{Y}_{t-1} + \underset{(2.51)}{1.9652} \dot{Y}_{t-2} + \underset{(1.17)}{0.8209} \dot{Y}_{t-3} \quad (4.27)$$

$\bar{R}^2 = 0.85; DW = 1.96; h = 0.133;$

$ESS = 0.1101; V(e) = 0.0092;$

$E = 0.76.$

This model is also not acceptable because of the same reasons as given in case of Model 4.

Model 6 :

$$\ln S_t = -0.1799 + \underset{(1.07)}{0.2315} \ln Y_t + \underset{(4.61)}{0.7280} \ln S_{t-1}$$

$$+ \underset{(0.58)}{0.4360} \dot{Y}_t$$

$$\underset{(0.92)}{0.7534} \dot{Y}_{t-1} + \underset{(3.19)}{2.3575} \dot{Y}_{t-2} + \underset{(2.00)}{1.4265} \dot{Y}_{t-3} + \underset{(1.90)}{1.2339} \dot{Y}_{t-4} \quad (4.28)$$

$\bar{R}^2 = 0.88; DW = 2.44; h = -1.311;$

$ESS = 0.0829; V(e) = 0.0075; E = 0.85.$

This model is also not acceptable because of the same reasons as given in case of Model 4.

Model 7 :

$$\ln S_t = -1.0970 + \underset{(2.02)}{0.3680} \ln Y_t + \underset{(4.95)}{0.6483} \ln S_{t-1}$$

$$+ \underset{(1.64)}{1.0619} \dot{Y}_t + \underset{(1.97)}{1.3911} \dot{Y}_{t-1} + \underset{(4.64)}{2.9780} \dot{Y}_{t-2}$$

$$\underset{(3.55)}{2.4967} \dot{Y}_{t-3} + \underset{(3.48)}{2.3320} \dot{Y}_{t-4} + \underset{(2.63)}{1.7486} \dot{Y}_{t-5}$$

$$\bar{R}^2 = 0.92;\ DW = 2.35;\ h = -0.903; \qquad (4.29)$$

$$ESS = 0.049;\ V(e) = 0.0049;$$

$$E = 1.05.$$

With the addition of Y_{t-5} as an independent variable, there are many changes over the previous models as listed below :

i. The estimated coefficients of all the independent variables are significant at 95 per cent level of confidence (except that of $\dot{Y}_t$, which is significant at 90 per cent level of confidence);
ii. $\bar{R}^2$ attains the maximum value as compared to the six previous models;
iii. Long term elasticity (E) attains a value greater than unity;
iv. ESS and V(e) show a sudden and steep decline; and
v. h-statistic lies within the critical limits at 95 per cent level of confidence.

The above merits of Model 7 clearly indicate that this model describes the behaviour of steel consumption in India vis-a-vis its GNP in a plausible manner. This model is straightaway acceptable, on strength of its own merits, as the best fit model.

Model 7 clearly explains the lagged effect of growth rate of GNP on steel consumption and also the length of this lag. Apart from current year's level of GNP and last year's level of steel consumption, the current year's steel consumption is also determined by the growth rates of GNP during the current and the five immediately preceding years. The impact curve exhibiting the impact coefficients of GNP growth rates during these years on current year's level of steel consumption is of inverted-V type as shown in Fig. 4.7.

Fig. 4.7 Impact of Current and Lagged GNP Growth Rates on Current Steel Consumption

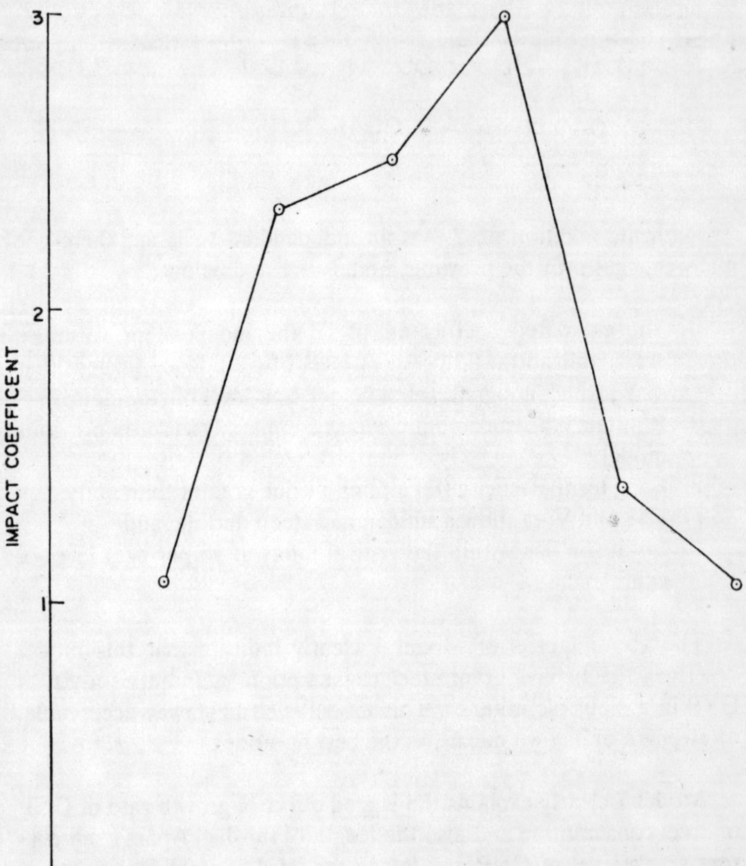

The impact coefficients are the coefficients of current and lagged GNP growth rates as estimated in equation (4.30). The impact coefficient corresponding to the variable $\dot{Y}_{t-i}$ may be defined as the elasticity of steel consumption with respect to the ratio of Y_{t-i} to Y_{t-i-1} (i varies from 0 to 5).

It is clear from Fig. 4.7 that if the impact of growth rates of GNP on steel consumption is analysed from $\dot{Y}_t$ backwards, the impact goes on increasing and $\dot{Y}_{t-2}$ has the maximum impact on current steel consumption. This impact gradually decreases corresponding to the years t-3, t-4 and t-5. This also implies that the growth rate of GNP during the current year shall continue to have an impact on the level of steel consumption during the next five years and the third future year shall experience this impact with maximum intensity.

To examine the sensitivity of the model, it may be important to test as to what happens to Model 7 when $\dot{Y}_{t-6}$ is added as an additional independent variable. The estimated results are given below :

Model 8 :

$$\ln S_t = -0.6769 + \underset{(1.42)}{0.2981} \ln Y_t + \underset{(4.70)}{0.6920} \ln S_{t-1}$$

$$+ \underset{(1.58)}{1.0519} \dot{Y}_t + \underset{(1.52)}{1.1839} \dot{Y}_{t-1} + \underset{(3.57)}{2.7075} \dot{Y}_{t-2}$$

$$+ \underset{(2.58)}{2.1813} \dot{Y}_{t-3} + \underset{(2.07)}{1.8973} \dot{Y}_{t-4} + \underset{(1.41)}{1.3031} \dot{Y}_{t-5}$$

$$- \underset{(-0.72)}{0.5336} \dot{Y}_{t-6}$$

$$\bar{R}^2 = 0.92; DW = 2.39; h = -1.081; \tag{4.30}$$

$$ESS = 0.0463; V(e) = 0.0051;$$

$$E = 0.97.$$

It can be easily seen that the strength and merits of Model 7 start breaking down as soon as the variable Y_{t-6} is added as an independent variable. It may be observed that :

i. Elasticity (E) becomes less than unity;
ii. The coefficient of ln Y_t becomes statistically insignificant;

iii. Residual variance, V(e), increases;
iv. The coefficient of $\dot{Y}_{t-6}$ has an unexpected sign; and
v. The coefficients of $\dot{Y}_{t-1}$ and Y_{t-5} are now significant only at 90 per cent level of confidence.

The above weaknesses seem to have arisen from the possibility that Y_{t-6} is an irrelevant variable in explanation of the current year's level of steel consumption and that the form specified in Model 7 is the truth under Indian conditions.

Apart from these weaknesses, a degree of freedom is lost without any extra benefit. Thus, there is absolutely no benefit gained by adding $\dot{Y}_{t-6}$ as an independent variable to the form specified in Model 7. Model 7 is, therefore, validated and its authenticity further reinforced. Thus, it is now clear that the growth rate of GNP during a particular year can have a meaningful impact on the steel consumption during the next five years.

In order to increase the number of degrees of freedom, the form specified in Model 7 is estimated on 22 years data of steel consumption (1956 to 1977). The estimated model is given below :

Model 7A :

$$\ln S_t = -1.6571 + \underset{(1.85)}{0.3673} \ln Y_t + \underset{(5.69)}{0.7109} \ln S_{t-1}$$

$$+ \underset{(1.63)}{1.1166} \dot{Y}_t + \underset{(2.30)}{1.7559} \dot{Y}_{t-1} + \underset{(4.25)}{3.0361} \dot{Y}_{t-2}$$

$$+ \underset{(3.34)}{2.5846} \dot{Y}_{t-3} + \underset{(3.04)}{2.2559} \dot{Y}_{t-4} + \underset{(2.14)}{1.5576} \dot{Y}_{t-5} \quad (4.31)$$

$$\bar{R}^2 = 0.94; DW = 1.85; h = 0.434;$$

$$ESS = 0.08; V(e) = 0.0062; E = 1.2704.$$

The results are quite similar to the ones obtained in case of Model 7. Model 7A as estimated in equation (4.32) has all the merits of Model 7 as estimated in equation (4.30). Further, the degrees of freedom have increased from 10 to 13.

To ensure that the Model 7A is still the most appropriate model estimated on 22 years data (1956 to 1977) of steel consumption, following two experiments are done :

i. Study the effect of deleting the variable $\dot{Y}_{t-5}$ from the form estimated in equation (4.32); and

ii. Study the effect of adding the variable $\dot{Y}_{t-6}$ to the form estimated in equation (4.32).

The estimated equation, when the variable $\dot{Y}_{t-5}$ is deleted from the form specified for Model 7A, is given below :

Model 6A :

$$\ln S_t = -0.7396 + \underset{(1.18)}{0.2518} \ln Y_t + \underset{(5.56)}{.7637} \ln S_{t-1}$$

$$+ \underset{(0.83)}{0.5935} \dot{Y}_t + \underset{(1.39)}{1.0916} \dot{Y}_{t-1} + \underset{(3.32)}{2.4594} \dot{Y}_{t-2}$$

$$+ \underset{(2.30)}{1.6310} \dot{Y}_{t-3} + \underset{(1.94)}{1.2621} \dot{Y}_{t-4}$$

$$\bar{R}^2 = 0.93;\ DW = 2.14;\ h = -0.429; \qquad (4.32)$$

$$ESS = 0.1083;\ V(e) = 0.0077;$$

$$E = 1.0658.$$

The model form estimated in equation (4.33) has the following weaknesses :

i. The coefficients of $\ln Y_t$ and $\dot{Y}_t$ are statistically insignificant;

ii. V(e) shows an increase; and

iii. $\bar{R}^2$ declines marginally.

Fig. 4.8 Observed Versus Estimated Steel Consumption in India During 1956 to 1977 (Equation (4.32))

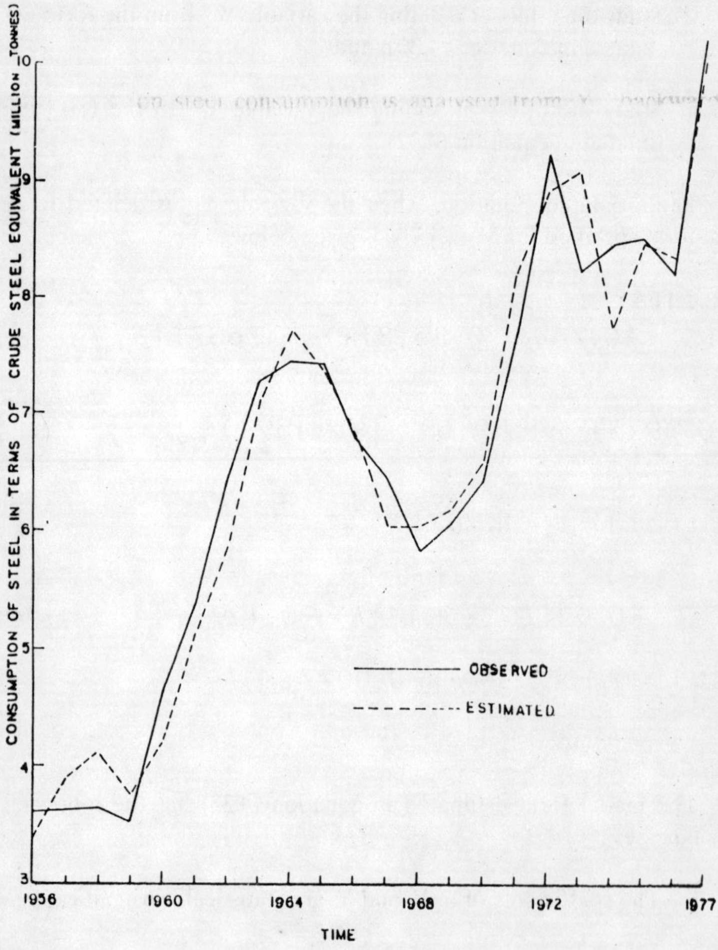

Thus, model form estimated in equation (4.33) is not acceptable when compared to the one estimated in equation (4.32).

The effect of adding the variable $\dot{Y}_{t-6}$ to the form specified for Model 7 is estimated below :

Model 8A :

$$\ln S_t = -1.0401 + \underset{(1.15)}{0.2613} \ln Y_t + \underset{(5.40)}{0.7787} \ln S_{t-1}$$

$$+ \underset{(1.61)}{1.1061} \dot{Y}_t + \underset{(1.75)}{1.4549} \dot{Y}_{t-1} + \underset{(3.23)}{2.6525} \dot{Y}_{t-2}$$

$$+ \underset{(2.30)}{2.1129} \dot{Y}_{t-3} + \underset{(1.63)}{1.6257} \dot{Y}_{t-4} + \underset{(0.93)}{0.9227} \dot{Y}_{t-5}$$

$$- \underset{(-0.95)}{0.7621} \dot{Y}_{t-6} \qquad (4.33)$$

$$\bar{R}^2 = 0.94;\ DW = 1.89;\ h = 0.350;$$

$$ESS = 0.0744;\ V(e) = 0.0062;$$

$$E = 1.1808.$$

The model form estimated equation (4.34) has certain weaknesses as compared to one estimated in equation (4.32), as enumerated below :

i. The coefficients of In Y_t and $\dot{Y}_{t-5}$ are statistically insignificant;
ii. Sign of the coefficient of $\dot{Y}_{t-6}$ is not as expected; and
iii. A degree of freedom is lost at no extra gain in $\bar{R}^2$ or V(e).

Going through the above analysis, it may be concluded that Model 7A, as estimated in equation (4.32), is the most appropriate representation of the steel consumption function (in terms of GNP of India) in Indian economy.

The behaviour of the observed apparent steel consumption of India (in terms of crude steel equivalent) and that of the estimated one from equation (4.32) are shown in Fig. 4.8.

4.7 ESTIMATING A GNP FUNCTION FOR INDIAN ECONOMY

As observed earlier from equation (4.11), the GNP of India has grown exponentially over time as shown in Fig. 4.4.

It is assumed that the GNP function is of the following general form :

$$Y_t = f\left(Y_{t-1}, \dot{Y}_{t-1}, \dot{Y}_{t-2}, \ldots, \dot{Y}_{t-i}, \ldots, \dot{Y}_{t-n}\right) \tag{4.34}$$

To be more specific, the following general form has been assumed :

$$\ln Y_t = \alpha + \beta_1 \ln Y_{t-1} + \sum_{i=1}^{n} \beta_{i+1} \dot{Y}_{t-1} \tag{4.35}$$

In estimating an appropriate GNP function a similar strategy is adopted as was done for estimating the steel consumption function under sub-section 4.6.2. The growth rates of GNP in the past years are successively added as independent variables and the effects analysed.

Initially, various models are tried on 19 years data (1959 to 1977) because in this case also the number of appropriate lags in the past are not known a priori. The following are the results of estimating various model forms (t=1 for 1959, and t = 19 for 1977) :

Model I :

$$\ln Y_t = -0.0300 + \underset{(21.37)}{1.0064} \ln Y_{t-1}$$

$$\bar{R}^2 = 0.96;\ DW = 2.47;\ h = -1.042; \tag{4.36}$$

$$ESS = 0.0245;\ V(e) = 0.0014.$$

Model II :

$$\ln Y_t = -0.0037 + \underset{(21.81)}{1.0050} \ln Y_{t-1} - \underset{(-1.33)}{0.3161} \dot{Y}_{t-1}$$

$$\bar{R}^2 = 0.96;\ DW = 2.02;\ h = -0.044; \tag{4.37}$$

$$ESS = 0.0220;\ V(e) = 0.0014$$

Model III :

$$\ln Y_t = -0.0304 + \underset{(21.31)}{1.0083} \ln Y_{t-1} - \underset{(-1.43)}{0.3721} \dot{Y}_{t-1} - \underset{(-0.61)}{0.1518} \dot{Y}_{t-2} \tag{4.38}$$

$$\bar{R}^2 = 0.96; DW = 1.94; h = 0.134;$$

$$ESS = 0.0215; V(e) = 0.0014.$$

Model IV :

$$\ln Y_t = 0.0053 + \underset{(20.88)}{1.0059} \ln Y_{t-1} - \underset{(-1.55)}{0.4228} \dot{Y}_{t-1} - \underset{(-0.84)}{0.2341} \dot{Y}_{t-2} - \underset{(-0.73)}{0.2024} \dot{Y}_{t-3} \tag{4.39}$$

$$\bar{R}^2 = 0.96; DW = 1.96; h = 0.089; ESS = 0.0207; V(e) = 0.0015.$$

Model V :

$$\ln Y_t = 0.0441 + \underset{(20.37)}{1.0035} \ln Y_{t-1} - \underset{(-1.63)}{0.4621} \dot{Y}_{t-1} - \underset{(1.00)}{0.2966} \dot{Y}_{t-2} - \underset{(-0.94)}{0.2930} \dot{Y}_{t-3} - \underset{(-1.68)}{0.1963} \dot{Y}_{t-4} \tag{4.40}$$

$$\bar{R}^2 = 0.96; DW = 2.06; h = -0.134;$$

$$ESS = 0.0200; V(e) = 0.0015$$

Model VI

$$\ln Y_t = 0.2552 + \underset{(22.74)}{0.9880} \ln Y_{t-1} - \underset{(-2.41)}{0.6196} \dot{Y}_{t-1} - \underset{(-1.74)}{0.4696} \dot{Y}_{t-2} - \underset{(-1.93)}{0.5748} \dot{Y}_{t-3} - \underset{(-1.77)}{0.5035} \dot{Y}_{t-4} - \underset{(-2.26)}{0.5984} \dot{Y}_{t-5} \tag{4.41}$$

$$\bar{R}^2 = 0.97; DW = 2.12; h = -0.266;$$

$$ESS = 0.0140; V(e) = 0.0012.$$

Model VII :

$$\ln Y_t = 0.3639 + \underset{(21.75)}{0.9806} \ln Y_{t-1} - \underset{(-2.47)}{0.7314} \dot{Y}_{t-1}$$

$$- \underset{(-1.88)}{0.5999} \dot{Y}_{t-2} - \underset{(2.06)}{0.6809} \dot{Y}_{t-3} - \underset{(-1.89)}{0.6607} \dot{Y}_{t-4}$$

$$- \underset{(-2.28)}{0.7535} \dot{Y}_{t-5} - \underset{(-0.80)}{0.2546} \dot{Y}_{t-6} \qquad (4.42)$$

$$\bar{R}^2 = 0.97;\ DW = 2.08;\ h = -0.178;$$

$$ESS = 0.0132;\ V(e) = 0.0012.$$

Model VIII :

$$\ln Y_t = 0.5043 + \underset{(22.01)}{0.9730} \ln Y_{t-1} - \underset{(-2.72)}{0.7947} \dot{Y}_{t-1}$$

$$- \underset{(-2.32)}{0.8259} \dot{Y}_{t-2} - \underset{(-2.48)}{0.9091} \dot{Y}_{t-3} - \underset{(-2.31)}{0.8756} \dot{Y}_{t-4}$$

$$- \underset{(-2.66)}{1.0406} \dot{Y}_{t-5} - \underset{(-1.44)}{0.5676} \dot{Y}_{t-6} - \underset{(-1.29)}{0.4145} \dot{Y}_{t-7} \qquad (4.43)$$

$$\bar{R}^2 = 0.97;\ DW = 1.96;\ h = 0.089;$$

$$ESS = 0.0114;\ V(e) = 0.0011.$$

Model IX :

$$\ln Y_t = 0.5657 + \underset{(20.31)}{0.9693} \ln Y_{t-1}$$

$$- \underset{(-2.53)}{0.8341} \dot{Y}_{t-1} - \underset{(-2.17)}{0.8734} \dot{Y}_{t-2}$$

$$- \underset{(-2.09)}{0.9998} \dot{Y}_{t-3} - \underset{(-1.97)}{0.9674} \dot{Y}_{t-4} \qquad (4.44)$$

$$- \underset{(2.28)}{1.1283} \dot{Y}_{t-5} - \underset{(-1.26)}{0.6761} \dot{Y}_{t-6}$$

$$- \underset{(-1.13)}{0.5106} \dot{Y}_{t-7} - \underset{(-0.32)}{0.1165} \dot{Y}_{t-8}$$

$$\bar{R}^2 = 0.97;\ DW = 1.88;\ h = -0.421;$$

$$ESS = 0.0112;\ V(e) = 0.0013.$$

Before starting a discussion regarding the above estimated model forms of GNP function for Indian economy, it may be mentioned that the DW-statistic corresponding to the exponential trend equation (4.11) of the GNP of India is 2.01. This value of the DW-statistic is a proof of the fact that error terms in equation (4.11) are not serially correlated. Thus, even though the behaviour of GNP exhibits cyclical fluctuations around its trend, as shown in Fig. 4.4, the cycles are of random nature.

The nine models which have been estimated, as given in equations (4.37) through (4.45), are an attempt in search of a model which can best explain the trend and random behaviour of the GNP. It is readily admitted that the above trials do not claim to be an exercise in the well established theory of distributed lag models. However, these trials attempt to capture the random component of the behaviour of GNP over time in the best possible manner.

As far as Model I is concerned, theoretically, there is nothing wrong when it is estimated in equation (4.37). The coefficient of the independent variable is statistically significant, $\bar{R}^2$ is quite high, and the error terms are not serially correlated, as is clear from the value of the h-statistic. In fact, the main aim of the above trial is to reduce the residual variance, V(e), to the minimum possible value. Even though the residual sum of squares (ESS) necessarily decreases with addition of a variable, the residual variance, V(e), need not, because V(e) takes into consideration information about the degrees of freedom (128). In fact, there is a one-to-one correspondence between the two statistics, $\bar{R}^2$ and V(e), because of the definition of $\bar{R}^2$. The search for a GNP function with the minimum possible V(e) is important because the steel consumption function estimated in equation (4.32) contains Y_t and $\dot{Y}_{t-i}$ (i = 0, 1, ..., 5) as independent variables. Thus, when the simulation of the system is undertaken, any errors in the simulated GNP series for future shall pass on to the simulated series of future steel consumption requirements. It is, therefore, necessary that only that GNP function should be accepted in which the estimated GNP series follows the observed one as closely as possible, even though some cost may have to be paid in the form of losing some degrees of freedom or in the form of not following the rigorous norms of the theory of distributed lag models.

The forms estimated in equations (4.38) through (4.41) are not accepted because the residual variance goes up by approximately 7 per cent. The $\bar{R}^2$ seems to have remained constant at 0.96 because the specified values are given with only two significant digits after the decimal point. Moreover, most of the estimated coefficients are not statistically significant in these model forms (Model II to Model V).

Model VI, as estimated in equation (4.42), shows a sudden improvement over the previous ones. The residual variance declines by approximately 20 per cent as compared to estimated Model V and all the estimated coefficients become significant at 90 per cent level of confidence.

When the estimated equations of the forms, as specified in Models VII, VIII and IX, are analysed, it is found that Model VIII is the ideal representation of the GNP function. Model VII is not accepted because the estimated coefficient of $\dot{Y}_{t-6}$ is not statistically significant in equation (4.43) and moreover, the residual variance can further be reduced in the next model. Model IX is also not accepted as the value of residual variance goes up by approximately 18 per cent in equation (4.45) as compared to the residual variance of equation (4.44), and a degree of freedom is also lost. Model VIII as estimated in equation (4.44), seems to be the best fit model. Out of the nine estimated model forms, equation (4.44) has the minimum residual variance. It goes down by approximately 8 per cent as compared to that of equation (4.43) of Model VII, and by approximately 21 per cent as compared to equation (4.37) of Model I. All the estimated coefficients in equation (4.44) are statistically significant at 95 per cent level of confidence, except the ones corresponding to $\dot{Y}_{t-6}$ and $\dot{Y}_{t-7}$. However, the coefficient of $\dot{Y}_{t-6}$ is significant at 80 per cent and that of $\dot{Y}_{t-7}$ at 70 per cent levels of confidence.

In order to increase the number of degrees of freedom, the form specified in Model VIII is estimated on 24 years data of GNP (1956 to 1979). The estimated model is given below :

Fig. 4.9 Observed Versus Estimated GNP of India During 1956 to 1979 (Equation (4.46))

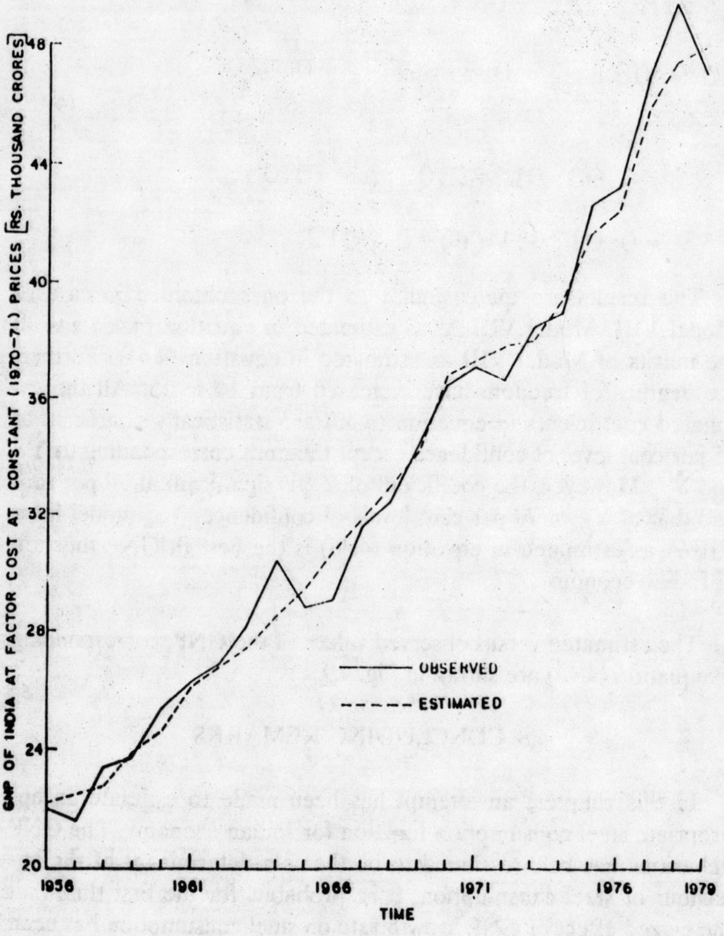

Model VIII A :

$$\ln Y_t = 0.2303 + \underset{(33.73)}{0.9994} \ln Y_{t-1} - \underset{(-3.33)}{0.8456} \dot{Y}_{t-1}$$

$$- \underset{(-2.77)}{0.8664} \dot{Y}_{t-2} - \underset{(-2.41)}{0.8055} \dot{Y}_{t-3} - \underset{(-3.08)}{0.9807} \dot{Y}_{t-4}$$

$$- \underset{(-2.77)}{0.9708} \dot{Y}_{t-5} - \underset{(-1.91)}{0.6182} \dot{Y}_{t-6} - \underset{(-1.14)}{0.3307} \dot{Y}_{t-7} \quad (4.45)$$

$$\bar{R}^2 = 0.98; DW = 2.02; h = -0.05;$$

$$ESS = 0.0174; V(e) = 0.0012.$$

The results are quite similar to the ones obtained in case of Model VIII. Model VIII-A, as estimated in equation (4.46) has all the merits of Model VIII as estimated in equation (4.44). Further, the degrees of freedom have increased from 10 to 15. All the estimated coefficients in equation (4.46) are statistically significant at 95 per cent level of confidence except the ones corresponding to $\dot{Y}_{t-6}$ and $\dot{Y}_{t-7}$. However, the coefficient of $\dot{Y}_{t-6}$ is significant at 90 per cent and that of $\dot{Y}_{t-7}$ at 70 per cent levels of confidence. The model form VIII-A as estimated in equation (4.46) is the best fit GNP function of Indian economy.

The estimated versus observed values of the GNP, corresponding to equation (4.46) are shown in Fig. 4.9.

4.8 CONCLUDING REMARKS

In this chapter, an attempt has been made to estimate an appropriate steel consumption function for Indian economy. The GNP behaviour has been assumed to be the sole determinant of the behaviour of steel consumption. It is, probably, for the first time that the lagged effect of GNP growth rate on steel consumption has been analysed. The consumption function estimated in this chapter will be used to simulate the future steel requirements of Indian economy. A GNP function has also been estimated which will simulate the future GNP behaviour of India. This sub-model will be dovetailed into the overall simulation model of Indian steel industry in Chapter VI.

FIVE

THE STEEL PRODUCTION SUB-MODEL

5.1 INTRODUCTION

The theory of production attempts to analyse the behaviour of a firm in combing the services of various productive inputs in order to produce a pre-determined quantity of a particular commodity at minimum cost. The basic concepts of the theory are assumed to be the same when it is used in an aggregate manner in case of an industry. Two sets of issues are involved in this process :

i. Characteristics of the commodity and the input markets; and

ii. Technical constraints which limit the range of feasible productive processes.

As far as the first set of issues is concerned, the present study assumes that there is perfect competition in both commodity and input markets. This assumption is necessary to facilitate the analysis, in spite of its being too simplistic. Most of the studies which analyse the production process of a firm or an industry, implicitly make this assumption.

The second set of issues with reference to Indian steel industry is, in fact, the subject matter of the present chapter. The technical constraints faced by Indian steel industry may be analysed with the help of two different approaches which are dual to each other, namely production function approach and cost function approach.

The concepts of a production function and an aggregate production function, evolution of the theory of production function along with the recent developments in this theory have already been discussed and reviewed in Chapter II. The concept of a cost function was also introduced in Chapter II.

There are two broad classes of production functions, fixed and variable-proportions production functions. In case of a fixed proportions production function, each level of output technologically requires a unique combination of inputs. The production process is characterised by fixed input coefficients if the technologically determined input-output ratio is independent of the scale of production for each input and the production function is homogeneous of degree one. The fixed-proportions production function is homogeneous if all the pairs of input ratios are constant even though the input-output ratios are not independent of scale.

A variable-proportions production function is one in which the same level of output may be produced by two or more combinations of inputs. Variable-proportions production functions are always assumed to be smoothly continuous for the sake of convenience (46). The essential technological feature of variable-proportions is preserved under the above assumption, i.e. one input may be substituted for another while maintaining a constant level of output. It may, however, be mentioned that the production coefficients are still 'fixed' due to economic considerations (say, cost minimisation), given a set of input prices.

The time-series of output and various inputs in Indian steel industry, for the period 1951 to 1977, are already given in Tables 3.1 and 3.2. It may be observed that over the period of 27 years, output of steel in India has gone up by 6.5 times, labour-input by 3.25 times, capital-input by 13.13 times, fuels-input has roughly doubled and raw-materials input has gone up by 5.22 times. It may be inferred from this analysis that the production process in Indian steel industry is of variable proportions type.

The present chapter formulates and estimates the cost minimising demand functions for various inputs and the relevant cost function. An approximate production function has also been derived corresponding to the estimated cost function.

5.2 SOME BASIC CONCEPTS IN PRODUCTION FUNCTION THEORY

5.2.1 Average and Marginal Productivity of a Factor of Production

A typical production function, as described in equation (2.2), may be written in the following form :

$$Q = F(\overline{X}, t) \tag{5.1}$$

where,

Q is the output;

$\vec{x}$ is the vector of services of various inputs, x_1, x_2, ..., x_n (there are n inputs; x_i denotes the service of the ith input $\overline{X} = X_i$); and

t denotes time (it is assumed that technological progress is a function of time).

The average productivity (AP) of a factor of production, say, X_i, is defined as the ratio between total output, Q, and the quantity of input X_i, such that :

$$AP_i = \frac{Q}{X_i} \tag{5.2}$$

The marginal productivity (MP) of input X_i is defined as the ratio between changes in output (resulting from a very small change in the quantity of X_i) and the change in x_i, keeping all other factors constant, such that :

$$MP_i = \frac{\partial Q}{\partial x_i} \tag{5.3}$$

The average and marginal productivities of a factor of production, say X_i, are related to its output elasticity. The output elasticity of X_i, denoted by W_i, is defined as the proportionate rate of change of Q with respect to X_i, such that

$$w_i = \frac{\partial Q / Q}{\partial x_i / x_i} = \frac{x_i \, \partial Q}{Q \, \partial x_i} = \frac{MP_i}{AP_i} \tag{5.4}$$

Output elasticity of an input may, thus, be expressed as a ratio between its marginal and average productivities. W_i is positive if MP_i and AP_i are positive. W_i may be greater than, equal to or less than unity if the corresponding MP_i is respectively greater than, equal to or less than AP_i.

5.2.2 Rate of Technical Substitution and Elasticity of Substitution

The rate of technical substitution (RTS) or the marginal rate of substitution is the rate at which an input X_i must be substituted for X_j (or X_j for X_i), the levels of all other inputs as well as the level of output remaining the same, that is :

$$RTS_{ij} = -\frac{\partial x_j}{\partial x_i} \tag{5.5}$$

If the levels of X_i and X_j are so altered that the level of output does not change (the levels of all other inputs remaining the same), then,

$$dQ = dx_i \left(\frac{\partial Q}{\partial x_i} \right) + dx_j \left(\frac{\partial Q}{\partial x_j} \right) = 0 \tag{5.6}$$

The equation (5.6) implies that :

$$-\frac{\partial x_j}{\partial x_i} = -\frac{\partial Q / \partial x_i}{\partial Q / \partial x_j} = -\frac{MP_i}{MP_j} = RTS_{ij} \tag{5.7}$$

The marginal rate of substitution (or RTS) as a measure of the degree of substitutability of factors has a serious defect as it depends on the units of measurement of the factors. A better measure of the ease with which two factors may be substituted is provided by the elasticity of substitution. The elasticity of substitution (σ_{ij}) between factors X_i and X_j is defined as the percentage change in the ratio of the quantities of two inputs, divided by the percentage change in RTS_{ij}, all other inputs remaining at the same level, that is,

$$\sigma_{ij} = \frac{\text{Percentage change in } X_j / X_i}{\text{Percentage change in } RTS_{ij}} \tag{5.8}$$

5.3 LAWS OF PRODUCTION

5.3.1 Long Run Analysis of Production

The level of output can be increased in various technically possible ways. In the long run, output can be increased by changing all factors of production, while, in the short run, only the use of variable factors can be increased, while fixed capital (and may be some other factors) does not change.

Long run analysis of production is a study of laws of returns to scale. It is in the long run that all the factors of production may be varied and the effects of scale relationships become important. All the factors of production may be varied in the same proportion or in different proportions. The term 'returns to scale' refers to the changes in output when all factors change in the same proportion.

A production function is homogeneous such that if each of the inputs is multiplied by a real number, say k, then k can be completely factored out of the function. The power h of k is called the degree of homogeneity of the function and is a measure of the returns to scale.

Let,

$$Q = f(x_1, x_2, \ldots, x_n) \tag{5.9}$$

The technological change is not being considered here, and if,

$$Q k^h = f(kx_1, kx_2, \ldots., kx_n). \tag{5.10}$$

then, the function 'f' given in equation (5.9) is homogeneous of degree h.

The production function, 'f', exhibits :

i. constant returns to scale if $h = 1$;

ii. decreasing returns to scale if $h < 1$; and

iii. increasing returns to scale if $h > 1$.

If k cannot be completely factored out of the function 'f', then the production function is non-homogeneous.

5.3.2 Short Run Analysis of Production

It is not possible to alter the level of fixed capital (buildings, plant and machinery, etc.) in the short run. Such inputs are called fixed inputs. If the level of a variable input, say X_i, is increased (keeping the other inputs at fixed levels), then, both average productivity and marginal productivity of X_i(AP_i and MP_i) increase and then decline. This is the almost universal law of diminishing marginal productivity, i.e. MP_i shall eventually decline as x_i is slowly increased, keeping the levels of all other inputs unchanged. This law is not applicable if the levels of two or more inputs are increased simul taneously.

The basic theory of production usually concentrates on the range of output over which marginal productivities of factors, although positive, decrease. Alternatively, the theory of production concentrates on levels of employment of the factors over which their marginal productivities are positive but decreasing (92).

If the production function is homogeneous with constant or decreasing returns to scale, the variable factors must exhibit diminishing productivities. In case there are increasing returns to scale, the diminishing returns from a variable factor may be offset if returns to scale are considerable. However, the productivity of a single variable factor is generally diminishing, all other things remaining constant.

5.4 TECHNOLOGICAL PROGRESS AND PRODUCTION FUNCTION

The existing technology provides all the technical information about the combination of inputs necessary for production of a predetermined quantity of output. It includes all physical possibilities. A given combination of various productive inputs may be utilised in a number of different ways under the existing technology and these can yield a number of different output levels. The production function differs from technology as it pre-supposes technical efficiency and defines the maximum output obtainable from every possible input combination. The best utilisation of a given input combination is a technical and not an economic problem. The selection of the best input combination to produce a given level of output is done in order to minimise the total cost of production and is the subject of economic analysis.

Technology itself is variable and it changes as knowledge of new and more efficient methods of production becomes available. Furthermore, the efficiency of all existing methods of production may increase as a result of new inventions. Some of the existing techniques become obsolete and are dropped out. These changes in technology constitute technological progress. As already mentioned in Chapter II, the technological progress has been assumed to be a function of time, in the case of the present study.

There are two general types of technological changes - neutral and non-neutral (15).

A neutral technical change neither saves nor uses a particular input, say X_i; it is one which causes a variation in the production relation itself but does not affect the rate of technical substitution between factors X_i and X_j.

A non-neutral technical change alters the production function and saves one factor at the cost of the other. Consider a production function in which there are only two factors of production, capital and labour. If the production function is altered in such a way that the marginal productivity of capital rises relative to the marginal productivity of labour for each combination of capital and labour, this is considered to be a capital-using (labour-saving) technological change. A capital-saving change occurs when the rate of technical substitution of labour for capital is lowered at every combination of capital and labour (66).

5.5 COST FUNCTION AND INPUT DEMAND FUNCTIONS

5.5.1 Introduction

The duality relation between production and cost functions has been discussed in detail in Chapter II. Under the cost minimising conditions, it is possible to deduce either of the two functions, given the other. It may again be emphasised that a cost function contains all the information necessary to reconstruct the structure of production possibilities of the production system under consideration.

Consider that a firm (or an industry) chooses to utilise the service of n inputs ($X_1, X_2, ..., X_n$) to produce an output level of, say, $\bar{Q}$ The total cost to the firm (or industry) is given as follows :

$$C = \sum_{i=1}^{n} p_i x_i \tag{5.11}$$

where,

C = total cost of production Q;

p_i = price of input X_i; and

x_i = level of input X_i.

A rational firm (or industry) shall aim to choose the levels of various inputs ($x_1, x_2, ..., x_n$) such that the total cost, C, is minimised subject to the production function constraint given in equation (5.1).

5.5.2 Some Properties of Cost Minimising Input Demand Functions

The input demand functions may be written in the following general form :

$$x_i = g_i\left(\overline{Q}, p_1, p_2, \ldots, p_n\right) \tag{5.12}$$

for i=1, 2, ..., n.

where x_i is the demand for the ith input in order to produce $\overline{Q}$.

Assuming that the firm (or industry) under consideration behaves in a rational manner as explained in sub-section 5.5.1 (i.e. attempts to produce $\overline{Q}$ at minimum cost), then, Dixon et al. (39) have shown that the input demand functions as given in equation (5.12) exhibit the following properties :

i. Homogeneity Restriction :

The input demand functions are homogeneous of degree zero in prices, i.e. for any $\alpha > 0$,

$$g_i\left(\overline{Q}, \alpha p_1, \alpha p_2, \ldots, \alpha p_n\right) = g_i\left(\overline{Q}, p_1, p_2, \ldots, p_n\right) \quad \ldots. \tag{5.13}$$

The homogeneity restriction implies that if the prices of all the inputs increase (or decrease) in the same proportion, all other things remaining the same, the firm (or industry) sees no reason to alter the pre price-change cost minimising inputs combination.

The homogeneity restriction may be established as follows :

$$\sum_{j=1}^{n} \frac{\partial g_i}{\partial p_j} p_j = 0 \text{ ; for } i = 1, 2.., n \tag{5.14}$$

ii. Symmetry Restriction

$$\frac{\partial g_i}{\partial p_j} = \frac{\partial g_j}{\partial p_i} \text{ ; for all } i \neq j \tag{5.15}$$

iii. Case of Linear Homogeneous Production Function

If the production function, F, given in equation (5.1) is homogeneous of degree one (constant returns to scale) then g_i is homogeneous of degree one in Q. The input demand functions may be written as :

$$x_i = \overline{Q} G_i(p_1, p_2, \ldots, p_n); \text{for all i} \quad (5.16)$$

iv. Own Price Substitution Effect

The own price substitution effect is non-positive, that is :

$$\frac{\partial g_i}{\partial p_i} \leq; \text{for all i} \quad (5.17)$$

5.5.3 Some Properties of Cost Functions

Let the minimum cost of producing the output Q be given by

$$C = C(\overline{Q}, p_1, p_2, \ldots, p_n) \quad (5.18)$$

Dixon et al. (39) have shown that the following properties hold good for such a cost function :

i. C is a non-decreasing function of Q and the p_i's. It is homogeneous of degree one in prices, i.e.

$$C(\overline{Q}, \alpha p_1, \alpha p_2, \ldots, \alpha p_n) = \alpha C(\overline{Q}, p_1, p_2, \ldots, p_n)$$

$$\text{for any } \alpha > 0. \quad (5.19)$$

ii. If the production function, 'f', is homogeneous of degree one, then, the input demand functions, g_i's, are homogeneous of degree one in $\overline{Q}$. Hence, it can be shown that C is homogeneous of degree one with respect to Q, i.e.

$$C(\alpha \overline{Q}, p_1, p_2, \ldots, p_n) = \alpha C(\overline{Q}, p_1, p_2, \ldots, p_n)$$

$$\text{for any } \alpha > 0. \quad (5.20)$$

iii. It can be shown that the Shephard's lemma holds good, i.e.

$$\frac{\partial C(\overline{Q}, p_1, p_2, \ldots, p_n)}{\partial p_i} = g_i(\overline{Q}, p_1, p_2, \ldots, p_n) \tag{5.21}$$

$$= x_i \text{ for all i}$$

where x_i is the cost minimising level of ith input.

5.6 DIRECT SPECIFICATION OF INPUT DEMAND FUNCTIONS

One of the most important purposes of analysing a production function is to derive the corresponding input demand functions. Given the production function (or cost function), the input demands can be derived which explain the variations in various input demands with respect to the changes in levels of output and prices of inputs.

The difficulty in deriving the input demand functions from a given production function has already been explained in sub-section 2.3.4. The input demand functions may, however, be easily derived from a cost function by applying the Shephard's lemma as expressed in equation (5.21).

The input demand functions derived from a production function (or cost function) may be quite restrictive and of not much practical use. This is so because there are some limitations in the estimation of a production function (or cost function). These limitations arise because of the use of the method of ordinary least squares, since it is a case of estimating a single equation. Further, certain restrictions are implicitly imposed on the elasticities of substitution between different inputs when a pre-specified form of production function (or cost function) is estimated. These limitations and restrictions are passed on to the derived input demand functions.

As mentioned in sub-section 2.3.4, a recent step in the generalisation of production function forms is the introduction of flexible forms. In case of a flexible form, no prior restrictions are imposed on the elasticities of substitution between different inputs except those which arise from their definition or from assumption of optimising behaviour. The translog form is the most flexible form. The limitation of using this form is that only input share equations can be estimated and not the input demand equations.

Thirsk (148) has used a direct specification of input demand functions in his study on factor substitution in Colombian agriculture using cross-section data. The theoretical specification of his model is as given in the following equation :

$$x_i(t) = K_i Q(t) \left(\prod_{j=1}^{n} p_j(t)^{\eta_{ij}} \right) \epsilon_i(t) \tag{5.22}$$

for $i = 1, 2, \ldots, n$.

where K_i and η_{ij} are the parameters to be estimated; η_{ij} is the elasticity of demand for the ith input with respect to changes in the price of the jth input. $X_i(t)$, $Q(t)$ and $P_j(t)$ are the t-th observations of the level of farm use of the ith input, the level of farm output and price of the jth input. $\epsilon_i(t)$ is a disturbance term with an expected value of unity. In order to get more precise parameter estimates, Thirsk (148) imposed, a priori, the following cost minimising restrictions :

i. Homogeneity Restriction :

$$\sum_{j=1}^{n} \eta_{ij} = 0 \text{; for all i} \tag{5.23}$$

This result is obtained by applying the homogeneity restriction given in equation (5.14) to the input demand specification given in equation (5.22), as shown below :

$$\frac{\partial g_i}{\partial p_j} = \frac{\partial x_i}{\partial p_j} = \frac{\eta_{ij}}{p_j} x_i \text{; for all i.} \tag{5.24}$$

Substituting equation (5.24) into equation (5.14), it may be seen that :

$$\sum_{j=1}^{n} \frac{\eta_{ij}}{p_j} x_i p_j = 0 \text{; for all i}$$

It implies that,

$$\sum_{j=1}^{n} \eta_{ij} = 0 \text{ ; for all i}$$

which is the same as equation (5.23).

ii. Symmetry Restriction :

$$\frac{\eta_{ij}}{\overline{S}_j} = \frac{\eta_{ji}}{\overline{S}_i} \text{ ; for all } i \neq j \tag{5.25}$$

where S_i is the average over all observations of the cost share of the ith input. Thus,

$$\overline{S}_i = \frac{1}{T} \sum_{t=1}^{T} \left(\frac{p_i(t)\, x_i(t)}{\sum_{j=1}^{T} p_j(t)\, x_j(t)} \right) \tag{5.26}$$

where T is the number of farms.

The result expressed in equation (5.25) is obtained by modifying the symmetry restriction given in equation (5.15). The numerator and the denominator of the left hand side of equation (5.15) are both multiplied by P_j and those of the right hand side by P_i. Both the sides are also multiplied by $C/g_i\, g_j$ to obtain the following result :

$$\frac{\partial g_i}{\partial p_j} \cdot \frac{p_j}{g_i} \cdot \frac{C}{g_j p_j} = \frac{\partial g_j}{\partial p_i} \cdot \frac{p_i}{g_j} \cdot \frac{C}{g_i p_i} \tag{5.27}$$

Equation (5.27) implies that :

$$\frac{\eta_{ij}}{\overline{S}_j} = \frac{\eta_{ji}}{\overline{S}_i} \text{ ; for all } i \neq j$$

which is same as equation (5.25).

The specification for input demand functions given in equation (5.22) is very useful from an econometric point of view as it is linear in logs. This specification has been criticised as it has not been derived from an underlying model in which cost minimising input demand functions are estimated subject to a production function constraint. This criticism of the said specification is, however, not well founded. The inputs chosen according to this specification shall minimise the cost of producing a given output level as both the restrictions of cost minimisation (homogeneity and symmetry) have been imposed, a priori, on this specification. In fact, the relevant cost function may easily be derived using equation (5.11) and the production function can be worked back once the input demand equations have been estimated. The limitation of the cost and production functions thus estimated is that these are more accurate when the cost shares of various inputs are closer to their respective means over all observations.

5.7 ESTIMATING INPUT DEMAND FUNCTIONS IN INDIAN STEEL INDUSTRY

A specification similar to the one used by Thirsk (148), given in equation (5.22), has been used to estimate the input demand functions in Indian steel industry. There are two major differences between the two specifications. Firstly, Thirsk assumes the production function to be homogeneous of degree one and, as a corollary, each input demand function is homogeneous of degree one in output. The present study does not a priori make this assumption. Secondly, Thirsk uses cross-section data which is not so in case of the present study as it is a study at industry level and not of different steel manufacturing units. This study uses the time-series data and 't' in equation (5.22) refers to the time-period of one year.

Three different theoretical specifications are conceived of in case of Indian steel industry and are given as follows :

Specification 1 :

$$x_i(t) = K_i Q(t)^{\eta_{iQ}} \left(\overset{n}{\underset{j=1}{\pi}} p_j(t)^{\eta_{ij}} \right) \epsilon_i(t) \tag{5.28}$$

for i = 1,2, ..., n

Specification 2 :

$$x_i(t) = K_i Q(t)^{\eta_{iQ}} \left(\prod_{j=1}^{n} p_j(t)^{\eta_{ij}} t^{\eta_{it}} \epsilon_i(t) \right) \tag{5.29}$$

for i = 1, 2, ..., n

Specification 3 :

$$x_i(t) = K_i Q(t)^{\eta_{iQ}} \left(\prod_{j=1}^{n} p_j(t)^{\eta_{ij}} e^{r_i t} \epsilon_i(t) \right) \tag{5.30}$$

for i = 1, 2, ..., n

The interpretation of all the specifications is similar to that given for the specification expressed in equation (5.22) except for the following additional parameters :

η_{iQ} : elasticity of demand for the ith input with respect to the changes in output;

η_{it} : elasticity of demand for the ith input with respect to the change in time; and

r_i : exponential trend in the demand for ith input.

These specifications can also be written in the following log linear forms :

Specification 1 :

$$\ln x_i(t) = A_i + \eta_{iQ} \ln Q(t) + \sum_{j=1}^{n} \eta_{ij} \ln p_j(t) + E_i(t) \tag{5.31}$$

Specification 2 :

$$\ln x_i(t) = A_i + \eta_{iQ} \ln Q(t) + \sum_{j=1}^{n} \eta_{ij} \ln p_j(t) + \eta_{ij} \ln t + E_i(t) \tag{5.32}$$

Specification 3 :

$$\ln x_i(t) = A_i + \eta_{iQ} \ln Q(t) + \sum_{j=1}^{n} \eta_{ij} \ln p_j(t)$$

$$+ r_i t + E_i(t) \quad (5.33)$$

where

$A_i = \ln K_i$;

$E_i(t) = \ln(\epsilon_i(t))$;

$\ln$ is an abbreviation for natural logarithm.

The present chapter analyses the production behaviour of Indian steel industry during the period 1951 to 1977. The time series of production of steel in India is identified in terms of crude steel equivalent as given in Table 3.1. Various inputs which interact with one another to produce steel have been divided into four major categories, namely labour, capital, fuels and raw-materials. The identified series of the levels of these inputs are given in Table 3.2 and are denoted by L, K, F and M, respectively. The identified input price series are denoted by P_L, P_K, P_F and P_M, respectively and are given in Table 3.3.

It may be observed from Tables 3.1 and 3.2 that the raw-materials are being transformed into output at a more or less fixed conversion ratio. The elasticity of raw-materials usage with respect to the changes in output is nearly equal to unity as shown by the estimated coefficient of the independent variable ln Q(t) in the following equation:*[1]

$$\ln M(t) = 1.6635 + 0.9343 \ln Q(t) \quad (5.34)$$

$\bar{R} = 0.96$

The similar equations in case of the other three inputs are as given below :

---

1. * The equations estimated in this chapter use the data in the form specified in Tables 3.1, 3.2 and 3.3.

$$\ln L(t) = 2.9340 + 0.6335 \ln Q(t)$$
$$\bar{R}^2 = 0.92 \tag{5.35}$$

$$\ln K(t) = -1.2269 + 1.4688 \ln Q(t)$$
$$\bar{R}^2 = 0.97 \tag{5.36}$$

$$\ln F(t) = -0.5146 + 0.5566 \ln Q(t)$$
$$\bar{R}^2 = 0.90 \tag{5.37}$$

It may be observed that the estimated coefficient of ln Q(t) is not near unity in any of the above three inputs. Thus, the raw-materials variable seems to be a dominant variable with respect to output if all the four factors of production are considered to be mutually substitutable. In fact, raw-materials may not be substitutable with any of the other three inputs. The inclusion of a dominant variable leaves no room for the effects of the other inputs to be significant. The inclusion of a dominant variable cannot be ascertained on a priori basis and it must be ascertained by investigation as there is no rule of thumb which can solve this problem (128).

To begin with, it is assumed that there exists a production function with all the four inputs being mutually substitutable. This type of production function may be written in the following functional form :

$$Q = F(L, K, F, M) \tag{5.38}$$

To increase the precision of the parameter estimates of the specifications given in equations (5.31), (5.32) and (5.33) some restrictions are imposed a priori. Three different sets of restrictions are attempted and their validity tested with the help of an F-test (93). In the four-inputs case the average cost shares during 1951 to 1977 are as given below :

$S_L = 0.1786$; $S_K = 0.2200$; $S_F = 0.1210$; and $S_M = 0.4804$

such that,

$$\bar{S}_L + \bar{S}_K + \bar{S}_F + \bar{S}_M = 1 \tag{5.39}$$

The following are the three alternative restriction sets :

Restriction Set A :

a. Cost Minimising Restrictions

i. Homogeneity Restriction as given in equation (5.23) ; and
ii. Symmetry Restriction as given in equation (5.25).

b. Linear Homogeneous Production Function, that is, η_{iQ} is unity for all i (as was assumed by Thirsk (148)).

Restriction Set B :

a. Cost Minimising Restrictions : Same as under Restriction Set A(a) ; and

b. Homogeneous Production Function, that is, $\eta_{iQ} > 0$ and is same for all i.

Restriction Set C :

Only Cost Minimising Restrictions : Same as under Restriction Set A(a).

Firstly, one may consider the specification 1 as given in equation (5.31) and test the validity of each of the three restriction sets with reference to the identified series of output, four inputs and the corresponding input prices as given in Tables 3.1, 3.2 and 3.3. The same is then repeated for specifications 2 and 3 as given in equations (5.32) and (5.33), respectively. Each of the three specifications comprises four equations if the production function is assumed to have a form as given in equation (5.38). The simultaneous estimation and testing of the validity of different restriction sets was done by using 'Zellner's Seemingly Unrelated Regressions Technique' (166) under SYSREG (Systems Regression) procedure of SAS (Statistical Analysis System) software (64) available in IBM-360 computer system of University of Delhi.

While testing the validity of a restriction set on a particular specification the null hypothesis to be tested is as follows :

H_o : all restrictions are true;

against the alternative hypothesis

H_1 : not all restrictions are true.

The null hypothesis, H_o, is accepted if the F*-value (F-ratio calculated with the help of SAS software) is less than the critical F-value at the chosen level of signficance (5 per cent or 1 per cent) corresponding to the degrees of freedom in the numerator and denominator (n_1 and n_2, respectively). It is concluded that the restrictions are compatible with the observed ones in the real world data. The null phypothesis is, however, rejected if the F*-value is greater than the critical F-value. It is, then, concluded that the restrictions are not supported by the sample (93).

TABLE 5.1
Tests of Validity of Various Restriction Sets with regard to Specification 1 (4-inputs case)

Restriction Set	n_1	n_2	$F_{0.05}$ (n_1, n_2)	$F_{0.01}$ (n_1, n_2)	F*
A	14	84	1.81	2.31	18.80
B	13	84	1.84	2.36	18.87
C	10	84	1.94	2.54	7.16

TABLE 5.2
Tests of Validity of Various Restriction Sets with regard to Sepcification 2 (4 inputs case)

Restriction Set	n_1	n_2	$F_{0.05}$ (n_1, n_2)	$F_{0.01}$ (n_1, n_2)	F*
A	14	80	1.82	2.32	4.94
B	13	80	1.85	2.37	5.16
C	10	80	1.95	2.55	3.62

TABLE 5.3
Tests of Validity of Various Restriction Sets with regard to Specification 3 (4-inputs case)

Restriction Set	n_1	n_2	$F_{0.05}(n_1, n_2)$	$F_{0.01}(n_1, n_2)$	F*
A	14	80	1.82	2.32	15.60
B	13	80	1.85	2.37	11.31
C	10	80	1.95	2.55	8.03

The F-statistic depends on two parameters: the number of restrictions, n_1 (called the number of degrees of freedom in the numerator), and the number of degrees of freedom of the equations-set in the specification when no restrictions are imposed on their estimation, n_2 (called the number of degrees of freedom in the denominator). As the n_1 and n_2 change, the distribution of F-statistic changes when the null-hypothesis is true. Under the assumption that the errors are normally distributed, the theoretical properties of F-statistic follow Snedecor's F-distribution values of n_1 and n_2 (128).

Table 5.1 shows the estimated F*-values when the validity of the three alternative restriction sets is tested with regard to specification 1 given in equation (5.31). Tables 5.2 and 5.3 specify the similar F*-values with regard to the specifications 2 and 3 given in equations (5.32) and (5.33), respectively.

It is observed from Table 5.1 that F*-values estimated in case of all the three restriction sets are greater than the corresponding critical F-values not only at 5 per cent level of signficance but even at 1 per cent level of significance. Thus, all the restrictions given under restriction set A are not true and compatible with the ones observed in the real world data with regard to specification 1. The same may be said regarding the restrictions given under restriction sets B and C, respectively.

Tables 5.2 and 5.3 exhibit the similar phenomena in case of specifications 2 and 3, respectively, as explained for Table 5.1, with regard to specification 1.

Thus, none of the theoretical specifications given in equations (5.31), (5.32) and (5.33) is acceptable when all the four inputs (L, K, F and M) are assumed to be mutually substitutable with one another.

This result strengthens the observation that the raw-materials are being transformed into output of steel at a more or less fixed conversion ratio and are, therefore, a dominant variable in explaining the output of steel when all the four inputs are considered together in the explanation of steel production in India.

A restrictive assumption on the structure of production in Indian steel industry is hence required to be made. It is assumed that captial, labour and fuels are, as a group, weakly separable from the fourth input, raw-materials. Weak separability implies that the marginal rate of substitution between any two of the first three inputs (L, K and F) is independent of the quantity of raw-materials used (125). This is a necessary and sufficient condition for the production function to be of the following form :

$$Q = F(f(L, K, F); M) \tag{5.40}$$

This implies that the production function in Indian steel industry is of three-input type and the demand for raw-materials depends upon the quantity of steel to be produced and the existing technology, such that :

$$M = M(Q, t) \tag{5.41}$$

Each of the three specifications given in equations (5.31), (5.32) and (5.33) now comprises of three equations only as the production function form now assumed is as given in equation (5.40). The validity of the three restriction sets (A, B and C) is separately tested with regard to each of the three specifications. In this case, the average cost shares during 1951 to 1977 are as given below :

$$\bar{S}_L = 0.3458; \bar{S}_K = 0.4166; \text{and} \quad \bar{S}_F = 0.2376$$

such that,

$$\bar{S}_L + \bar{S}_K + \bar{S}_F = 1 \tag{5.42}$$

Tables 5.4, 5.5 and 5.6 are similar to the Tables 5.1, 5.2 and 5.3, except that these correspond to the three-input type of production function instead of the earlier four-input type.

It may be observed from Tables 5.4, 5.5 and 5.6 that neither of the restriction sets A and B is true and compatible with the restrictions observed in the real world data with regard to the three specifications. The restrictions under restriction set C are also not supported by the observed data with regard to specification 1. However, it is observed that these restrictions are true when tested with regard to specifications 2 and 3. The validity of restriction set C with regard to specification 2 is upheld at 1 per cent level of significance (Table 5.5) and at 5 per cent level of significance with regard to specification 3 (Table 5.6) as the F*-values are less than the corresponding critical F-values.

TABLE 5.4

Tests of Validity of Various Restriction Sets with regard to Specification 1 (3-inputs case)

Restriction Set	n_1	n_2	$F_{0.05}(n_1, n_2)$	$F_{0.01}(n_1, n_2)$	F*
A	9	66	2.02	2.70	15.60
B	8	66	2.08	2.79	16.26
C	6	66	2.24	3.09	3.76

TABLE 5.5

Tests of Validity of Various Restriction Sets with regard to Specification 2 (3-inputs case)

Restriction Set	n_1	n_2	$F_{0.05}(n_1, n_2)$	$F_{0.01}(n_1, n_2)$	F*
A	9	63	2.03	2.71	6.06
B	8	63	2.09	2.80	5.92
C	6	63	2.24	3.09	2.31

TABLE 5.6
Tests of Validity of Various Restriction Sets with regard to Specification 3 (3-inuts case)

Restriction Set	n_1	n_2	$F_{0.05}$ (n_1, n_2)	$F_{0.01}$ (n_1, n_2)	F*
A	9	63	2.03	2.71	9.04
B	8	63	2.09	2.80	6.45
C	6	63	2.24	3.09	1.53

It may, thus, be concluded that under the assumption that Indian steel industry aims at cost minimisation, the acceptable form of production function is as given in equation (5.40). The production function is non-homogeneous as both the restriction sets A and B, which include the assumption that production function is homogeneous, are not validated with regard to any of the three specifications. It may also be concluded that technology (assumed to be a function of time) is a significant variable in the production function of Indian steel industry as restriction set C is validated with regard to the specifications 2 and 3 and both these specifications include the time variable which is assumed to represent the state of technology.

The estimated input demand equations when cost minimising restriction set C is imposed on specification 2 are given as follows:

$$\begin{aligned}\ln L(t) = {} & 2.1616 + \underset{(7.14)}{0.6969} \ln Q(t) \\ & - \underset{(-3.17)}{0.2063} \ln P_L(t) \\ & + \underset{(2.02)}{0.0694} \ln P_k(t) + \underset{(2.42)}{0.1369} \ln P_F(t) \\ & - \underset{(-0.49)}{0.0335} \ln t\end{aligned} \tag{5.43}$$

$$\begin{aligned}\ln K(t) = {} & 0.0063 + \underset{(11..19)}{1.2434} \ln Q(t) \\ & + \underset{(2.02)}{0.0576} \ln P_L(t)\end{aligned}$$

$$+\underset{(-3.96)}{0.0995}\ln P_k(t)+\underset{(1.88)}{0.0419}\ln P_F(t)$$

$$+\underset{(1.55)}{0.0959}\ln t \tag{5.44}$$

$$\ln F(t) = -1.8977+\underset{(9.98)}{0.9148}\ln Q(t)$$

$$+\underset{(2.42)}{0.1993}\ln P_L(t)$$

$$+\underset{(1.88)}{0.0734}\ln P_k(t)-\underset{(-3.2)}{0.2727}\ln P_F(t)$$

$$-\underset{(-2.97)}{0.1669}\ln t \tag{5.45}$$

The value given in parenthesis below an estimated coefficient is its t-ratio value.

Weighted R^2 for the system = 0.95

Weighted MSE for the system = 1.4326
(69 degrees of freedom)

MSE is the abbreviated form of Mean Square Error.

Equations (5.43), (5.44) and (5.45) constitute the estimated Model I.

When the restriction set C is imposed on specification 3, the estimated input demand equations are given as follows:

$$\ln L(t) = 3.8444+\underset{(4.79)}{0.4912}\ln Q(t)$$

$$-\underset{(-2.64)}{0.1586}\ln P_L(t)$$

$$+\underset{(2.22)}{0.0909}\ln P_k(t)+\underset{(1.67)}{0.0677}\ln P_F(t)$$

$$-\underset{(2.14)}{0.0187}\,t \tag{5.46}$$

$$\ln K(t) = \underset{}{1.6591} + \underset{(8.87)}{1.0960} \ln Q(t) + \underset{(2.22)}{0.0754} \ln P_L(t)$$

$$- \underset{(-0.03)}{0.0011} \ln P_k(t) - \underset{(-2.45)}{0.0743} \ln P_F(t)$$

$$- \underset{(3.39)}{0.0351}\, t \tag{5.47}$$

$$\ln F(t) = -\ 1.4438 + \underset{(6.85)}{0.6479} \ln Q(t)$$

$$+ \underset{(1.17)}{0.0986} \ln P_L(t)$$

$$- \underset{(-2.45)}{0.1303} \ln P_k(t) + \underset{(0.28)}{0.0317} \ln P_F(t)$$

$$- \underset{(-2.38)}{0.0207}\, t \tag{5.48}$$

Weighted R^2 for the system = 0.95

Weighted MSE for the system = 1.3448

(69 degrees of freedom)

Equations (5.46), (5.47) and (5.48) constitute the estimated Model II.

Out of the two estimated models, Model I appears to be more appropriate as compared to Model II. Firstly, the coefficient of ln $P_F(t)$ in equation (5.47) of Model II is negative implying thereby that capital and fuels are complements. On the contrary, it may be observed from Table 3.2 that the technology in Indian steel industry has been highly capital using and saves on labour and fuels. Capital and fuels are, thus, expected to be substitutes and not complements. Secondly, the coefficient of ln $P_F(t)$ in equation (5.48) of Model II is positive (even though statistically insignificant) implying thereby that steel industry may demand a higher quantity of fuels when their price increases, all other things remaining the same. This is a result contrary to the intuition and the common law of demand.

The estimated Model I has no such weaknesses. The signs of all the estimated coefficients are as expected and statistically significant. The three inputs (L, K and F) are substitutable with one another. The estimated coefficient of time variable is negative (even though statistically insignificant) in equation (5.43). This coefficient is negative in equation (5.45) also. However the coefficient of time variable is positive in equation (5.44). These results imply that the technology in Indian steel industry has been capital using and has saved on labour and fuels. This is a fact observed in Indian steel industry.

The above analysis puts forward ample evidence in favour of the production function form specified in equation (5.40). It may also be concluded that the production function is non-homogeneous and there is a non-neutural technical change (as explained in section 5.4) in Indian steel industry.

The demand function form for raw-materials is already specified in equation (5.41). The following are the two different models of raw-materials demand estimated on the basis of the functional form specified in equation (5.41):

$$\ln M(t) = 2.8692 + \underset{(7.58)}{0.7642} \ln Q(t) + \underset{(1.50)}{0.0150}\, t$$

$$\bar{R}^2 = 0.96 \tag{5.49}$$

$$\ln M(t) = 1.0295 + \underset{(12.09)}{1.0355} \ln Q(t) - \underset{(-1.31)}{0.874} \ln t$$

$$\bar{R}^2 = 0.96 \tag{5.50}$$

The model estimated in equation (5.49) is not acceptable as the coefficient of time variable is positive which means that there have been raw-materials wastages over time. The model estimated in equation (5.50) is acceptable because of the following reasons :

i. The coefficient of ln Q(t) is nearly equal to unity proving thereby the proportionality between M and Q; and
ii. The coefficient of time variable is negative.

Thus, the cost minimising demand functions for all the four inputs have been directly estimated in the present section.

5.8 WORKING BACK THE PRODUCTION FUNCTION FROM THE ESTIMATED INPUT DEMAND FUNCTIONS

An approximate production function may be worked back from the estimated cost minimising input demand functions given in equations (5.43), (5.44) and (5.45) by using a method similar to the one suggested by Dixon et al. (39). The production function thus derived is a local approximation in the region where the input cost shares are close to their respective average values over all observations. As one moves away from the average cost shares, the symmetry restriction given in equation (5.25) is violated.

The cost function may be formulated by substituting the estimated input demand functions into equation (5.11). In order to do this, the estimated input demand functions corresponding to labour, capital and fuels have to be converted into the specification form mentioned in equation (5.29) by taking the exponentials of both left and right hand sides of each of the equations (5.43), (5.44) and (5.45), respectively. The cost function may now be written as follows:

$$C = 8.6849\,Q(t)^{0.6969}\,P_L(t)^{0.7937}\,P_K(t)^{0.0694}$$

$$P_F(t)^{0.1369}\,t^{-0.0335} + 1.0063\,Q(t)^{1.2434}$$

$$P_L(t)^{0.0576}\,P_K(t)^{0.9005}\,P_F(t)^{0.0419}\,t^{0.0959}$$

$$+\,0.1499\,Q(t)^{0.9148}\,P_L(t)^{0.1993}\,P_K(t)^{0.0734}$$

$$P_F(t)^{0.7273}\,t^{-0.1669} \tag{5.51}$$

Given the existing technology, the cost C in equation (5.51) represents the minimum cost of producing the output Q(t). Conversely, given the cost constraint and the existing input prices, Q(t) is the maximum output that can be produced.

It may be assumed that there is a restriction that total cost to be incurred on the three inputs is equal to one rupee, such that, C = Re. 1.

The respective shares of labour, captial and fuels in the total cost during the year t may be written in the following way :

$$S_L(t) = \frac{P_L(t)L(t)}{C(t)} = P_L(t)L(t) \tag{5.52}$$

$$S_K(t) = \frac{P_K(t)K(t)}{C(t)} = P_K(t)K(t) \tag{5.53}$$

$$S_F(t) = \frac{P_F(t)F(t)}{C(t)} = P_F(t)F(t) \tag{5.54}$$

as C(t) = Re. 1.

It has been assumed in Section 5.7 that the input cost shares remain equal to their respective averages over all observations. It follows, therefore, that :

$$S_L(t) = \overline{S}_L = 0.3458 \tag{5.55}$$

$$S_K(t) = \overline{S}_K = 0.4166 \tag{5.56}$$

$$S_F(t) = \overline{S}_F = 0.2376 \tag{5.57}$$

for all t.

Substituting these values of $S_L(t)$, $S_K(t)$ and $S_F(t)$ into equations (5.52), (5.53) and (5.54), respectively, it follows that:

$$P_L(t) = \frac{0.3458}{L(t)} \tag{5.58}$$

$$P_K(t) = \frac{0.4166}{K(t)} \tag{5.59}$$

$$P_F(t) = \frac{0.2376}{F(t)} \tag{5.60}$$

Substituting these values of $P_L(t)$, $P_K(t)$ and $P_F(t)$ into equation (5.51) along with the restriction C(t) = 1, it follows that :

$$\frac{2.89\,Q(t)^{0.6969}\,t^{-0.0335}}{L(t)^{0.7937}\,K(t)^{0.0694}\,F(t)^{0.1369}}$$

$$+\frac{0.4051\,Q(t)^{1.2434}\,t^{0.0959}}{L(t)^{0.0576}\,K(t)^{0.9005}\,F(t)^{0.0419}}$$

$$+\frac{0.04\,Q(t)^{0.9148}\,t^{-0.1669}}{L(t)^{0.1993}\,K(t)^{0.0734}\,F(t)^{0.7273}}=1 \qquad \text{.......(5.61)}$$

Equation (5.61) may be written in the following form:

$$A(t)Q(t)^{0.6969}+B(t)Q(t)^{1.2434}$$

$$+C(t)(Q(t))^{0.9148}-1=0 \qquad (5.62)$$

Where A(t), B(t) and C(t) are functions of the levels of three inputs used and the technology (time), such that :

$$A(t)=\frac{2.89\,t^{-0.0335}}{L(t)^{0.7937}\,K(t)^{0.0694}\,F(t)^{0.1369}} \qquad (5.63)$$

$$B(t)=\frac{0.4051\,t^{0.0959}}{L(t)^{0.0576}\,K(t)^{0.9005}\,F(t)^{0.0419}} \qquad (5.64)$$

$$C(t)=\frac{0.04\,t^{-0.1669}}{L(t)^{0.1993}\,K(t)^{0.0734}\,F(t)^{0.7273}} \qquad (5.65)$$

Given the availabilities of the three inputs (L, K and F), the value of Q(t) computed from equation (5.62) is the maximum output that can be produced. In accordance with the concept of production function as defined in sub-section 2.3.1, equation (5.62) represents the production function corresponding to the input demand functions given in equations (5.43), (5.44) and (5.45). It may be observed that the output, Q(t), is not an explicit function of the levels of three inputs and time. Given the availability of three inputs during a particular year, Q(t) may be calculated such that the left hand side of equation (5.62) is equal to zero. It is implicitly assumed that raw-materials are always available according to their demand function given in equation (5.50). The production function thus derived will be validated in the subsequent chapter.

5.9 CONCLUDING REMARKS

The production structure of Indian steel industry has been analysed in the present chapter. The basic concepts and characteristics underlying a typical production function and its dual, the cost function, have been discussed. The main emphasis is on formulation and estimation of cost minimising input demand functions. These functions are directly estimated under the cost minimising restrictions, thus avoiding the difficulties and limitations of deriving the input demand functions from an estimated production or cost function. It is found that labour, capital and fuels are mutually substitutable with one another and are, as a group, weakly separable from raw-materials. Raw-materials requirement depends upon the level of steel production and the technology. The production function in Indian steel industry is found to be a non-homogeneous function of labour, capital and fuels. There has been a non-neutral technical change which is capital using, labour saying and fuels saving. The production sub-model developed in this chapter will be incorporated in the simulation model to be developed in the subsequent chapter.

SIX

SIMULATION MODEL OF INDIAN STEEL INDUSTRY

6.1 INTRODUCTION

The present chapter is concerned with the development of a computer simulation model of Indian steel industry. This is an economic application of the simulation technique because the language of economists, economic theory, has been used as a basis to analyse the system of Indian steel industry. The simulation of an economic system begins with a verbal description of the system, which is then translated into a set of mathematical models (142). The most popular way to translate the verbal description into mathematical models has been the use of econometric models which provide the least ambiguous descripion of the economic system under consideration (26). A simulation model is then formulated, based on the estimates of the econometric models.

As is true with any non-laboratory science, controlled experimentation and testing are very difficult in the study of an economic system. However, the computers have extended the possibilities of such experimentation and testing. Computer models can be made as complex and realistic as the theory permits, since analytical solutions to these models are not required. Simulation techniques enable one to trace out the consequences of such complex models (26).

It is important to compare econometric models with simulation models in order to understand the similarities and differences between the two. An econometric model describes the economic system with the help of a set of simultaneous equations expressing all the inter-relationships among the measurable economic magnitudes relevant to the system's behaviour (89). The measurable economic magnitudes or the system variables may be classified into two main types - endogenous and exogenous. The endogenous variables are determined within the model of the economic system while the exogenous variables represent the forces outside the confines of this system. Given the econometric model of the system to be simulated, simulation is simply the mathematical solution of the model (124).

Cohen (26, 27) was among the first writers to clearly differentiate between these two forms of analyses. Econometric models are usually interpreted as 'one-period-change' models. The lagged values of the endogenous variables are treated as exogenous variables. The values of the endogenous variables are determined for a given time period and new values would have to be assigned to the lagged endogenous variables in order to determine the values of the endogenous variables for the next period. Thus, an econometric model generally determines changes which take place in an economic system from one period to another (27).

Computer simulation models of economic systems are called 'process-models' and differ from econometric models primarily in the treatment of lagged endogenous variables. The mathematically specified model, together with the observed time paths of exogenous variables, are treated as a closed dynamic system; each period, the values of the lagged endogenous variables are the values generated by the model, not the known or actually observed values (26).

The estimated GNP function and consumption function (Chapter IV) together with the estimated input demand functions (Chapter V) form the core of the econometric model of the system of Indian steel industry. In the present chapter, various sub-models are put together in a logical arrangement and a simulation model of the overall system is developed. The simulation model has been retrospectively validated and has also been used to forecast various endogenous variables upto 2005 A.D.

Fig. 6.1 Flow Chart: Simulation Model of Indian Steel Industry

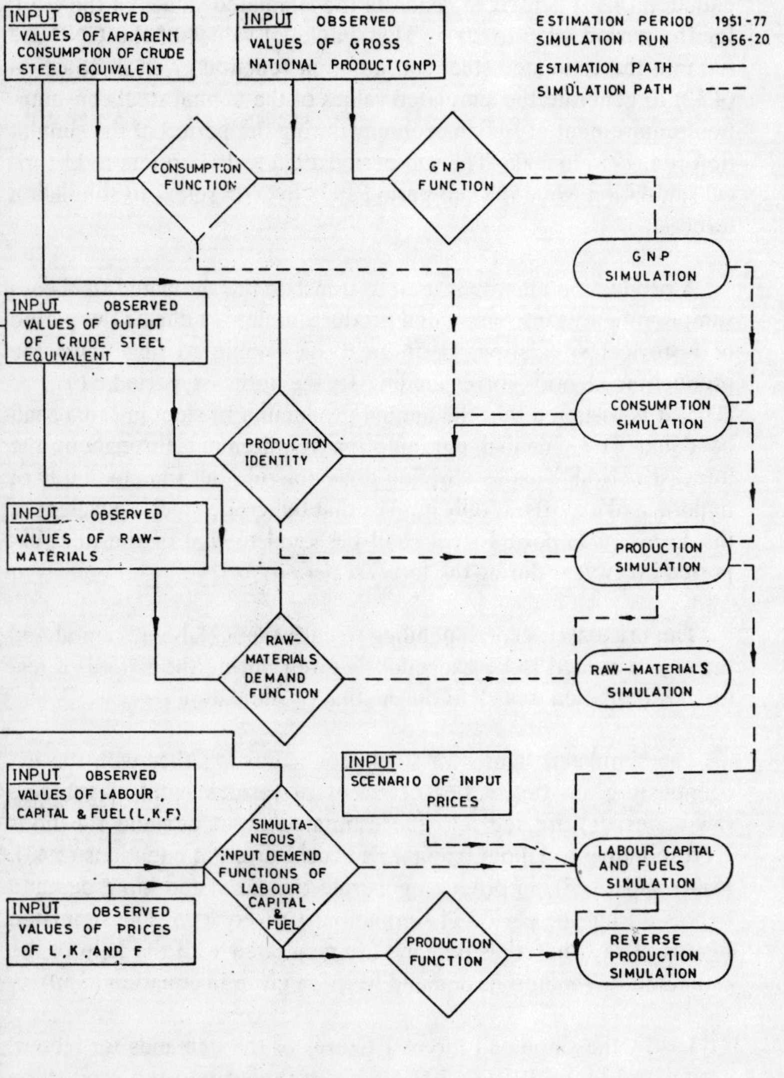

6.2 FLOW CHART OF THE SIMULATION MODEL

A detailed flow-chart of the simulation model used in the present chapter is given in Fig. 6.1. The estimated GNP function given in equation (4.46) is used to generate the simulated values of the GNP for the period 1956 to 2005. The simulated values of the GNP are fed into the estimated steel consumption function given in equation (4.32) to generate the simulated values of the annual steel consumption requirement of Indian economy during the period of the simulation run, 1956 to 2005. The sub-period 1956 to 1977 refers to historical simulation while the sub-period 1978 to 2005 refers to simulation forecast.

A production identity is used to translate the simulated steel consumption figures into simulated production figures during the period of historical simulation, 1956 to 1977. While writing down the production identity corresponding to the forecast period, 1978 to 2005, it is assumed that the annual production of steel in India shall be equal to its annual consumption requirement throughout the forecast period. This assumption does not rule out the possibility of imports and exports. It only implies that the crude steel equivalent of the forms of imported steel shall be equal to that of the ones exported every year during the forecast period.

The price-series corresponding to each input (labour, capital and fuels) is assumed to be exogenously given during the period of historical simulation as well as during that of simulation forecast.

The simulated figures of steel production together with the exogenously given time-series of prices of various inputs (excluding raw-materials) are fed into the estimated input demand functions corresponding to labour, capital and fuels, given in equations (5.43), (5.44) and (5.45), in order to generate the simulated input demand figures during the period of simulation, 1956 to 2005. The simulated figures of raw-materials demand are generated with the help of the estimated raw-materials demand function given in equation (5.50).

Lastly, the simulated forecast figures of the demands for labour, capital and fuels (1956 to 2005) are substituted into the production function that has been derived from the estimated input demand functions (Chapter V). It is assumed that the raw-materials are not a constraint. The estimated figures of steel production are observed to be identical with the simulated production forecast figures. This test validates the derivation of the production function in Chapter V.

The endogenous variables of the simulation model are as given below :

i. GNP
ii. Steel Consumption Requirement
iii. Production of Steel
iv. Demand for Labour
v. Demand for Capital
vi. Demand for Fuels
vii. Demand for Raw-Materials

The exogenous variables are the price series corresponding to the inputs of labour, capital and fuels, respectively.

6.3 GNP SIMULATION

The simulated GNP figures, for the period 1956 to 2005, are generated on the basis of the estimated GNP function given in equation (4.46). In order to facilitate the discussion under this section, the estimated GNP function is reproduced, as follows :

$$\ln Y_t = 0.2303 + 0.9994 \ln Y_{t-1} - 0.8456 \dot{Y}_{t-1}$$

$$- 0.8665 \dot{Y}_{t-2} - 0.8055 \dot{Y}_{t-3} - 0.9807 \dot{Y}_{t-4}$$

$$- 0.9708 \dot{Y}_{t-5} - 0.6182 \dot{Y}_{t-6} - 0.3307 \dot{Y}_{t-7}$$

Where,

Y_t = GNP during the year t ; and

$\dot{Y}_{t-i}$ = growth rate of GNP during the year (t-i) such that it is equal to ($\ln Y_{t-i}$ - $\ln Y_{t-i-1}$), for i = 1,2,...... 7.

It may be observed from the GNP function that in order to generate the simulated Y_{1956} value, the knowledge of the simulated GNP values corresponding to the eight years period prior to 1956 is required, i.e. simulated values of Y_{1948} through Y_{1955}. It may, however, be mentioned that the simulation run begins from 1956 and the simulated GNP values for the years prior to 1956 are not available. It is, therefore, assumed that the simulated Y_{1956} is equal to the Y_{1956} value estimated on the basis of the observed GNP values for the years 1948 through 1955.

In order to generate the simulated Y_{1957}, the observed Y_{1948} is no more required. The observed GNP values of only seven years period, 1949 to 1955, are used and for the eighth year, i.e. 1956, the simulated Y_{1956} is used. Similarly, to generate the simulated Y_{1958} value, only six observed values of GNP are needed (1950 to 1955) and for the remaining two years, 1956 and 1957, the simulated GNP values are utilised. The requirement of the number of observed GNP values gradually goes down as the simulated GNP values for years further ahead of 1958 are generated, and, completely vanishes in case of the year 1964. The simulated Y_{1964} is generated on the basis of the GNP values corresponding to the years 1956 through 1963, all of which are available as simulated figures. Similarly, the simulated Y_{1965} value is arrived at on the basis of the simulated Y_{1957} through Y_{1964}. This process of generating the successive GNP values continues upto the year 2005.

The simulated GNP values corresponding to the period of historical simulation, 1956 to 1977, are given in Table 6.1 and shown in Fig. 6.2. The observed GNP values for the same period are also shown in Fig. 6.2. The simulation forecast of the GNP during the period 1978 to 2005 is given in Table 6.3 and shown in Fig. 6.9.

6.4 SIMULATING STEEL CONSUMPTION REQUIREMENTS

The simulated values of the annual steel consumption requirement of Indian economy are generated for the period 1956 to 2005, on the basis of the estimated steel consumption function given in equation (4.32). In order to facilitate the discussion under this section, the estimated steel consumption function is reproduced, as follows :

$$\ln S_t = -1.6571 + 0.36734 \ln Y_t + 0.7109 S_{t-1} + 1.1166 \dot{Y}_t + 1.7559 \dot{Y}_{t-1} + 3.0361 \dot{Y}_{t-2} + 2.5846 \dot{Y}_{t-3} + 2.2559 \dot{Y}_{t-4} + 1.5576 \dot{Y}_{t-5}$$

where,

S_t = steel consumption requirement for the year t.

All other variables have already been explained in Section 6.3.

In order to generate the simulated S_{1956} value, the knowledge of the simulated S_{1955} value, the simulated Y_{1956} value, and the simulated GNP values corresonding to the six years period prior to 1956 are required, i.e. Y_{1950} through Y_{1955}. As the simulated values corresponding to Y_t and S_t are not available for the years prior to 1956, it is assumed that the simulated S_{1956} value is equal to the S_{1956} value estimated with the knowledge of the simulated Y_{1956} value, observed S_{1955} value, and the observed values of Y_{1950} through Y_{1955}.

The simulated S_{1957} value is generated with the knowledge of the simulated Y_{1957} and S_{1956} values along with the observed values of Y_{1951} through Y_{1955}. As in Section 6.3, the requirement of the number of observed GNP values gradually decreases, as the simulated S_t values for the years further ahead of 1957 are generated, and completely vanishes in case of the year 1962. The simulated S_{1962} value is generated with the knowledge of the simulated S_{1961} value and the simulated GNP values, Y_{1956} through Y_{1962}. The simulated S_{1963} value is generated with the knowledge of the simulated S_{1962} value and the simulated values Y_{1957} through Y_{1963}. This process of generating the successive simulated values of the annual steel consumption requirement continues upto the year 2005.

It may be pointed out that the two simulation programmes explained in sections 6.3 and 6.4 are recursive in nature. The simulation programme of steel consumption requirements can begin only when the GNP values have been simulated for all the years, 1956 through 2005.

The simulated values of the annual steel conumption requirement, corresponding to the period of historical simulation, 1956 to 1977, are given in Table 6.1 and shown in Fig. 6.3. The corresponding observed values are also shown in Fig. 6.3. The simulation forecast of the annual steel consumption requirement during the period 1978 to 2005 is given in Table 6.3 and shown in Fig. 6.10.

6.5 SIMULATING STEEL PRODUCTION

Simulation of the annual steel production values begins only when the simulation programme for steel consumption requirements has completed its run, i.e. when the simulated values of annual steel consumption requirement have been generated for all the years, 1956 through 2005.

The annual simulated production values, corresponding to the period 1956 to 1977, are obtained on the basis of an assumption that the ratio between the simulated production and consumption values is equal to that between the observed production and consumption values, for every year during this period. This is termed as production identity for the period 1956 to 1977 and is given as follows :

$$\frac{Simulated\, Q_t}{Simulated\, S_t} = \frac{Observed\, Q_t}{Observed\, S_t} \qquad (6.1)$$

where,

Q_t = steel production during the year t; and
t = 1956, 1957, ..., 1977.

The simulated S_t values have already been generated as explained in Section 6.4. The simulated Q_t values can, thus, be obtained in the following way :

$$Simulated\,Q_t = \frac{Observed\,Q_t}{Observed\,S_t} \cdot Simulated\,S_t \qquad (6.2)$$

for t = 1956, 1957 1977

The simulated values of the annual steel production, corresponding to the period 1956 to 1977, are given in Table 6.1 and shown in Fig. 6.4. The corresponding observed values are also shown in this figure.

Further, it is assumed that the annual production of steel in the economy is equal to its annual consumption requirement (in terms of crude steel equivalent) during the period of simulation forecast, 1978 to 2005. Therefore, during this period the following production identity holds true :

$$Simulated\,Q_t = Simulated\,S_t \qquad (6.3)$$

As already pointed out in Section 6.2, this assumption does not rule out the possibility of imports and exports. The assumption, however, implies that the net imports of steel per annum, in terms of crude steel equivalent, shall be equal to zero during the forecast period.

The simulation forecast of the annual steel production is same as that of its annual consumption requirement as given in Table 6.3 and shown in Fig. 6.3.

TABLE 6.1
Historical Simulation of GNP, Consumption and Production of Steel in India (1956-1977)

Year	GNP at Factor Cost (Rs. crores at constant (1970-71) prices)	Consumption (thousand tonnes of crude steel equivalent)	Production (thousand tonnes of crude steel equivalent)
1956	22179	3427	1685
1957	22514	4009	1930
1958	22906	4449	2253
1959	23831	4492	3152
1960	24680	4561	3228
1961	25766	4755	3606
1962	26959	4945	3956

1963	27922	5464	4417
1964	28834	6120	4961
1965	29524	6503	5669
1966	30333	6662	6540
1967	31516	6640	6638
1968	32847	6653	7426
1969	34291	6949	7471
1970	35690	7513	7342
1971	36796	8256	6828
1972	37783	8902	6664
1973	38854	9176	8197
1974	40179	9192	7332
1975	41859	9212	8589
1976	43702	9489	10771
1977	45472	10173	9900

TABLE 6.2

Historical Simulation of Inputs of Labour, Capital, Fuels and Raw-materials Used in Indian Steel Induatry (1956-1977)

Year	Labour (Lakh man-hours:all employees)	Capital (Gross fixed capital in Rs. lakhs at constant 1960 prices)	Fuels (Lakh tonnes of coal replacement equivalent)	Raw-Materials (Rs. lakhs at constant 1960 prices)
1956	2156	16156	34.52	5252
1957	2332	20008	36.69	5964
1958	2554	25376	39.76	6920
1959	2985	40180	55.95	9697
1960	3073	42746	52.82	9848
1961	3396	49057	56.28	10953
1962	3620	57239	57.03	11964
1963	3948	66302	60.85	13317
1964	4284	76519	67.48	14922
1965	4570	91577	77.31	17030
1966	4933	114079	84.40	19635
1967	4951	118308	83.48	19835
1968	5320	138330	90.40	22167
1969	5217	141990	90.85	22201
1970	5012	140217	91.43	21706
1971	4773	133197	79.54	20049
1972	4651	127361	80.67	19471
1973	5466	164856	94.76	24034
1974	5439	141291	78.96	21333
1975	6059	176332	87.49	25042
1976	7141	235177	105.21	31549
1977	6496	220295	95.58	28815

Fig. 6.2 Observed Versus Simulated GNP of India

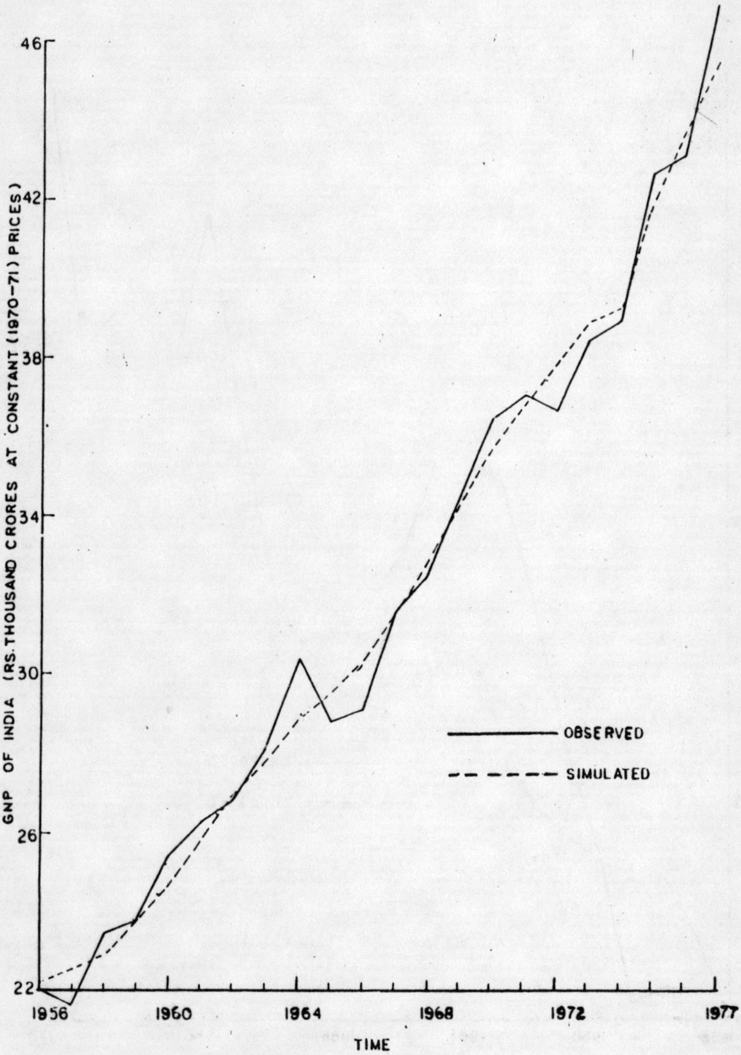

Fig. 6.3 Observed Versus Simulated Steel Consumption in India

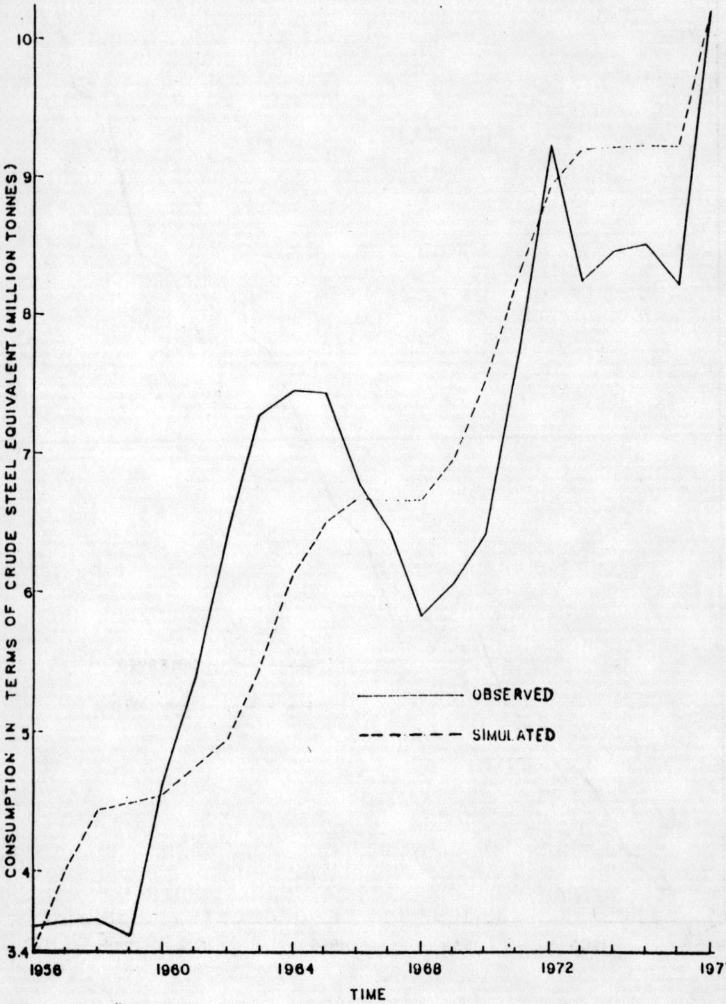

Fig. 6.4 Observed Versus Simulated Steel Production in India

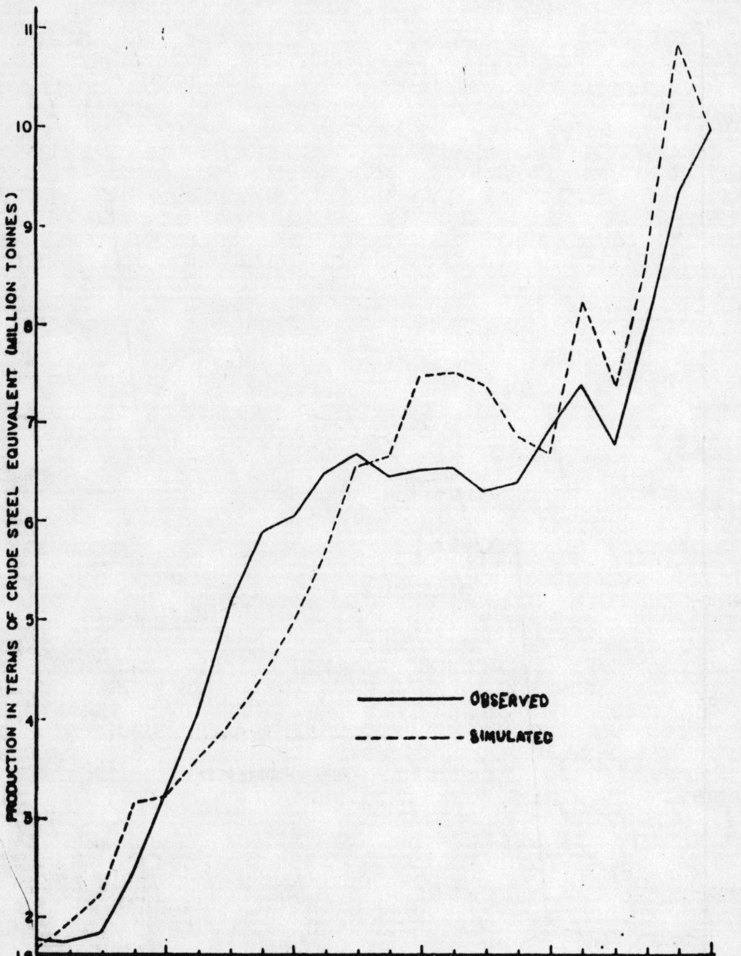

Fig. 6.5 Observed Versus Simulated Input of Labour

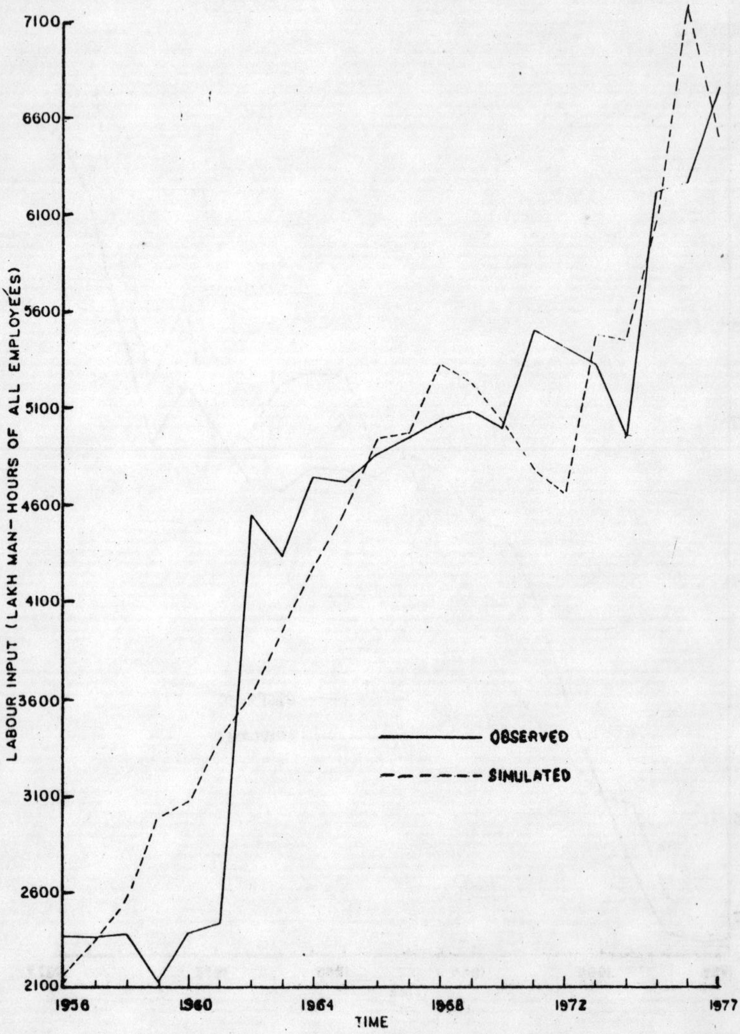

Fig. 6.6 Observed Versus Simulated Input of Capital

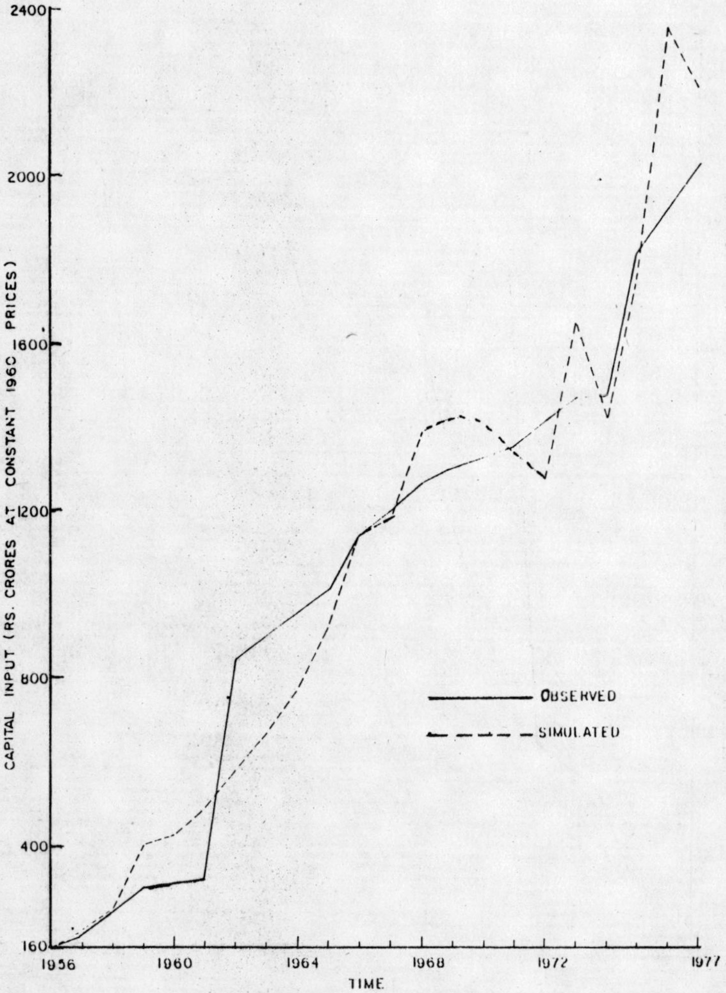

Fig. 6.7 Observed Versus Simulated Input of Fules

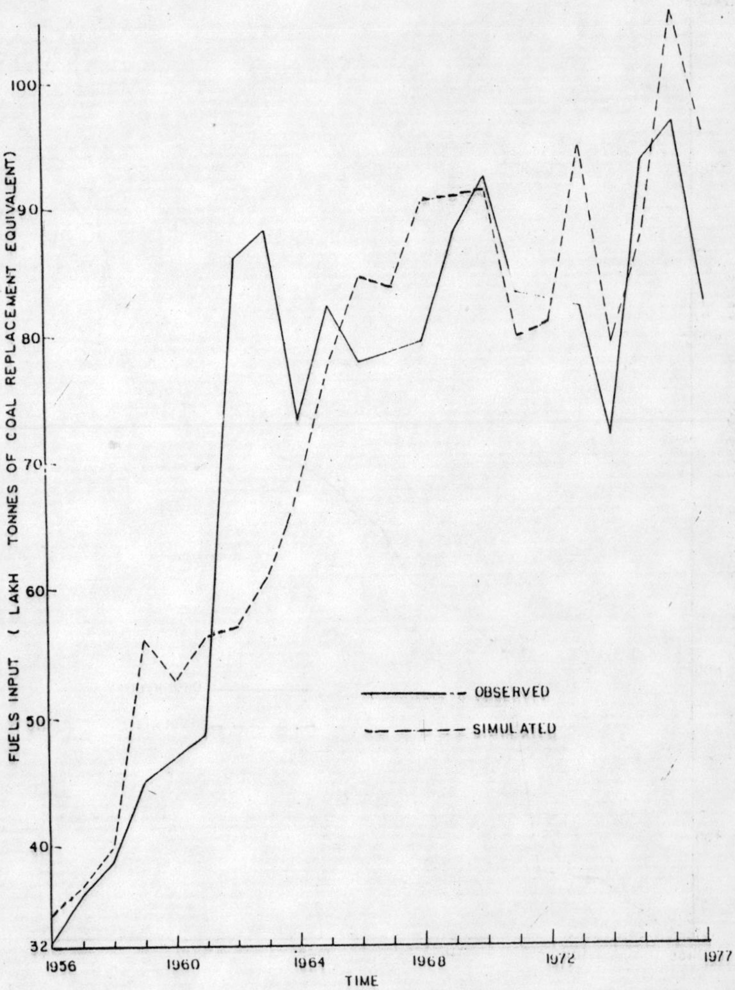

Fig. 6.8 Observed Versus Simulated Input of Raw Materials

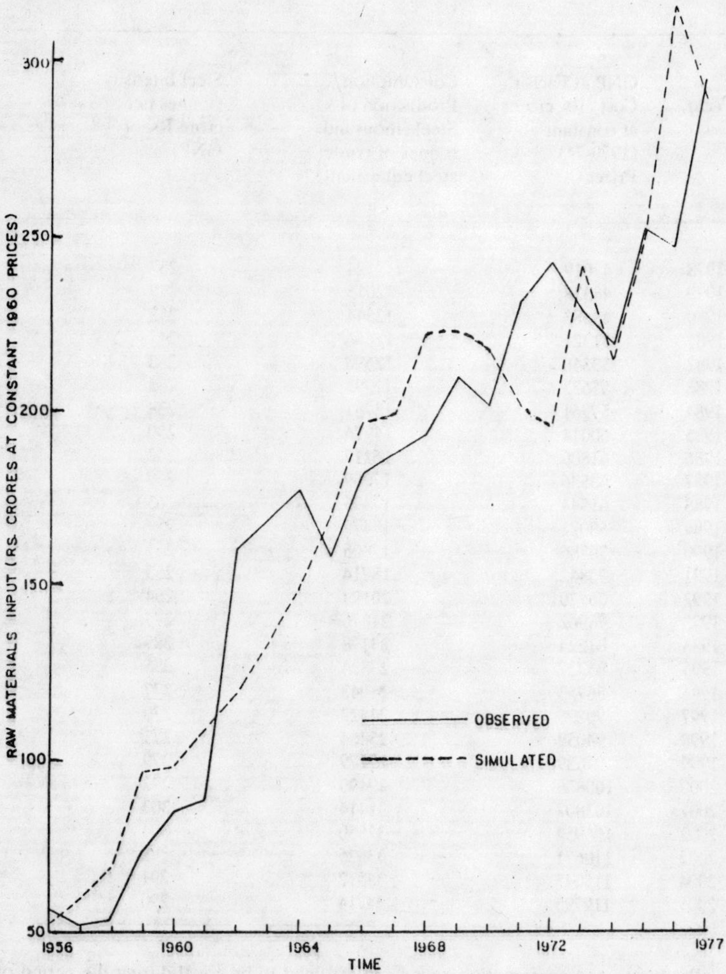

TABLE 6.3

Simulation Forecast of GNP, Consumption/Production* of Steel and Steel Intensity in India (1978-2005)

Year	GNP at Factor Cost (Rs. crores at constant (1970-71) Prices	Consumption/ Production of Steel (thousand tonnes of crude steel equivalent)	Steel Intensity (tonnes per crore Rs. of GNP)
1978	47019	11124	237
1979	48338	12015	249
1980	49683	12544	252
1981	51321	12666	247
1982	53346	12690	238
1983	55655	12995	233
1984	57961	13781	238
1985	60014	14976	250
1986	61800	16217	262
1987	63536	17069	269
1988	65544	17395	265
1989	68021	17479	257
1990	70886	17805	251
1991	73842	18714	253
1992	76570	20194	264
1993	78962	21876	277
1994	81224	23178	285
1995	83727	23824	285
1996	86753	24043	277
1997	90298	24422	270
1998	94059	25464	271
1999	97639	27279	279
2000	100836	29490	292
2001	103802	31414	303
2002	106952	32550	304
2003	110671	33025	298
2004	115045	33512	291
2005	119795	34714	290

* Producion and consumption have been assumed to be equal during the period of forecast.

TABLE 6.4

Simulation Forecast of Demands for Labour, Capital, Fuels and raw-Materials* Under Normal Input Price Conditions (Indian Steel Industry) (1978-2005)

Year	Labour (Lakh man-hours:all employees)	Capital (Gross fixed capital in Rs. lakhs at constant 1960 prices)	Fuels (Lakh tonnes of coal replacement equivalent)	Raw-Materials (Rs. lakhs at constant 1960 prices)
1978	7146	251119	106.59	32409
1979	7530	278567	112.81	34994
1980	7750	296203	115.78	36482
1981	7793	302109	115.26	36744
1982	7794	305134	113.95	36714
1983	7915	316649	114.95	37527
1984	8237	343175	119.75	39776
1985	8719	383362	127.59	43244
1986	9206	426337	135.52	46844
1987	9531	457642	140.26	49277
1988	9648	471883	140.97	51035
1989	9671	478079	139.88	50271
1990	9787	492623	140.56	51129
1991	10116	528243	145.25	53719
1992	10650	585250	153.78	58002
1993	11240	651185	163.34	62855
1994	11687	705515	170.16	66628
1995	11895	735682	172.35	68417
1996	11953	749808	171.69	68936
1997	12065	770362	172.06	69930
1998	12403	817592	176.62	72888
1999	12994	897383	185.86	78133
2000	13699	996109	197.23	84551
2001	14295	1085585	206.50	90114
2002	14632	1143032	201.82	93332
2003	14760	1172406	211.14	94585
2004	14890	1202721	211.50	95873
2005	15239	1265790	215.90	99277

* Demand for raw-materials is independent of the prices of inputs.

Fig. 6.9 Simulation Forecast of GNP of India

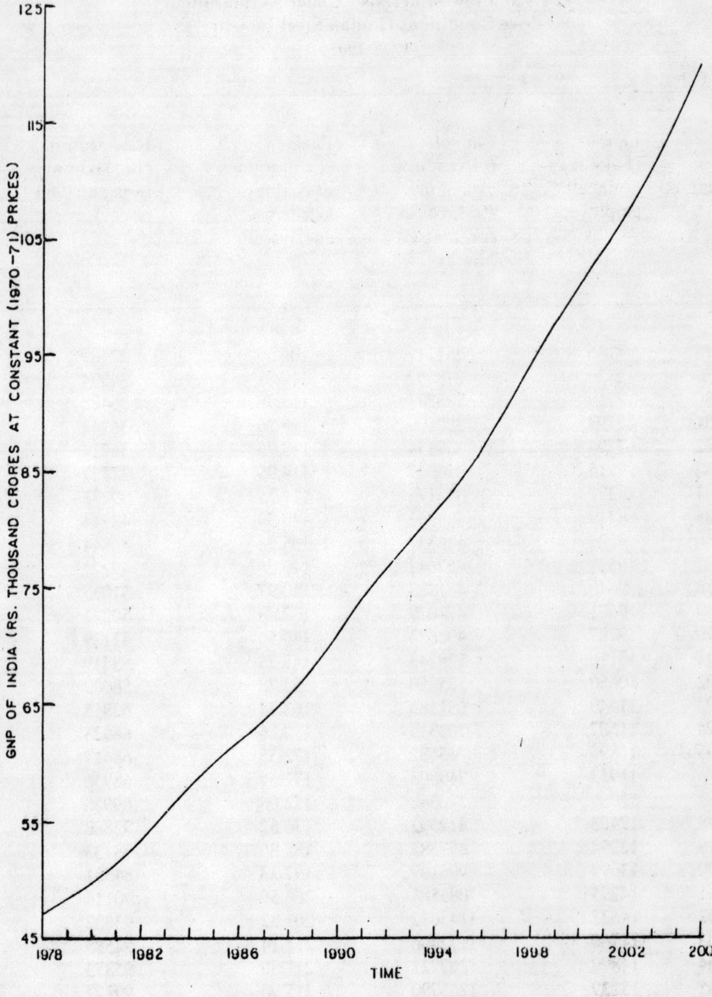

Fig. 6.10 Simulation Forecast of Steel Consumption/Steel Production in India

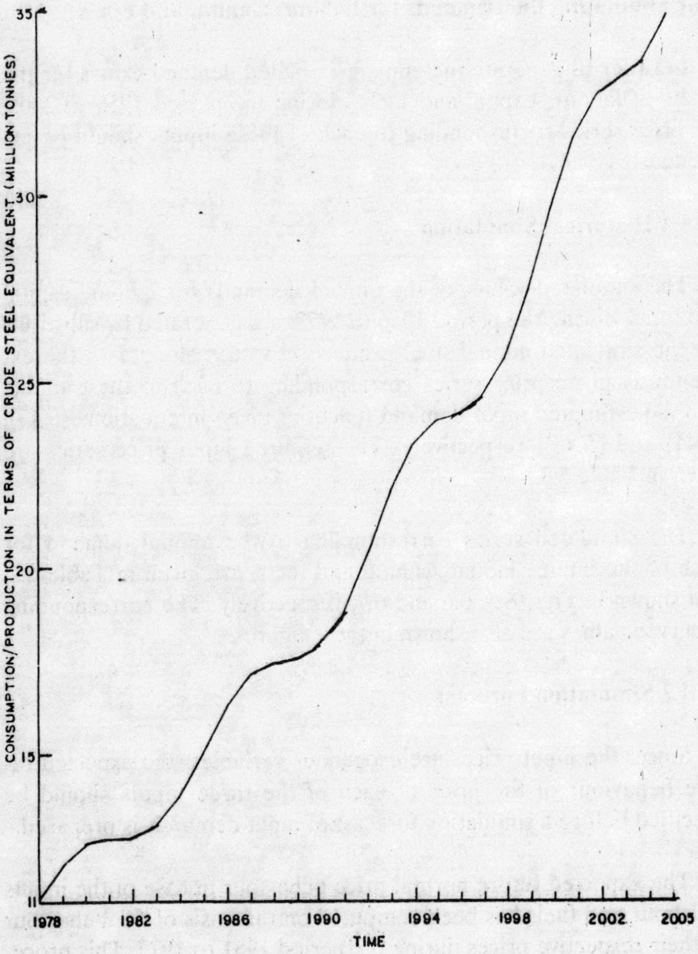

6.6 SIMULATING INPUT DEMANDS

The simulated values of annual demands for various inputs, during the period 1956 to 1977, can be generated with the knowledge of the simulated values of annual production during the same period.

6.6.1 Simulating the Demands for Labour, Capital and Fuels

In order to generate the annual simulated demand values for the inputs of labour, capital and fuels, during the period 1956 to 2005, the price series corresponding to each of these inputs should be exogenously given.

6.6.1.1 Historical Simulation

The simulated values of the annual demands for labour, capital and fuels, during the period 1956 to 1977, are generated by substituting the simulated annual steel production values along with the exogenously given price series corresponding to each of these inputs into the estimated input demand functions given in equations (5.43), (5.44) and (5.45), respectively. The required input price series are given in Table 3.3.

The simulated series corresponding to the annual demand for each of the inputs, labour, capital and fuels, are given in Table 6.2, and shown in Figs. 6.5, 6.6 and 6.7, respectively. The corresponding observed values are also shown in these figures.

6.6.1.2 Simulation Forecast

Since, the input prices are exogenous variables, the expected future behaviour of the price of each of the three inputs should be specified before a simulation forecast of input demands is prepared.

The expected future normal price behaviour in case of the inputs of labour and fuels has been computed on the basis of the behaviour of their respective prices during the period 1951 to 1977. This procedure has been adopted with regard to the prices of labour and fuels inputs and not with regard to capital input, because the prices of the first two have grown roughly with an exponential trend during the period 1951 to 1977, while the price of capital input has not exhibited a uniform trend. The average annual growth rate in the price series (1951 to 1977) corresponding to each of the two inputs (labour and fuels) is estimated and it is assumed that under normal conditions the respective price series shall grow at this rate during the forecast period, 1978 to 2005.

The average annual growth rate in the price of labour input, during the period 1951 to 1977, is computed with the help of the following estimated regression equation :

$$\ln P_L(t) = -0.5422 + 0.0696\,t \tag{6.4}$$

$$\bar{R}^2 = 0.94$$

Where,

$P_L t$ = price of labour input during the year t; and
t = 1, 2, ..., 27 (i.e., 1951, 1952, ..., 1977)

To show that the estimated coefficient of variable t is the average annual growth in labour-price, equation (6.4) is transformed into the following form by taking the exponential of both the sides of this equation, so that:

$$P_L(t) = 0.5815\, e^{.0696\, t} \tag{6.5}$$

It is, thus, estimated that the price of labour input grew at an average annual rate of 6.96 per cent (approximately 7 per cent). It is assumed that during the forecast period (1978 to 2005) the normal expected price series corresponding to labour input shall grow at an annual rate of 7 per cent, taking the observed labour-price during the year 1977 as the base.

The average annual growth rate in the price of fuels input, during the period 1951 to 1977, is computed with the help of the following estimated regression equation :

$$\ln P_F(t) = 2.76 + 0.098\,t \tag{6.6}$$

$$\bar{R}^2 = 0.96$$

where,

$P_F(t)$ = price of fuels input during the year t; and
t is same as explained in case of equation (6.4).

Thus, the series of fuels-price grew at an average annual rate of 9.8 per cent during the period 1951 to 1977. A point to be noted is that the fuels prices grew with a smooth exponential trend during the years 1951 through 1973, but grew at an abnormaly high rate during the years 1973 through 1977. It is, however, expected that this abnormally high rate of growth would settle at a lower value in the long run. The average annual growth rate in fuels prices may settle somewhere near the one corresponding to the period 1951 to 1973.

The average annual growth rate in the price of fuels input, during the period 1951 to 1973, is computed with the help of the following estimated regression equation :

$$\ln P_F(t) = 2.8915 + 0.0829\,t \qquad (6.7)$$

$$\bar{R}^2 = .99$$

It may, thus, be observed that the price series of fuels input grew at an average annual rate of 8.29 per cent during the years 1951 through 1973. It has been assumed that during the forecast period (1978 to 2005) the normal expected price series corresponding to fuels input shall grow at an annual rate of 9 per cent, taking the observed price of fuels input during the year 1977 as the base.

The price series corresponding to the capital-input, as given in Table 3.3, has not exhibited a uniform trend during the period 1951 to 1977. The price of capital (written in percentage terms) rose at a rapid rate during the years 1951 through 1956, from around 8 per cent in 1951 to around 24 per cent in 1956. It, then, declined to around 8 per cent in 1962, and rose to around 11 per cent in 1965. During the years 1966 through 1972, the price of capital fluctuated around 8 per cent level. It rose to around 17 per cent in 1974 and remained around 15 per cent in 1975 and 1976. It was around 11 per cent in 1977. Thus, no general trend can be attributed to the behaviour of the price of capital.

The price of capital, as defined in sub-section 3.5.4, is the average rate of return to the gross fixed stock of capital (at constant 1960 prices). It is expected that the price of capital shall grow from 11 per cent onwards during the period of forecast. It has been a judgemental assumption that the normal expected rate of growth in the price of capital, during the period 1977 to 1990, shall be 3 per cent per annum, so that the price of capital rises to around 16 per cent in 1990. For the period 1990 to 2005, it has been assumed that this price shall grow at the rate of 2 per cent per annum and shall be around 22 per cent in 2005.

The simulation forecasts corresponding to the annual demands for labour, capital and fuels, during the period 1978 to 2005, are generated by substituting the simulation forecast values of the annual steel production along with the exogenously given price series corresponding to each of these inputs into the estimated input demand functions given in equations (5.43), (5.44) and (5.45). The value of variable t on the right hand side of each function shall take values as given below :

$$t = 28 \text{ for } 1978 \text{ ; } t = 29 \text{ for } 1979 \text{ ; ... ; } t = 55 \text{ for } 2005.$$

The simulated forecast series corresponding to the annual demand for each of the inputs, labour, capital and fuels are given in Table 6.4.

6.6.2 Simulating the Demand for Raw-Materials

The simulated values of the annual demands for raw-materials, during the period 1956 to 2005, are generated by substituting the simulated annual steel production values into the estimated raw-materials demand function given in equation (5.50). The values of t are taken such that $t=6$ for year 1956, $t=7$ for year 1957, ..., and $t=55$ for year 2005.

The simulated raw-materials demand series during the period 1956 to 1977 is given in Table 6.2 and shown in Fig. 6.8. The corresponding observed values are also shown in this figure.

The simulated forecast series of raw-materials demand (1978 to 2005) is given in Table 6.4.

6.7 VALIDATING THE DERIVED PRODUCTION FUNCTION

A check to test the validity of the production function derived from the estimated input demand functions (for labour, capital and fuels), in Chapter V, has been explained in this section. It has been assumed that there is no raw-materials constraint.

The simulated values of demands for labour, capital and fuels, corresponding to a particular year, are substituted into the production function equation (5.62) for each year during the period 1956 to 1977 and also during 1978 to 2005. The series of steel production during the period 1956 to 2005 is, thus, re-simulated. This process has been termed as the 'reverse production simulation'. The re-simulated steel production series corresponding to the period 1956 to 1977 is given in Tables 6.5 and 6.6.

In order to test that the steel production series re-simulated through the use of production function is identical to the originally simulated steel production series of Section 6.5, the re-simulated series is regressed over the originally simulated series corresponding to the periods of historical simulation and of simulation forecast, respectively. The following are the estimated regression equations :

For the period 1956 to 1977 :

$$RSQ_t = 5.22 + 0.998\, SQ_t \qquad \bar{R}^2 = 1.00 \tag{6.8}$$

and,

For the period 1978 to 2005 :

$$RSQ_t = 167.59 + 0.986\, SQ_t \qquad \bar{R}^2 = 1.00 \tag{6.9}$$

where,

RSQ_t = re-simulated steel production value for the year t; and
SQ_t = originally simulated value.

It may be observed that the coefficient of SQ_t in equation (6.8) is practically equal to unity and same is the case with equation (6.9). Further, the $\bar{R}^2$ = 1, in both the equations, proves that the two series corresponding to SQ_t and RSQ_t are identical in both the periods under consideration.

TABLE 6.5

A Comparison Between the Simulated Production (of steel) Series and the Re-Simulated Production (of Steel) Series during the Period of Historical Simulation (1956-1977)

Year	Simulated Production of Steel (thousand tonnes of crude steel equivalent)	Re-simulated Production of Steel (thousand tonnes of crude steel equivalent)
1956	1685	1682
1957	1930	1928
1958	2253	2252
1959	3152	3149
1960	3228	3227
1961	3606	3605
1962	3956	3956
1963	4417	4416
1964	4961	4959
1965	5669	5668
1966	6540	6539
1967	6638	6637
1968	7426	7424
1969	7471	7469
1970	7342	7340
1971	6828	6820
1972	6664	6660
1973	8197	8194
1974	7332	7326
1975	8589	8576
1976	10771	10750
1977	9900	9877

TABLE 6.6

A Comparison Between the simulated Production (of Steel) Series and the Re-Simulated Production (of Steel) Series During the Forecast Period (1978-2005)

Year	Simulated Production of Steel (thousand tonnes of crude steel equivalent)	Re-Simulated Production of Steel(thousand tonnes of crude steel equivalent)
1978	11124	11103
1979	12015	11989
1980	12544	12515

1981	12666	12634
1982	12690	12656
1983	12995	12958
1984	13781	13739
1985	14976	14926
1986	16217	16158
1987	17069	17002
1988	17395	17323
1989	17479	17403
1990	17805	17723
1991	18714	18622
1992	20194	20087
1993	21867	21742
1994	23178	23036
1995	23824	23670
1996	24043	23880
1997	24422	24247
1998	25462	25271
1999	27279	27059
2000	29490	29238
2001	31414	31130
2002	32550	32240
2003	33025	32696
2004	33512	33163
2005	34714	34335

6.8 VALIDATING THE SIMULATION MODEL DEVELOPED

6.8.1 A Brief Theoretical Background

Validation or verification of the results obtained from the simulation model of an economic system is a highly elusive problem. It is difficult to establish a set of criteria which can differentiate between the models which are 'true' and models which are 'not true'. However, if a particular model can serve the purpose, for which it has been designed and experimented with, to a reasonalbe level of satisfaction, it should be accepted to be the relevant model.

According to Friedman (50), the validity of an economic model depends not on the validity of the assumptions on which the model rests but rather on the ability of the model to predict the behaviour of endogenous variables which are treated by the model. Although conformity to observed behaviour is a desirable check on the validity of an economic model, Friedman has been criticised for maintaining such a position (115).

Before choosing a particular method of verifying the results, it is important to know the purpose which the model is expected to serve. There are two important uses which may be made of simulation models, namely explanatory analysis and normative analysis. The motivation underlying these two types of analysis is quite different. When the computer simulation model of an economic system is used for explanatory (or positive) analysis, its primary concern is to explain the behaviour of this system. The results obtained from such a model must be subjected to direct empirical observation for verification. On the other hand, the concern of a simulation model used for normative (or prescriptive) analysis is to recommend certain guidelines or courses of action keeping in view the defined system objectives. The implementation of the recommended policy may provide a means of testing the validity of the model (115).

There are two alternative approaches available to test the degree to which the data generated by a computer simulation model of an economic system conform to observed data, namely historical verification and verification by forecasting. the essence of both these procedures is prediction - historical forecasting is concerned with retrospective predictions while forecasting is concerned with prospective predictions (117).

6.8.2 Historical Verification

The following tests have been carried out in order to test the degree of conformity between the data generated by the simulation model of the system of Indian steel industry and the observed data corresponding to each of the seven endogenous variables (as defined in Section 6.2) of this system, during the period of historical simulation (1956 to 1977) :

i. Graphical Analysis
ii. Regression Analysis
iii. Mann-Whitney U-Test

i. Graphical Analysis

Figures 6.2 through 6.8 contain a comparison of the time paths of the actual data and simulated data for each of the seven endogenous variables in the simulation model of Indian steel industry given in Tables 6.1 and 6.2. These figures show a good degree of agreement between the actual and simulated data for each endogenous variable, thus confirming the validity of the simulation model developed.

ii. Regression Analysis

To check for the goodness of fit between the simulated and actual series, one may compute a simple regression of the simulated series as a function of the corresonding observed series. Cohen and Cyert (27) state that the two series are said to be in agreement if the intercept in the resulting equation is not significantly different from zero and the slope is not significantly different from unity. Thus, the restrictions to be tested in case of each regression equation are :

a. Intercept = 0 ; and
b. Slope = 1.

1. GNP (Y) :

$$SIMY_t = 343.58 + 0.9895\, OY_t \tag{6.10}$$

$$\bar{R}^2 = 0.99\ ;\ F-ratio = 0.09$$

where,

$SIMY_t$ = simulated GNP value for year t; and
OY_t = observed GNP value for year t; and

F-ratio = F-test for checking the validity of imposed restrictions; intercept = 0, and slope = 1. The test has already been explained in Section 5.7.

2. Steel Consumption Requirement (S) :

$$SIMS_t = 394.27 + 0.9576\, OS_t \tag{6.11}$$

$$\bar{R}^2 = 0.81\ ;\ F-ratio = 0.26$$

3. Production of Steel (Q) :

$$SIMQ_t = 228.85 + 1.0632\, OQ_t \tag{6.12}$$

$$\bar{R}^2 = 0.91 ; = 0.67$$

4. Demand for Labour Input (L) :

$$SIML_t = 598.18 + 0.8737\, OL_t \tag{6.13}$$

$$\bar{R}^2 = 0.87 ; F-ratio = 1.41$$

5. Demand for Capital Input (K) :

$$SIMK_t = -4297.83 + 1.0615\, OK_t \tag{6.14}$$

$$\bar{R}^2 = 0.94 ; F-ratio = 0.72$$

6. Demand for Fuels Input (F) :

$$SIMF_t = 10.83 + 0.8605\, OF_t \tag{6.15}$$

$$\bar{R}^2 = 0.73 ; F-ratio = 0.48$$

7. Demand for Raw-Materials Input (M) :

$$SIMM_t = 1139.11 + 0.9498\, OM_t \tag{6.16}$$

$$\bar{R}^2 = 0.87 ; F-ratio = 0.31$$

where the pre-fixes SIM and O refer to the simulated and observed values of the input variables, respectively.

While computing the F-ratio for each equation, the degrees of freedom in the numerator are equal to 2, while those in the denominator are equal to 20, i.e. $n_1 = 2$, $n_2 = 20$. The corresponding critical F-value at 5 per cent level of significance, $F_{0.05,\,2.20}$, is obtained from the standard tables and is equal to 3.49.

It may be observed that the F-ratio computed for each of the equations, 6.10 through 6.16, is less than the critical (tabulated) F-value at 5 per cent level of significance. The two restrictions, namely intercept = 0, and slope = 1 are, thus, valid in case of all the regression equations, (6.10) through (6.16).

It may, therefore, be concluded that the simulated and observed series, corresponding to each of the seven endogenous variables, are in agreement with each other.

iii. Mann-Whitney U-Test :

It is a non-parametric test. In case of a non-parametric test, its model does not specify conditions about the parameters of the population from which the sample was drawn (144). Certain assumptions are associated with most non-parametric statistical tests, but these are fewer and weaker than those associated with a parametric test.

In this sub-section, the Mann-Whitney U-Test is used to compare the simulated and observed series coresponding to each of the seven endogenous variables. As this test is applied in case of two unrelated samples, it is assumed that the simulated and observed series corresponding to each endogenous variable are independent samples. This test is used to test whether two independent samples have been drawn from the same population. This is one of the most powerful non-parametric tests (144).

As the sample size is greater than 20, the normal approximation to the sampling distribution of U is made to carry out the above test (144). The standard normal 'z' -values, as computed with the help of a computer programme under the SAS package (64), corresponding to various endogenous variables, are given in Table 6.7.

All the 'z'-values are within the limits of critical z-value at 5 per cent level of significance. This value is $\pm$ 1.96 (under two tailed-test) and is obtained from the table of the standardised normal distribution (128). It may, thus, be concluded that the simulated and observed series corresponding to each endogenous variable have been drawn from the same population.

TABLE 6.7
Comparison Between the Observed and Simulated Values of Various Endogenous Variables For the Period 1956 to 1977
Mann-Whitney U-Test ('z' - Values)

S. No.	Variable Name	z-Value
1	GNP	- 0.0352
2	Steel Consumption	- 0.1995
3	Steel Production	- 0.4812
4	Labour Input	- 0.0704
5	Capital Input	- 0.1056
6	Fuels Input	- 0.2230
7	Raw-Materials Input	- 0.1056

On the basis of retrospective verification reported under (i), (ii) and (iii) above it may, thus, be concluded that there is a reasonable degree of conformity between the data generated by the simulation model and the observed data corresponding to each of the seven endogenous variables. The simulation model has thus been historically validated.

6.8.3 Verification by Forecasting

The ultimate test of a computer simulated model is the degree of accuracy with which the model predicts the behaviour of the actual system (which is being simulated) for the future (115). In fact, the ability of the computer simulation models to accurately forecast the future is the major source of justification for the use of computer simulation as a tool of analysis. If the policy and guidelines recommended by a computer simulation model are implemented, this in itself provides a means of testing the validity of this model.

In the present study, the period of forecast has been chosen to be 1978 to 2005 which is almost equal to the period of analysis (1951 to 1977) of the system of Indian steel industry.

The data on the endogenous variables GNP and apparent steel consumption are now available for the years 1978 through 1984. The values of observed and simulated GNP and apparent steel consumption are given in Tables 6.8 and 6.9, respectively. The percentage difference between the observed and simulated values has been computed for each year in case of both the endogenous variables, such that :

$$\text{Percentage Difference} = \frac{\text{Observed Value - Simulated Value}}{\text{Simulated Value}}$$

These percentage differences are also given in Tables 6.8 and 6.9. The observed and simulated values are found to be in agreement with each other during the years 1978 through 1984 for each of the two endogenous variables.

A check on the performance of the simulation model developed in this chapter may be made from time to time in future and corrective measures may be introduced in case the performance turns out to be poor as compared to the observed system behaviour. Such a procedure of dynamic checks will be detailed out in the subsequent chapter.

TABLE 6.8

Observed and Simulated Values of GNP* of India at Factor Cost (Rs. Crores at Constant (1970-71) prices) (1978 - 1984)

Year	Observed GNP	Simulated GNP	Percentage Difference
1978	49559	47019	5.24
1979	47233	48338	-2.29
1980	50793	49683	2.23
1981	53467	51321	4.18
1982	54836	53346	2.79
1983	59043	55655	6.09
1984+	61201	57961	5.59

Provisional

+ Quick Eestimates

Source : Economic Survey, 1985-86

TABLE 6.9
Observed and Simulated Values of Apparent Steel Consumption in India (Million Tonnes of Crude Steel Equivalent) (1978 - 1984)

Year	Observed Steel Consumption	Simulated Steel Consumption	Percentage Difference
1978	10.90	11.12	-1.98
1979	13.29	12.01	10.66
1980	11.97	12.54	-4.55
1981	14.70	12.67	16.02
1982	14.08	12.69	10.95
1983	12.75	13.00	-1.92
1984	13.05	13.78	-5.30

Source: Steel Statistical Yearbook 1985, International Iron and Steel Institute, Brussels.

6.9 CONCLUDING REMARKS

In this chapter, various estimated sub-models have been woven together into a single simulation model of Indian steel industry. The model generates the simulated series corresponding to each of the seven endogenous variables for the period of historical simulation as well as for the period of simulation forecast. The input prices have been assumed to be exogenous variables; their values are known for the period of historical simulation, while certain judgemental assumptions are made regarding their behaviour during the period of forecast. The simulation model has been historically validated and certain intermittent checks on the future performance of the model have been recommended. The sensitivity analysis of the simulated behaviour with respect to change in various variables will be reported in the next chapter together with the projections of various scenarios of Indian steel industry upto the year 2005.

SEVEN

ANALYSIS OF RESULTS

7.1 INTRODUCTION

The analysis of results obtained during the course of the present study is an important exercise which facilitates formulation of the major future policy guidelines with regard to the growth and development of Indian steel industry. This analysis brings forth various possibilities and their outcome in case the actual future behaviour of endogenous variables deviates from their respective simulation forecasts or in case the exogenous variables do not follow their respective assumed paths. However, this chapter admits of the need for a dynamic follow-up of the reported simulation model and its performance.

7.2 ANALYSIS OF FORECASTS OF GNP, STEEL CONSUMPTION REQUIREMENT AND PRODUCTION OF STEEL

As already mentioned in Section 3.9, the analysis in the present study is based on the annual data from 1951 to 1977. Therefore, the period 1978 to 2005 is termed as the forecast period, even though the years 1978 to 1986 have already passed. In fact, the forecast for the period 1978 till today is called the ex post forecast and that from today to 2005 the ex ante forecast (126). However, the observed data on GNP and steel consumption are now available for the years 1978 to 1984, which have already been compared with the simulated data under sub-section 6.8.3.

7.2.1 Forecast of GNP

The simulation forecast (1978 to 2005) of the GNP of India at factor cost (at constant (1970-71) prices) has already been given in Table 6.3 and shown in Fig. 6.9. It has been estimated to be Rs. 47,019 crores during 1978 and Rs. 119,795 crores during 2005. It may be observed from Fig. 6.9 that the GNP is expected to grow with an exponential trend during the period of forecast. The compound annual rate of growth computed with the help of the forecast GNP values corresponding to the initial and the terminal years (1978 and 2005, respectively) is 3.52 per cent.

The forecast period, 1978 to 2005, may be divided into eight sub-periods on the basis of rate of growth in GNP. Table 7.1 depicts these sub-periods along with the compound annual rates of growth corresponding to the respective sub-periods. The compound annual rate of growth corresponding to a sub-period has been computed with the help of the forecast GNP values corresponding to the initial and the terminal years of the sub-period under consideration. It may be observed from Table 7.1 that each sub-period of three to four years of duration with rapid growth of GNP (as compared to the long run GNP growth rate of 3.52 per cent) is expected to be followed by an approximately equal sub-period of slow growth in GNP.

The growth rate of Gross Domestic Product (GDP) envisaged in Sixth Plan (80) was 5.2 per cent per annum for the period 1979-80 to 1984-85, and 5.5 per cent during the subsequent decade, that is 1984-85 to 1994-95. This appears to be an unrealistic target. In fact, many radical and fundamental changes are required to be introduced in India's socio-economic structure in order to achieve a long-run growth rate of 5 per cent or more. With the existing socio-economic conditions, the GNP is expected to grow as depicted in Table 7.1. An international study by Chase Econometrics (121) has recently been reported regarding the world steel outlook upto 1990. This study is of the opinion that the GDP of India is expected to grow at the average annual rate of 3.5 per cent during the 1980s. This appears to be a realistic foreacast and is very much in agreement with the long run rate of growth of India's GNP, projected to be 3.52 per cent per annuam by the present study.

TABLE 7.1
Sub-Periods of Rate of Growth of GNP (Forecast)

S. No.	Sub-Period	Compound Annual Rate of Growth (%)
1	1978 to 1981	2.96
2	1981 to 1984	4.14
3	1984 to 1988	3.12
4	1988 to 1992	3.96
5	1992 to 1995	3.02
6	1995 to 1999	3.92
7	1999 to 2003	3.18
8	2003 to 2005	4.04

TABLE 7.2
Sub-Periods of Rate of Growth of Steel Consumption Requirement (Forecast)

S. No.	Sub-Period	Compound Annual Rate of Growth (%)
1	1978 to 1979	8.01
2	1979 to 1983	0.60
3	1983 to 1987	7.06
4	1987 to 1990	1.42
5	1990 to 1994	6.82
6	1994 to 1997	1.76
7	1997 to 2002	5.91
8	2002 to 2005	2.17

7.2.2 Forecast of Steel Consumption Requirement

The simulatin forecast of steel consumption requirement has already been given in Table 6.3 and shown in Fig. 6.10. The steel consumption requirement or the demand for steel in Indian economy is expected to grow from 11.124 million tonnes (in terms of crude steel equivalent) in 1978 to 34.714 million tonnes in 2005. It may be observed from Fig. 6.10 that the future demand for steel is expected to grow somewhat with an exponential trend. The compound annual rate of growth computed with the help of the forecast values of the steel demand corresponding to the initial and the terminal years (1978 and 2005, respectively) is 4.31 per cent.

The forecast period, 1978 to 2005, may be divided into eight sub-periods on the basis of rate of growth of steel demand in the economy as depicted in Table 7.2. It may be observed from Tables 6.3 and 7.2 that the steel consumption is expected to increase during 1979 as compared to 1978. Further, it is also expected that there would be stagnation or a very slow rise in steel consumption requirement of Indian economy during the sub-period 1979 to 1983. In fact, both these phenomena have actually been observed not only in case of India but also in case of the world steel consumption (121). It is expected that there shall be a period of improvement in steel consumption of Indian economy during the post-1983 years. The alternate sub-periods of improvement and stagnation (or slow growth) have been depicted in Table 7.2.

The Sixth Plan (80) forecasts for the steel demand were 12.9 million tonnes of saleable steel (plain carbon) by 1984 and 18.4 million tonnes by 1989. These values are approximately equal to 16.125 and 23.0 million tonnes, respectively in terms of crude steel equivalent. The Seventh Five Year Plan (1985-90) forecasts demand for finished steel at 13.86 million tonnes (17.32 million ingot tonnes) by 1989, 17.76 million tonnes (22.20 million ingot tonnes) by 1994 and 22 million tonnes (27.5 million ingot tonnes) by the year 2000. Table 7.3 compares these forecasts with those reported by Chase Econometrics (121) and the present study. It may be observed that the forecasts reported by Chase Econometrics and the present study are much in agreement. The forecast of steel demand reported in Sixth Plan appears to be highly overestimated. The Seventh Plan seems to have revised the demand projections in coherence with what this study had already predicted in 1983.

Further, the period of forecast in the study by Chase Econometrics (121) is 1982 to 1990. The steel consumption in India is expected to grow with a compound annual rate of 4.62 per cent during this period. The present study estimates this rate to be 4.32 per cent, which is, again, in agreement with the results reported by Chase Econometrics.

7.2.3 Forecast of Production of Steel

The desired targets of production of steel during the period 1978 to 2005 have been fixed to be equal to the annual steel consumption requirements during the same period. This has already been explained in Section 6.5. Therefore, the simulation forecast of steel production (targets) is the same as that for steel consumption requirements, given in Table 6.3 and shown in Fig. 6.10.

TABLE 7.3
A Comparison of Various Estimates of Steel Consumption Requirement (Steel Demand) of Indian Economy for the Years 1984 and 1989

Year	Forecast Estimates of Steel Demand (Million tonnes in crude steel terms)			
	Present Study	Chase Econometrics	Sixth Plan	Seventh Plan
1984	13.78	14.14	16.13	-
1989	17.48	17.41	23.00	17.32
1994	23.18	-	-	22.20
2000	29.49	-	-	27.50

Sources : 1. Chase Econometrics (121)
2. Sixth Five Year Plan (1980-85)
3. Seventh Five Year Plan (1985-90).

The Sixth Plan (80) forecasts the producion of steel to be approximately equal to 21.75 million tonnes (in terms of crude steel equivalent) by 1989. The study reported by Chase Econometrics (121) forecasts steel production (in crude steel terms) to be 14.51 million tonnes in 1989. The present study fixes the target of steel production (in terms of crude steel equivalent) at 17.48 million tonnes in 1989. Thus, the forecast of steel production during 1989, as reported by the present study, lies between the forecasts reported in Sixth Plan and Chase Econometrics. The Seventh Plan expects the steel production by the turn of the century to be below 25 million tonnes of crude steel equivalent.

It has already been pointed out in Section 1.2 that the ingot steel capacity of Indian economy is expected to be approximately 26 million tonnes by the end of 1990. The study by Chase Econometrics (121), however, forecasts this capacity at 21.70 million tonnes and the rate of capacity utilisation at approximately 72 per cent, thus estimating the steel production at 15.68 million tonnes in 1990. The target of steel production expected in the present study is 17.81 million tonnes, which is higher than the production expected by Chase Econometrics and lower than the production expected by Sixth Plan document (for 1989). However, if the capacity target of 26 million tonnes is fulfilled by 1990 and if the capacity utilisation is slightly more optimistic than expected by Chase Econometrics (say, 75 per cent), then it is possible to produce about 19.5 million tonnes of steel. In the case of a pessimistic rate of capacity utilisation of say, 65 per cent, it is possible to produce about 16.9 million tonnes of steel. It may, thus, be seen that the production target for 1990 set by the present study (17.81 million tonnes) is well within the feasible limits if the planned capacity is actually installed by 1990. The forecast of steel production for 1989 as estimated by Sixth Plan document (21.75 million tonnes) seems to be an overestimate and the foreacast by Chase Econometrics for 1990 (15.68 million tonnes) an underestimate of the likely production possibility in 1990.

However, the study reported by Chase Econometrics (121) does not explain the methodology underlying the reported results. The production structure of Indian steel industry has not been analysed. Further, it gives forecasts of GNP, steel consumption and steel production only upto 1990.

7.2.4 Forecast of Steel Intensity of GNP

The steel intensity of GNP has already been defined (in Section 4.4) as a ratio between steel consumption (S) and GNP (Y). The behaviour of observed annual steel intensity has also been shown in Fig. 4.5. The values of steel intensity during the period of forecast (1978 to 2005) have already been given in Table 6.3. The forecast of steel intensity values have been plotted in Fig. 7.1. The steel intensity is expected to grow with a linear trend from about 237 tonnes per crore rupees of GNP at factor cost (at constant (1970-71) prices) during 1978 to about 290 tonnes during 2005. It may be observed from Fig. 7.1 and Table 7.2 that the steel intensity is rising during the sub-period in which there is an improvement in steel consumption. Steel intensity is stagnant or declining during the sub-period in which steel consumption is stagnant or rising slowly.

Fig. 7.1 Simulation Forecast of Steel Intensity of GNP (GNP: At Factor Cost At Constant (1970-71) Prices)

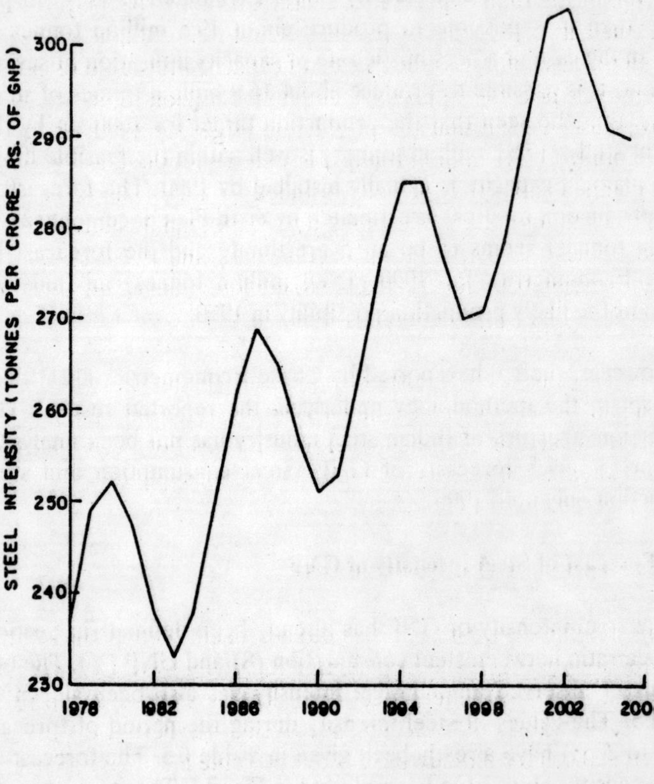

7.3 PRICE ELASTICITIES OF INPUT DEMANDS AND PARTIAL ELASTICITIES OF SUBSTITUTION BETWEEN INPUTS

The knowledge of price elasticities of input demands and their partial elasticities of substitution facilitates the shaping of major policy decisions regarding the future plans of an industry. Allen (2) has shown that the partial elasticities of substitution between the ith and the jth inputs are analytically related to the price elasticities of demand between these two inputs in the following manner :

$$\eta_{ij} = \overline{S}\,\sigma_{ij} \tag{7.1}$$

for i, j = 1, 2, ..., n

where,

n = number of factors of production;

η_{ij} = the price elasticity of the ith input with respect to changes in price of the jth input;

σ_{ij} = the partial elasticity of substitution between the ith and the jth inputs (as defined in equation (5.8) of Section 5.2); and

$\overline{S}_j$ = the average cost share of the jth input over all observations.

Even though $\sigma_{ij} = \sigma_{ji}$ by definition, $\eta_{ij} \neq \eta_{ji}$, in general. It is only under the condition, $\overline{S}_i = \overline{S}_j$, that $\eta_{ij} = \eta_{ji}$.

The η_{ij}s have already been defined in Section (5.6) and estimated in Section (5.7). The values of the average cost shares (during the period 1951 to 1977) of labour, capital and fuels, in the total cost of these three inputs, have also been specified in Section (5.7) as given below :

$$\overline{S}_L = 0.3458;\ \overline{S}_K = 0.4166;\ \overline{S}_F = 0.2376;$$

$$\text{such that,}\quad \overline{S}_L + \overline{S}_K + \overline{S}_F = 1 \tag{7.2}$$

The partial elasticities of substitution between these three inputs (σ_{LK}, σ_{LF} and σ_{KF}) may now easily be computed by substituting the estimated values of η_{ij}s and $\overline{S}_j$s into equation (7.1).

The estimated price elasticities of input demands and partial elasticities of substitution between inputs are given in Table 7.4. It may be observed that the absolute value of the own price elasticity of capital (η_{KK}) is much less than the similar values corresponding to labour and fuels (η_{LL} and η_{FF}, respectively). The cross price elasticities between capital and any other input (η_{KL} and η_{KF}) and between any other input and capital (η_{LK} and η_{FK}) are much less than those between labour and fuels (η_{LF}) and between fuels and labour (η_{FL}).

TABLE 7.4
Estimated Price Elasticities of Input Demands and Partial Elasticities of Substitution Between Inputs of Labour, Capital and Fuels (1951 to 1977)

Type of Elasticity	Estimated Value
A. Price Elasticities	
η_{LL}	-0.21
η_{KK}	-0.10
η_{FF}	-0.27
η_{LK}	0.07
η_{KL}	0.06
η_{KF}	0.04
η_{FK}	0.07
η_{LF}	0.14
η_{FL}	0.20
B. Elasticities of Substitution	
σ_{LK}	0.17
σ_{KF}	0.18
σ_{LF}	0.58

The partial elasticity of substitution between labour and capital is quite small ($\simeq$ 0.17) and same is the case between fuels and capital ($\simeq$ 0.18). However, the elasticity of substitution between labour and fuels is comparatively high ($\simeq$ 0.58).

It has been implicitly assumed in the present study that these values of price and partial elasticities continue to remain the same during the period of forecast (1978 to 2005).

As the elasticity of substitution between capital and labour, or between capital and fuels is low, there is not much choice regarding the required level of capital input when the scale of steel production is increased over time. However, there exists some choice between installing new machinery and equipment which uses more labour but saves on fuels, or that which uses more fuels but saves on labour.

As far as the input of raw-materials in the production process of steel is concerned, it has already been shown in Section 5.7 that this input is not substitutable with any other input and its demand depends mainly on the output to be produced and to some extent on the changes in technology.

7.4 ELASTICITY OF OUTPUT WITH RESPECT TO INPUTS OF LABOUR, CAPITAL AND FUELS

It is an important exercise to analyse the effect of a small variation in the level of one input (keeping the levels of other inputs fixed) on output. It is also important to analyse the effect of a small equi-proportional increase (or decrease) in the levels of all the inputs on output. It may, however, be mentioned that only the levels of inputs of labour, fuels and raw-materials can be varied in a short-run period, while, in the long-run, the level of capital input can also be varied.

The elasticity of output with respect to an input X_i has already been defined in equation (5.4) as the ratio between marginal and average productivities of input X_i. The average productivity of input X_i, during a particular year, say 't', may be easily computed with the help of equation (5.2). In order to compute the marginal productivity of input X_i, during the year 't', an experiment may be performed on the computer. To begin with, the output of steel is estimated on the basis of the given combination of inputs during the year 't' with the help of the production function developed and methodology described in Section 5.8. The output value is then re-estimated by giving one per cent increment to the level of input X_i, keeping the levels of other inputs fixed. The marginal productivity of X_i may now be easily computed with the help of equation (5.3). The elasticity of output with respect to X_i may be computed with the help of equation (5.4). The values of average productivity, marginal prodctivity and output elasticity corresponding to each of the inputs, labour, capital and fuels (during the year 't'), may be computed by using a method similar to the one described above in case of input X_j. Another experiment is performed by re-estimating the output after giving one per cent simultaneous increment to all the three inputs. This experiment helps in determining the value of returns to scale in Indian steel industry.

The above experiments are repeated for some selected years during the period of analysis (using the observed data) and during the forecast period (using the simulated data).

The values of marginal and average productivities of labour and the elasticity of output with respect to labour are given in Table 7.5. The similar values corresponding to the inputs of capital and fuels are given in Tables 7.6 and 7.7, respectively. Table 7.7 also specifies the values of returns to scale in Indian steel industry.

TABLE 7.5

Average and Marginal Productivities of Labour Input and Elasticity of Steel Output with respect to Labour Input

(For some selected years)

Year	Average Productivity (Tonnes of crude steel equivalent per lakh employee man-hours)	Marginal Productivity (Tonnes of crude steel equivalent per lakh additional employee man-hours)	Elasticity of Steel Output with respect to Labour Input
1951*	737	275	0.37
1956	746	245	0.33
1962	1132	384	0.34
1967	1304	462	0.35
1972	1279	446	0.35
1977	1473	504	0.34
1978**	1557	539	0.35
1981	1625	561	0.35
1986	1762	604	0.34
1991	1850	635	0.34
1996	2001	686	0.34
2001	2198	750	0.34
2005	2278	779	0.34

* Observed data have been used for the years during the period 1951 to 1977.

** Simulated data (forecast) have been used for the years during the period 1978 to 2005.

TABLE 7.6

Average and Marginal Productivities of Capital Input and Elasticity of Steel Output with respect to Capital Input (For some selected years)

Year	Average Productivity (Tonnes of crude steel equivalent per lakh Rs. of gross fixed capital at constant 1960 prices	Marginal Productivity (Tonnes of crude steel equivalent per lakh additional Rs. of gross fixed capital 1960 prices	Elasticity of Steel Output with respect to Capital Input
1951*	99	40.3	0.41
1956	109	48.7	0.45
1962	61	26.8	0.44
1967	54	22.5	0.42
1972	49	20.6	0.42
1977	49	20.0	0.41
1978**	44	18.3	0.42
1981	42	17.4	0.41
1986	38	15.6	0.41
1991	35	14.3	0.41
1996	32	12.9	0.40
2001	29	11.6	0.40
2005	27	10.7	0.40

* Observed data have been used for the years during the period 1951 to 1977.

** Simulated data (forecast) have been used for the years during the period 1978 to 2005.

TABLE 7.7

Average and Marginal Productivities of Fuels Input, Elasticity of Steel Output with respect to Fuels Input, and the Measure of Returns to Scale (For some selected years)

Year	Average Productivity (Tonnes of crude steel equivalent per thousand tonnes of coal replacement equivalent)	Marginal Productivity (Tonnes of crude steel equivalent per thousand additional tonnes of coal replacement equivalent	Elasticity of Steel Output with respect to Fuels Input	Returns to Scale
1951*	344	87	0.25	1.04
1956	546	124	0.23	1.01
1962	598	138	0.23	1.01
1967	820	207	0.25	1.03
1972	836	210	0.25	1.03
1977	1204	325	0.27	1.03

1978**	1044	271	0.26	1.03
1981	1094	287	0.26	1.03
1986	1197	318	0.27	1.03
1991	1288	349	0.27	1.03
1996	1400	386	0.28	1.03
2001	1521	429	0.28	1.03
2005	1608	461	0.29	1.03

* Observed data have been used for the years during the period 1951 to 1977.
** Simulated data (forecast) have been used for the years during the period 1978 to 2005.

It may be observed from Tables 7.5, 7.6 and 7.7 that the average and marginal productivities corresponding to the inputs of labour and fuels have been rising during the period of analysis (1951 to 1977) and are expected to rise further during the forecast period. In case of capital input, the average and marginal productivities have been declining and are expected to decline further during the forecast period. It may, however, be observed that the values of elasticities of output with respect to different inputs have remained fairly stable during the period 1951 to 1977 and are expected to remain so during the forecast period. It may further be observed that these elasticities are of the order of respective average cost shares of different inputs, as specified in Section 7.3. This is an important result which validates the basic assumption made in some of the studies on total productivity (7, 52) that the relative cost shares of factors of production are equal to the respective elasticities of output with respect to corresponding inputs.

It may further be observed from Table 7.7 that the measure of returns to scale computed for each selected year is close to unity, even though the production function derived in Section 5.8 is non-homogeneous. The reason for this may be that the sample points of available data lie on that region of production function where constant returns to scale are operating.

The analysis reported in this section has important practical implications. If the availability of an input is less than its required level during a particular year in future, then, the corresponding elasticity of output provides the analyst with the measure of likely shortfall in the production of steel during that year. Suppose the availability of labour in the year 1991 turns out to be one per cent less than its desired availability, the output shall be less than its target level of

1991 by 0.343 per cent, provided the desired levels of capital and fuels are available. It has been implicitly assumed in the discussion under this section that there shall be no bottlenecks in the availability of the input of raw-materials during the forecast period and this input shall be available as specified in Table 6.4.

If the availabilities of more than one input are less than their respective desired levels during a particular year in future, the adverse effect of such a situation on output may be worked out by re-estimating the likely resultant output following the methodology already detailed out in this section.

7.5 SENSITIVITY ANALYSIS OF FORECASTS OF INPUT DEMANDS

7.5.1 Basis of Sensitivity Analysis

While doing the sensitivity analysis of the forecasts of input demands computed in Chapter VI (given in Table 6.4) it is assumed that the structural coefficients of the estimated input demand functions remain constant throughout the forecast period. The actual future demands for various inputs may differ from their forecast values because of the following two possibilities :

i. The future production targets of steel may deviate from their forecast path. This is a change in the expected schedule of an endogenous variable; and/or
ii. The future behaviour of prices of inputs of labour, capital and fuels may not follow their respective assumed normal paths. This results in the changes in assumed schedules of exogenous variables.

The effects of alterations in expected future schedules of endogenous variables and assumed future schedules of exogenous variables on the likely future schedules of input demands have been analysed independent of each other in this section.

7.5.2 Changes in the Schedule of Future Steel Production Targets

The actual future steel consumption requirements of the

economy may not be the same as depicted in Table 6.3. In case the actual future behaviour of the GNP deviates from its forecast path, it shall result in a changed schedule of the steel consumption requirements. As it has been assumed in Chapter VI that the schedule of future production targets (in terms of crude steel equivalent) is same as the schedule of future steel consumption requirements, a change in the schedule of steel consumption requirements of the economy also implies a changed future schedule of steel production targets. Secondly, the policy makers in steel industry may not fix production targets as being equal to steel consumption requirements and may fix the targets at a higher or lower level. This shall also lead to a different future schedule of production targets as compared to the one specified in Table 6.3.

The possibility of a changed schedule of future production targets may be taken care of by re-scheduling the input demands if the relevant indications are foreseen well in advance. In fact, it is easy to adjust production at a lower value than the pre-scheduled value even at a short notice by keeping a part of the available levels of capital and labour underemployed and using less than the pre-scheduled quantities of fuels and raw-materials. However, it is difficult to adjust production upward at a short notice, as this may only be possible if there are substitution possibilities between the fixed and the variable factors of production and there are no constraints on the supplies of variable factors of production. In general, a sufficient notice is needed to properly re-schedule the input requirements well in advance in order to meet the revised targets of steel production in future.

In this section, it is assumed that the exogenous variables (input prices) behave in the manner stipulated while computing the forecasts of input demands in Chapter VI. It is assumed that only the future targets of steel production are likely to change. It is easy to compute the revised schedules of input demands in future with the help of the input demand equations (5.43), (5.44), (5.45) and (5.50) estimated in Chapter V.

The elasticities of various input demands with respect to steel output may be computed from the respective estimated input demand equations in the following manner :

$$E_{LQ} = \frac{\partial \ln L}{\partial \ln Q} = 0.6969 \tag{7.3}$$

$$E_{KQ} = \frac{\partial \ln K}{\partial \ln Q} = 1.2434 \tag{7.4}$$

$$E_{FQ} = \frac{\partial \ln F}{\partial \ln Q} = 0.9148 \tag{7.5}$$

$$E_{MQ} = \frac{\partial \ln M}{\partial \ln Q} = 1.0355 \tag{7.6}$$

where E_{iQ} is the elasticity of the demand for ith input with respect to steel output and i = L, K, F and M.

Suppose there is a 10 per cent upward re-scheduling in the production targets starting from fifth year onwards in future, then,

$$\Delta \ln Q = \ln Q_R - \ln Q_S = \ln (Q_R/Q_S) \tag{7.7}$$

where

Q_R = rescheduled production target; and

Q_S = originally scheduled production target.

Equation (7.7) holds good for all the future years starting from fifth future year. As there is a 10 per cent upward scheduling in steel output,

$$\frac{Q_R}{Q_S} = 1.10 \tag{7.8}$$

and equation (7.7) takes the following form :

$$\partial \ln Q = \ln\left(\frac{Q_R}{Q_S}\right) = \ln(1.10) = 0.0953 \qquad (7.9)$$

Substituting this value of $\Delta\, \ell n$ Q into equation (7.3) the following result is obtained :

$$\partial \ln L = \ln L_R - \ln L_S = \ln(L_R / L_S) = 0.0664 \qquad (7.10)$$

where

L_R = re-scheduled labour demand; and

L_S = originally scheduled labour demand.

Taking the exponential of both sides of equation (7.10) one gets the following relationship :

$$\frac{L_R}{L_S} = \exp(0.0664) = 1.0687 \qquad (7.11)$$

The equation (7.11) points out that the labour demand should be re-scheduled upward by 6.87 per cent to cope up with 10 per cent increase in steel output targets.

The value of $\Delta\, \ell n$ Q as computed in equation (7.9) is then successively substituted into the equations (7.4), (7.5) and (7.6), and it is found that the planning for availabilities of various inputs should be done in such a manner that during the future years (starting from fifth future year) the capital input should be re-scheduled upward by 12.58 per cent, the fuels input by 9.11 per cent and the raw-materials input by 10.41 per cent.

It may, thus, be concluded that if the exogenous variables (input prices) behave in the same manner as assumed while computing the forecasts of cost minimising input demands, then a 10 per cent upward re-scheduling of future output targets shall be met by re-scheduling the demand levels of labour, capital, fuels and raw-materials by 6.87, 12.58, 9.11 and 10.41 per cent, respectively. It is possible only when a sufficiently advance notice regarding the upward re-scheduling of steel output is available.

TABLE 7.8
Effect of a Change in the Desired Target of Steel Production (for a future year) on Input Demands (in the corresponding year) : Sensitivity Analysis

Input	Percentage Changes* in Input Demands Corresponding to a Specified change (say m %) in Steel Production Target of, say nth Future Year			
	m = 5 %	m = 10 %	m = 15 %	m = 20 %
Labour	3.46	6.87	10.26	13.55
Capital	6.25	12.58	18.98	25.45
Fuels	4.56	9.11	13.64	18.15
Raw-Materials	5.18	10.41	15.57	20.78

* Percentage changes in input demands are positive or negative depending upon whether 'm' is positive or negative, respectively.

The analysis reported in this sub-section may be generalised for a prescribed upward or downward re-scheduling of the future steel production targets. Table 7.8 exhibits the results corresponding to the 5, 10, 15, or 20 per cent upward or downward change in the original schedule of future steel production targets, as specified in Table 6.3.

7.5.3 Effect of Variations in Future Prices of Inputs on Their Future Demands

It has already been mentioned under sub-section 6.6.1 that the input prices have been considered to be exogenous variables in the present study. The cost minimising demand functions for the inputs of labour, capital and fuels have already been estimated in equation (5.43), (5.44) and (5.45) under Section 5.7. The demand function for raw-materials, as estimated in equation (5.50), was found to be a function of steel production and technology only and independent of input prices. Given the steel production target series for the future, the annual cost-minimising combinations of the input of labour, capital and fuels depend upon the future price behaviour of these inputs. Thus, if the targets of steel output remain the same as specified in their computed forecast given in Table 6.3, then an expected variation in future input prices shall require the re-scheduling of the future input demands of labour, capital and fuels in order to achieve the production targets at the minimum costs. However, the demand series for raw materials remains unchanged as a result of variation in future input prices. In fact, it has been assumed and tested that there is no substitution possibility between the input of raw-materials and any other input.

The scenario of expected future normal price behaviour of labour, capital and fuels has already been explained in sub-section 6.6.1. The resulting cost-minimising combinations of labour, capital and fuels were simulated as given in Table 6.4.

Twelve different patterns or scenarios of possible future behaviour of prices of labour, capital and fuels have been visualised (including the scenario of normal price behaviour of sub-section 6.6.1) on the basis of intuitive judgement. This has been done in order to consider the effect of almost all possible extreme combinations of input prices. However, in the case of labour or fuels, the possibility of its price rising at a rate lower than the expected normal rate has not been visualised. But, in the case of capital, the possibility that its price does not rise during the period of forecast has been visualised. The effect of each price-scenario on cost-minimising input demands has been analysed in this sub-section.

Each price scenario has been defined on the basis of different assumed growth rates in input prices during the forecast period (1978-2005). The tweleve input price-scenarios visualised and analysed in the present study have been depicted in Table 7.9.

Input price scenario (IPS) I is the scenario of normal price behaviour as explained in sub-section 6.6.1. The input prices are assumed to grow at their respective expected normal rates.

Under IPS II, the price of labour is assumed to rise at a rate much faster than its expected normal rate while the prices of capital and fuels are assumed to grow at their respective expected normal rates.

Under IPS III, the price of capital is assumed to rise at a rate much faster than its expected normal rate while the prices of labour and fuels are assumed to grow at their respective expected normal rates.

TABLE 7.9
Assumed Growth Rates in Input Prices Under Different Price Scenarios (1977-2005)

Price Scenario	Percentage Price Rise Per Annum			
		Capital		
	Labour	1977-1990	1990-2005	Fuels
I	7	3	2	9
II	12	3	2	9
III	7	5	3	9
IV	7	3	2	15
V	12	5	3	9
VI	7	5	3	15
VII	12	3	2	15
VIII	12	5	3	15
IX	7	0	0	9
X	12	0	0	9
XI	7	0	0	15
XII	12	0	0	15

Under IPS IV, the price of fuels is assumed to rise at a rate much faster than its expected normal rate while the prices of labour and capital are assumed to grow at their respective expected normal rates.

Under IPS V, the prices of both labour and capital are assumed to grow at the rates much faster than their respective expected normal rates and only the price of fuels is assumed to rise at its expected normal rate.

It is assumed under IPS VI that the prices of both capital and fuels rise at the rates much faster than their respective expected normal rates and only the price of labour is assumed to grow at its expected normal rate.

Under IPS VII, the prices of both labour and fuels rise at the rates much faster than their respective expected normal rates and only the price of capital is expected to grow at its expected normal rate.

IPS VIII depicts the possibility when the prices of all the three inputs rise at the rates much faster than their respective expected normal rates.

It is assumed in each of the IPS IX through IPS XII that the price of capital does not rise and remains at its 1977 level throughout the period of forecast (1978 to 2005). The prices of both labour and fuels are assumed to rise at their respective expected normal rates under IPS IX and at much faster rates under IPS XII. It is assumed under IPS X that the price of labour rises at a rate much faster than its expected normal rate and the price of fuels at its expected normal rate. Under IPS XI, the price of labour is assumed to rise at its expected normal rate and that of fuels at a rate much faster than its expected normal rate.

The simulation forecasts of the targets of steel production during the period of forecast are given in Table 6.3. The simulation forecasts of cost minimising combinations of labour, capital and fuels corresponding to a particular price-scenario may be obtained by following the methodology already detailed out in sub-section 6.6.1. The results of such a simulation run corresponding to IPS I (normal price behaviour) have already been reported in Table 6.4. The results corresponding to the twelve input price scenarios are given in Table 7.10.

There is a one-to-one correspondence between the twelve input price-scenarios and twelve input demand scenarios. One and only one cost minimising input demand scenario corresponds to a particular input price scenario. Each input demand scenario specifies a series of combinations of the inputs of labour, capital and fuels (the raw-materials demand is independent of price scenarios and remains same under each price scenario) during the forecast period (1978 to 2005) such that the cost of producing the forecast targets of steel production is the minimum.

Further, there are twelve different combinations or packages of inputs of labour, capital and fuels during a particular forecast year which can produce the same quantity of steel provided the required quantities of raw-materials during that year are available. These alternative packages of inputs, corresponding to a particular forecast year, may be termed as 'isoquant' input packages. Thus, if the lack of desired availability of one or more input(s) in future years is foreseen at any point of time, the planners can immediately review the 'isoquant' input packages (and can even create more such packages) and attempt to substitute shortage(s) of some type(s) of input(s) by abundantly available input(s). However, the newly created input-package may not necessarily be the cost minimising one because the aim of achieving the production target may be considered to be more important than the aim of minimising the costs. Further, such adjustments may not be possible in a short period of time.

In order to analyse an input demand scenario the compound annual growth rates of the requirements of various inputs are computed with the help of the simulated input demand values of the initial and the terminal years (1978 and 2005). The compound annual growth rates in the demands for labour, capital and fuels are given in Table 7.10 corresponding to all the twelve price scenarios.

It may be observed from Table 7.10 that the variations in the likely future input price behaviour result in different future cost minimising schedules of input requirements. The compound annual growth rate in labour demand is minimum (1.71 per cent) corresponding to IPS X and maximum (3.641 per cent) corresponding to IPS VI. The compound annual growth rate in capital demand is minimum (6.117 per cent) corresponding to IPS III and maximum (6.949 per cent) corresponding to IPS XII. The growth rate in fuels demand is minimum (0.981 per cent) corresponding to IPS XI and maximum (3.628 per cent) corresponding to IPS V.

It may, thus, be concluded that the demand for capital input is not very responsive to variations in input prices while the demands for the inputs of labour and fuels are quite responsive to such variations.

TABLE 7.10
Compound Annual Growth Rates of Demand Forecasts of Labour, Capital and Fuels Under Different Price Scenarios

Price Scenario	Labour	Capital	Fuels
I	2.845	6.174	2.649
II	1.880	6.454	3.583
III	2.884	6.117	2.690
IV	3.602	6.413	1.160
V	1.919	6.396	3.628
VI	3.641	6.355	1.200
VII	2.631	6.693	2.085
VIII	2.669	6.635	2.126
IX	2.673	6.429	2.467
X	1.710	6.710	3.404
XI	3.429	6.668	0.981
XII	2.459	6.949	1.904

It may also be observed from Table 7.10 that under IPS X, when the labour demand grows at its minimum rate of 1.71 per cent, the demand for fuels grows at a very fast rate of 3.404 per cent per annum and the reverse behaviour is observed in case of IPS VI. When the fuels demand grows at its minimum rate of 0.981 per cent (under IPS XI), the demand for labour grows at a very fast rate of 3.429 per cent per annum and the reverse is true in case of IPS V. There is not much variation in the growth rate of demand for capital as it varies from a minimum of 6.117 per cent under IPS III to a maximum of 6.949 per cent per annum under IPS XII.

It may, thus, be concluded that there is very little substitution possible between capital and labour or between capital and fuels. A greater substitution is possible between labour and fuels. These results are in concurrence with the ones reported under Section 7.3 and given in Table 7.4.

7.6 NEED FOR A DYNAMIC FOLLOW-UP

The simulation model developed in Chapter VI is based on certain assumptions and is subject to certain limitations which shall be detailed out in Chapter IX. The model thus developed is not claimed to be the ultimate truth or applicable in all times to come in its present form. The basic purpose of this model is to provide to the national level planners of Indian steel industry with a broad long-term foresight of this industry. In fact, a check on the performance of this model has to be made from time to time in future. In case the predictions made through this simulation model turn out to be at variance with the actual system behaviour (when analysed at a future point of time) the model should be up-dated and improved upon. A procedure to carry out such dynamic checks and to introduce necessary corrective measures is suggested as follows.

It is suggested that the performance of the simulation model should be compared with the observed system behaviour in the year 1990. If the predicted and observed results are in agreement, the model gets validated to be used in future. If these results are not in agreement then suitable corrective steps must be taken. It is suggested that the sub-models estimated in Chapters IV and V should be re-estimated in 1990 incorporating the latest available data. The data of some of the initial years of the period of analysis (1951 to 1977) may be dropped out if it is felt that such data are no longer relevant. The simulation model can again be developed on the basis of the newly estimated sub-models and the forecast period can be pushed ahead upto the year 2015.

Such a procedure may then be repeated in the years 1995 and 2000 and the corresponding forecast periods pushed ahead to 2020 and 2025, respectively. Such a treatment shall keep the model up-to-date and necessary corrective actions can be taken well in advance. Thus, the model needs to be updated every five years (starting from 1990) to take into account the dynamics of the situation.

7.7 CONCLUDING REMARKS

The results obtained during the course of the present study and specially the ones obtained from the simulation model developed in Chapter VI have been analysed in the present chapter. It is expected that both GNP and steel consumption shall grow with exponential trends during the forecast period (1978 to 2005) exhibiting cyclical fluctuations around their respective trends. The GNP is expected to grow at a compound annual rate of 3.52 per cent and the steel consumption at 4.31 per cent. The steel intensity of GNP is expected to grow from 237 tonnes per crore rupees of GNP to about 290 tonnes per crore rupees of GNP during the forecast period. The desired targets of steel production have been fixed to be equal to the annual steel consumption requirements during the forecast period. Under the scenario of expected future normal price behaviour of inputs, the cost minimising demands for inputs of labour, capital and fuels are expected to grow with compound annual rates of 2.845, 6.174 and 2.649 per cent, respectively. It has been found that there is not much substitution possible between capital and labour or between capital and fuels, while labour and fuels are, to some extent, mutually substitutable. The effects of availability bottlenecks in one or more inputs on steel production have also been analysed in the present chapter. Finally, a sensitivity analysis of the forecasts of input demands has been performed with respect to changes in the schedule of future steel production targets (endogenous variable) and also with respect to variations in future input price behaviour (exogenous variables).

The analysis reported in this chapter has important practical implications and may be used by the national level planners of Indian steel industry. This analysis provides a very useful foresight of the likely behaviour of steel consumption requirements of the Indian economy, production targets, relevant input prices and their demands in Indian steel industry. A prognosis of the likely casualities in steel production due to input(s) availability bottleneck(s) has been carried out and the corrective measures have been prescribed to avoid such happenings. The need for a dynamic follow-up of the simulation model developd in Chapter VI has also been stressed in this chapter.

EIGHT

MAJOR FINDINGS AND CONTRIBUTIONS

8.1 INTRODUCTION

In the preceding chapters, a detailed account of the steel consumption requirements of Indian economy and the production structure of Indian steel industry has been reported along with a system simulation model of this industry. The study reported in this book is aimed to analyse the important elements of the system of Indian steel industry in order to help the planning process by supplying the input information in advance as to what are the likely annual requirements of steel in India upto the year 2005 and how much of each input (labour, capital, fuels, and raw-materials) shall be needed to produce the desired quantity of steel during each year at minimum possible cost. The purpose of this chapter is to summarise the major findings of this study and highlight the significant contributions made.

8.2 SUMMARY OF MAJOR FINDINGS

The major findings regarding the relevant literature, consumption behaviour of steel in Indian economy, production structure in Indian steel industry and the simulation forecasts of various relevant variables are discussed in this section.

8.2.1 Existing Relevant Literature

i. There has been a gradual evolution of a more realistic and sophisticated framework to analyse a firm or an industry.

ii. The available literature on Indian steel industry does not analyse this industry in its totality.
iii. Serious attention has not been paid to explore the possibility of applying global method to analyse and forecast steel consumption requirements of Indian economy.
iv. There have been very few attempts to estimate the production function in Indian steel industry. The models used are the crude forms of production function approach.
v. There seems to be no serious attempt to apply simulation modelling approach to analyse the system of Indian steel industry or any other industry.

8.2.2 Consumption Behaviour of Steel in Indian Economy (1951 to 1977)

i. Steel consumption in an economy is influenced by the level and behaviour of its GNP which is an overall economic indicator.
ii. The apparent consumption of steel in terms of crude steel equivalent has grown with a linear trend over time during the period of analysis (1951 to 1977). There have been marked cyclical fluctuations around the linear trend.
iii. The GNP has grown with an exponential trend during the period of analysis.
iv. The steel intensity of GNP has increased from about 100 tonnes of steel per crore rupees of GNP (at factor cost at constant (1970-71) prices) to above 200 tonnes in 1977, with wide annual fluctuations.
v. The elasticity of steel consumption with respect to GNP seems to be declining and tapering off around unity.
vi. The type of global model that was found to be appropriate in explaining and forecasting steel consumption in OECD contries (159) is inappropriate when tried on Indian data.
vii. The growth rate of GNP during a particular year has a lagged effect on steel consumption in Indian economy. The current year's level of steel consumption is determined by current and five immediately preceding years. The growth rate of GNP during (t-2)th year has the maximum impact on the level of steel consumption in the year t. The impact curve of the growth rates of GNP during the years t-5, t-4, ..., t-1, t vis-a-

vis the level of steel consumption during the year t is of inverted-V type with its peak corresponding to the (t-2)th year.

viii. Although the GNP has grown with a smooth exponential trend during the period of analysis, its random component seems to have been captured and explained, to a reasonable extent, by the growth rates of GNP during the seven immediately preceding years.

8.2.3 Production Structure in Indian Steel Industry (1951 to 1977)

i. The production function in Indian steel industry is non-homogeneous.

ii. There has been a non-neutral (biased) technical change in Indian steel industry such that it uses capital and saves labour and fuels.

iii. The inputs labour, capital and fuels are, as a group, weakly separable from the fourth input, raw-materials. The marginal rate of substitution between any two of the first three inputs is independent of the quantity of raw-materials used.

iv. The demand for each of the three inputs, labour, capital and fuels, is a function of output of steel, prices of these inputs and the state of technology. The demand for raw-materials is a function of output and the state of technology only.

v. The own price elasticity of demand (in absolute terms) for fuels is the maximum (-0.27) followed closely by that for labour (-0.21) and is the least for capital (-0.10).

vi. All the three inputs (labour, capital, and fuels) are mutually substitutable. Labour and fuels are found to be better substitutes than either labour and capital or capital and fuels. The partial elasticity of substitution is estimated to be 0.58 between labour and fuels, 0.17 between labour and capital, and 0.18 between capital and fuels. Raw-materials are not substitutable by any other input.

vii. The elasticities of demands for labour, capital, fuels, and raw-materials with respect to output of steel are estimated to be 0.70, 1.24, 0.91 and 1.04, respectively.

viii. The average and marginal productivities of the inputs of labour and fuels have been rising while those of capital input declining during the period of analysis. The value of the elasticity of output of steel with respect to each of the three inputs has remained fairly stable during the period of analysis.

ix. Although the production function is found to be non-homogeneous, the value of returns to scale has remained close to unity during the period of analysis.

8.2.4 Simulation Forecasts of the Relevant Variables (1978 to 2005)

8.2.4.1 Forecasts of GNP, Steel Consumption Requirement and Production of Steel

i. The GNP (at factor cost at constant (1970-71) prices) is expected to grow from Rs. 47019 crores in 1978 to Rs. 119795 crores in 2005, with a smooth exponential trend. The compound annual rate of growth is, thus, expected to be 3.52 per cent.

ii. The annual steel consumption requirement of the economy is expected to grow, somewhat with an exponential trend, from 11.124 million tonnes (in terms of crude steel equivalent) in 1978 to 34.714 million tonnes in 2005, with marked cyclical fluctuations around the trend. This implies a compound annual rate of growth of 4.31 per cent.

iii. The desired targets of production of steel during the period of forecast have been fixed to be equal to the annual steel consumption requirements during the same period. The simulation forecast of the annual steel production (targets) is the same as that for steel consumption requirements.

iv. The steel intensity of the GNP is expected to grow with a linear trend from about 237 tonnes of steel per crore rupees of GNP (at factor cost at constant (1970-71) prices) in 1978 to about 290 tonnes in 2005, with marked cyclical fluctuations.

v. The elasticity of steel consumption with respect to GNP is expected to remain at a constant value of 1.27 during the period of forecast.

8.2.4.2 Forecasts of Normal Behaviour of Input Prices

Under normal economic conditions during the forecast period it is expected that :

i. The price of labour input shall grow at an annual rate of 7 per cent.
ii. The price of fuels input shall grow at an annual rate of 9 per cent.
iii. The price of capital input shall grow at an annual rate of 3 per cent during the period 1978 to 1990 and thereafter at 2 per cent per annum upto 2005.
iv. The price of raw-materials input is not relevant for the purposes of the present study.

8.2.4.3 Forecasts of Input Demands

In case the set targets of steel production are to be achieved, the demands for the inputs of labour, capital and fuels are expected to behave in the following manner, under the assumption of normal price behaviour of these inputs. The demand for raw-materials is, however, independent of its own price and the prices of other inputs.

i. The demand for labour shall increase from about 7146 lakh employee man-hours in 1978 to about 15239 lakh employee man-hours in 2005. This implies a compound annual rate of growth of 2.84 per cent.
ii. The demand for capital, at constant 1960 prices, shall increase from about Rs. 2511 crores in 1978 to about Rs. 12658 crores in 2005. This implies a compound annual rate of growth of 6.17 per cent.
iii. The demand for fuels in terms of coal replacement equivalent shall increase from about 107 lakh tonnes in 1978 to about 216 lakh tonnes in 2005. This implies a compound annual rate of growth of 2.65 per cent.
iv. The demand for raw-materials, at constant 1960 prices, shall increase from about Rs. 324 crores in 1978 to about Rs. 993 crores in 2005. This implies a compound annual rate of growth of 4.23 per cent.

The forecasts of annual demands for all the four inputs exhibit cycles around their respective trends which are quite similar to the ones observed in the forecast of annual steel production targets (or steel consumption requirements).

8.3 SIGNIFICANT CONTRIBUTIONS MADE BY THE PRESENT STUDY

Steel plays a crucial role in the economic development of a nation. There is an urgent need for long term planning in steel industry of a developing country. This calls for the analysis of this industry in its totality. In the light of this, the study reported in this book may have considerable significance in the long term planning of this industry. The present study has resulted in the following significant contributions :

i The study reported in this book is perhaps the first attempt, though modest, to analyse Indian steel industry as a system. The steel consumption requirements of the economy have been analysed along with the production structure in this industry.

ii. The existing literature on forecasting steel consumption requirements of an economy (with special reference to India), the theory of production functions and its applications to Indian steel industry, and the technique of econometric simulation modelling has been discussed and critically reviwed. This can facilitate the researchers in the related areas to have a critical overview of the existing literature.

iii. It is for the first time that the concept of global modelling has been extensively explored to formulate the consumption function in Indian steel industry. The function thus estimated distinctly differs from the earlier attempts (with reference to some other countries) as it has been realised, perhaps for the first time that the growth rate of GNP has a current as well as lagged effect on steel consumption requirements of Indian economy.

iv. The latest developments in the production function theory have been incorporated while analysing the production structure of Indian steel industry. This study is a more realistic attempt as it has tested and accepted the existence of a non-homogeneous production function in Indian steel industry. The real behaviour of the production function has, thus, not been camouflaged by the assumption of a homogeneous production function, which is generally made for the sake of convenience.

v. It is for the first time that an attempt has been made to simultaneously estimate the cost minimising input demand functions and work back the corresponding production function (non-homogeneous) in case of an Indian industry.

vi. The use of a translog form has, perhaps, been made for the first time to analyse the inputs' substitution possibilities in case of Indian steel industry.

vii. The study performs a pioneering job by developing a simulation model of Indian steel industry. It is perhaps for the first time that this technique is used to analyse an Indian industry as a system.

viii. The forecasts of the expected behaviour of various endogenous variables have been computed, under different scenarios of the exogenous variables, in a long term period (1978 to 2005). These forecasts can facilitate the planning process for this industry at the national level.

The present study has, thus, made significant contributions towards developing a better methodology for research on Indian industries and has applied this methodology to analyse the system of Indian steel industry.

8.4 CONCLUDING REMARKS

An overview of the summary of major findings during the course of the present study and the significant contributions made have been discussed in this chapter. After going through these findings and contributions, it may be observed that this study has concentrated itself more on the practical aspects of the system of Indian steel industry. Some of the limitations/shortcomings of this study along with the suggestions for future extensions and modifications will be discussed in the subsequent chapter.

NINE

SUGGESTIONS FOR FUTURE RESEARCH

9.1 INTRODUCTION

The present study has taken the basic inspiration from Dixon et al. (39), Ellis and Ludwig (45), Nadiri (107), Naylor et al. (115), OECD study (124), Thirsk (148) and Vinell (157). The study reported in this book has its own limitations which are mentioned in this chapter. Considering the present study as a stratum, various possible extensions and modifications are suggested in this chapter.

9.2 LIMITATIONS OF THE STUDY

In its attempt to analyse the system of Indian steel industry in its totality, this study might have overlooked or ignored some finer and micro-economic aspects of this industry. These aspects could have been incorporated to make the models more sophisticated but at the cost of adversely affecting the constraints of available time, money and computational facilities. The following are the limitations/ shortcomings of the present study :

i. Different categories of finished steel have not been considered while analysing the consumption behaviour of steel in Indian economy and the production function in Indian steel industry. The analysis in this study is based on consumption and production of steel in terms of crude steel equivalent. In fact, it is the crude steel which is generally the bottleneck in the production process of the steel industry.

ii. The consumption of steel has been analysed in terms of apparent steel consumption and not in terms of actual steel consumption. This was done becaues of the lack of data on inventory changes in the system.

iii. Each factor of production has been considered to be a homogeneous sum of its components, thus implicitly assuming that all the components of an input make equal contributions to the production of steel. Although somewhat unrealistic, this assumption had to be made in the face of various constraints already mentioned in this section.

iv. In order to facilitate the analysis of production function in Indian steel industry, it has been implicitly assumed that there is perfect competition in the market for steel and also in the markets for the inputs of labour, capital, fuels and raw-materials. Though such assumptions are not completely true yet these have been made in most of the studies on production function analysis.

v. The most flexible form to analyse the production function (or cost function) of an industry is the translog form (25). Alathough this form could not be used for the purposes of this study, its application to Indian steel industry has been briefly explained in Appendix (1). The main limitation of using a translog form is that only input share equations can be estimated by this form and not the input demand (in real terms) equations.

vi. The production function worked back from the estimated input demand functions is a local approximation in the region where cost shares are around their average values (during the period of analysis). In spite of this weakness, the derived production function has proved to be a very good approximation to the actual production function.

vii. The imports of steel have been assumed to be equal to the exports (in terms of crude steel equivalent) during the period of forecast. The separate analysis of foreign trade of steel has not been attempted.

viii. The forecasts of different endogenous variables are conditional forecasts, valid under the following conditions :

a. The coefficients estimated in different sub-models are the true parameters and remain stable during the forecast period; and

b. The exogenous variables take their assumed values during the forecast period.

If these conditions hold good, then each of the endogenous variables should follow its forecast path. In spite of this, an unforeseen disturbance in the forecast behaviour of GNP, steel consumption requirements and steel production can cause disturbances in the forecasts of cost minimising input demands.

9.3 SUGGESTIONS FOR FUTURE RESEARCH

Some broad problem areas for future research regarding Indian steel industry (or any other industry) emerge directly from the inadequacy and limitations of the relevant literature discussed in Section 2.5. The same are not repeated here. However, the possible extensions and modifications of the present study are suggested here for future research work.

i. The GNP estimating procedure may be modified by developing an econometric model of the economy as a whole.
ii. A further exploration of the steel consumption function is suggested by trying some other functional forms or by changing the explanatory variable from GNP to some other macro-economic variable, such as industrial production, population, total fixed investments, etc. In fact, a number of different experiments were conducted during the course of the present study by taking industrial production, capital goods production and construction activity, individually and in combinations, as the explanatory macro-economic variables for estimating the steel consumption function in Indian economy. These trials have, however, not been reported as the same have not been found suitable for the purposes of the present study.
iii. A refinement in the reported steel consumption function may be introduced if the data on steel inventory changes are available. The actual steel consumption may then be used instead of apparent steel consumption in the estimation of the steel consumption function.
iv. The demand for various categories of finished steel may be analysed vis-a-vis the relevant economic indicators. The end-

use method may also be used for the analysis purpose. However, the efficacy of using this method for the purpose of forecasting is doubtful.

v. The substitution possibilities among various components of each input may be analysed with the help of a translog production (or cost) function. The basic idea of such a methodology may be taken from Pindyck's work (125). Pindyck has reported an international comparison of interfuel substitution possibilities and industrial demand for energy.

vi. There is a scope to analyse the effect of increasing use of substitutes of steel, such as plastics, aluminium, etc., on the demand for steel in the economy. Further, the effect of production of better and stronger qualities of steel may be analysed vis-a-vis its demand in terms of crude steel equivalent.

vii. A study of the existing and expected future availabilities of various inputs to the system of Indian steel industry may be a good complement to the present study.

viii. The simulation model developed in this study may be further refined by dropping the assumption of imports of steel being equal to its exports in terms of crude steel equivalent. The behaviour of imports and exports of steel may be extensively analysed with respect to various categories of finished steel.

ix. There exists a wide scope to study different industries in India from a system's point of view. Simulation modelling technique provides the convenient means to carry out such studies.

9.4 CONCLUDING REMARKS

The limitations of the present study have been discussed in this chapter. Various possible extensions and modifications of the present study have been summarised to facilitate the future research work. It is hoped that the work reported in this book would generate further interest in the study of Indian steel industry in its totality and would provide some useful material to the future researchers in the related areas.

BIBLIOGRAPHY

1. AGRAWAL GC (1976) Public Sector Steel Industry in India, Chaitanya Publishing House, Allahabad.
2. ALLEN RGD (1938) Mathematical Analysis for Economists, Macmillan and Co., London.
3. ALLEN RGD (1960) Mathematical Economics, Macmillan and Co., New York.
4. ARCHIBALD GC and LIPSEY RG (1977) An Introduction to a Mathematical Treatment of Economics, English Language Book Society, London.
5. ARROW KJ, CHENERY HB, MINHAS BS and SOLOW RM (1961) Capital-Labour Substitution and Economic Efficiency, Review of Economics and Statistics, 43 (3), 225-250.
6. ASCHER W (1978) Forecasting : An Appraisal for Policy Makers and Planners, The John Hopkins University Press, Baltimore.
7. BANERJI A (1975) Capital Intensity and Productivity in Indian Industry, The Macmillan Co. of India, Delhi.
8. BARNA T (1961) On Measuring Capital, Chapter V in The Theory of Capital (Eds. LUTZ FA and HAGUE DC), Macmillan and Co., London.
9. BARTEN AP (1969) Maximum Likelihood Estimation of a Complete System of Demand Equations, European Economic Review, 1 (1), 7-73.
10. BERNDT ER and CHRISTENSEN LR (1973) The Translog Function and the Substitution of Equipment, Structures, and Labour in U.S. Manufacturing 1929-68, Journal of

Econometrics, 1, 81-114.

11. BERNDT ER and WOOD DO (1975) Technology, Prices, and the Derived Demand for Energy, Review of Economics and Statistics, 57 (3), 259-268.
12. BHAGWATI JN and DESAI P (1970) India : Planning for Industrialisation and Trade Policies Since 1951, Oxford University Press, London.
13. BOULDING K (1956) The Skeleton of Science, Management Science, 2(3), 197-208.
14. BROUDE HW (1963) Steel Decisions and National Economy, Yale University Press, New Haven.
15. BROWN M (1966) On the Theory and Measurement of Technological Change, Cambridge University Press, Cambridge.
16. CHADHA R and PREM VRAT (1982a) The consumption Pattern of Steel in India : A Statistical Analysis, Proceedings of 24th National Convention of IIIE, New Delhi, 138-147.
17. CHADHA R and PREM VRAT (1982b) A Global Model of Steel Consumption in India, Journal of Engineering Production (ISME), New Delhi, 5(3), 11-15.
18. CHADHA R and PREM VRAT (1982c) A Translog Model of Energy Substitution in Indian Steel Industry, Proceedings of 15th Annual Convention of Operations Research Society of India, Kharagpur.
19. CHAKRABARTY D (1983) Translog Production Function - A Review Literature, Artha Vijnana, 25(2), 113-146.
20. CHAMBERS JC, MULLICK SK and SMITH DD (1974) An Executive's Guide to Forecasting, John Wiley and Sons, New York.
21. CHANDHOK HL (1978) Wholesale Price Statistics, India : 1947-78, Volume I, Economic and Scientific Research Foundation, New Delhi.
22. CHAUDHURI MR (1975) The Iron and Steel Industry of India, Oxford and India Book House, Delhi.
23. CHIANG AC (1974) Fundamental Methods of Mathematical Economics, McGraw Hill, Kogakusha, Tokyo.
24. CHRISTENSEN LR, JORGENSON DW and LAU LJ (1971) Conjugate Duality and the Transcendental Logarithmic Production Function, Econometrica, 39(4), 255-256.
25. CHRISTENSEN LR, JORGENSON DW and LAU LJ (1973) Transcendental Logarithmic Production Frontiers, Review of

Economics and Statistics, 55(1), 28-45.
26. COHEN KJ (1960) Computer Models of the Shoe, Leather, Hide Sequence, Prentice Hall, Englewood Cliffs, New Jersey.
27. COHEN KJ and CYERT RM (1961) Computer Models in Dynamic Economics, Quarterly Journal of Economics, 75(1), 112-127.
28. DASTUR MN (1961) Steel in India - Economic and Technological Possibilities, The Fourth Sir Visvesvaraya Lecture, Bombay.
29. DENISON EF (1957) Theoretical Aspects of Quality change, Capital Consumption and Net Capital Formation, in Part I of Problem of Capital Formation (A Report of the NBER, New York), Princeton University Press, Princeton.
30. DENISON EF (1961) Measurement of Labour Input : Some Questions of Definition and Adequacy of Data, in Part II of Output, Input and Prouctivity Measurement (A Report of the NBER, New York), Princeton University Press, Princeton.
31. DESAI BG (1978) Energy Policy of India, Jyoti, Vadodara.
32. DEUTSCH R (1969) System Analysis Techniques, Prentice Hall, Englewood Cliffs, New Jersey.
33. DHOLAKIA BH (1974) Sources of Economic Growth in India, Good Companions, Baroda.
34. DHOLAKIA BH (1977) Measurement of Capital Input and Estimation of Time Series Production Functions in Indian Manufacturing, Indian Economic Journal, 24(3), 333-355.
35. DHRYEMES P and KURZ M (1964) Technology and Scale in Electricity Generation, Econometrics, 32(3), 287-315.
36. DIEWERT WE (1971) An Application of the Shephard Duality Theorem : A Generalized Leontief Production Function, Journal of Political Economy, 79(3), 481-507.
37. DIEWERT WE (1973) Separability and the Generalized Cobb-Douglas Utility Functions, Mimeo, Department of Manpower and Immigration, Ottawa.
38. DIWAN RK (1968) Returns to Scale in Indian Industry : A Comment, Indian Economic Journal, 15(4), 496-500.
39. DIXON PB, BOWLES S and KENDRICK D (1980) Notes and Problems in Microeconomic Theory, Chapter 4, North Holland, Amsterdam.
40. DOUGLAS PH (1948) Are There laws of Production, American Economic Review, 38(1), 1-41.

41. DURBIN J and WATSON GS (1950) Testing for Serial Correlation in Least Squares Regression (Part I), Biometrika, 37(3,4), 409-428.
42. DURBIN J and WATSON GS (1951) Testing for Serial Correlation in Least Squares Regression (Part II), Biometrika, 38(1,2), 159-178.
43. DURBIN J (1970) Testing for Serial Correlation in Least Squares Regression When Some of the Regressors are Lagged Dependent Variables, Econometrica, 38(3), 410-421.
44. DUTT MM (1955) The Production Function for Indian Manufactures, Sankhya, 15(4), 417-426.
45. ELLIS DO and LUDWIG FJ (1962) Systems Philosophy, Prentice Hall, Englewood Cliffs, New Jersey.
46. FERGUSON CE (1969) The Neoclassical Theory of Production and Distribution, Cambridge University Press, Cambridge.
47. FORRESTER JW (1961) Industrial Dynamics, The MIT Press, Cambridge, Massachusetts.
48. FORRESTER JW (1969) Urban Dynamics, The MIT Press, Cambridge, Massachusetts.
49. FORRESTER JW (1971) World Dynamics, Wright Allen Press, Cambridge, Massachusetts.
50. FRIEDMAN M (1953) The Methodology of Positive Economics, Part I (Introduction) in Essays in Positive Economics (Ed. FRIEDMAN M), University of Chicago Press, Chicago.
51. FUSS M and McFadden d (Ed. 1978) Production Economics : A Dual Approach to Theory and Applications, 2 Volumes, North Holland, Amsterdam.
52. GOLDAR BN (1981) Some Aspects of Technological Progress in Indian Manufacturing Industry, Ph.D. Thesis, Delhi School of Economics, University of Delhi, Delhi.
53. GORDON G (1980) Systems Simulation, Prentice Hall, New Delhi.
54. GORMAN WM (1965) Production Functions in Which the Elasticities of Substitution Stand in Fixed Proportion to Each Other, Review of Economic Studies, 32, 217-224.
55. GRIFFIN JM and GREGORY PR (1976) An Intercountry Translog Model of Energy Substitution Responses, American Economic Review, 66(5), 845-857.
56. GRILICHES Z (1967) Production Functions in Manufacturing:

Some Preliminary Results, in the Theory and Empirical Analysis of Production (Ed. BROWN M), NBER, New York.

57. GRILICHES Z and RINGSTAD V (1971) Economies of Scale and the Form of Production Function, North Holland, Amsterdam.

58. GUJARATI D (1967) Sources of Output Growth in Indian Manufacturing, 1946-58, Indian Journal of Industrial Relations, 3(1), 41-48.

59. GUPTA GS (1973) Production Function and Factor Productivity in the Indian Cement Industry, Indian Journal of Industrial Relations, 8(3), 359-385.

60. GUPTA GS and PATEL K (1976) Production Function in Indian Sugar Industry, Indian Journal of Industrial Relations, 11(3), 315-337.

61. HANOCH G (1975) Production and Demand Models with Direct or Indirect Implicit Additivity, Econometrica, 43(3), 395-419.

62. HASHIM SR and DADI MM (1973) Capital-Output Relations in Indian Manufacturing, 1946-1964, M.S. University of Baroda, Baroda.

63. HEKMAN JS (1978) An Analysis of the Changing Location of Iron and Steel Production in the Twentieth Century, American Economic Review, 68(1), 123-133.

64. HELWIG JT and COUNCIL KA (Ed. 1979) SAS User's guide, SAS Institute, Cary, North Carolina.

65. HENDERSON JM and QUANDT RE (1971) Microeconomic Theory : A Mathematical Approach, McGraw Hill, New York.

66. HICKS JR (1963) The Theory of Wages, Macmillan and Co., London.

67. HILLIER LR and LIEBERMAN GJ (1967) Introduction to Operations Research, Holden Day, San Francisco.

68. HIRSCHMAN AO (1958) The Strategy of Economic Development, Yale University Press, London.

69. HOUGLUND B and WERLIN L (1964) The Production System of the Swedish Economy : An Input-Output Analysis, Almqvist and Wicksell, Stockholm.

70. HOPPE W (1974) Economic Forecasting in Steel Industry, in Method and Techniques of Business Forecasting (Eds. BULTER WF et al.), Prentice Hall, Englewood Cliffs, New Jersey.

71. HUMPHREY DB and MORONEY JR (1975) Substitution

Among Capital, Labour, and Natural Resource Products in American Manufacturing, Journal of Political Economy, 83(1), 57-82.

72. INDIA, CENTRAL STATISTICAL ORGANISATION (Annual Publication, 1946-1958) Census of Indian Manufactures, CSO, Calcutta.
73. INDIA, CENTRAL STATISTICAL ORGANISATION (Annual Publication, 1959 to 1977-78) Annual Survey of Industries (Census Sector), CSO, Calcutta..
74. INDIA, CENTRAL STATISTICAL ORGANISATION (Annual Publication, 1975 to 1980) National Accounts Statistics, CSO, New Delhi.
75. INDIA, GOVT. OF (Annual Publication, 1963 to 1986) Economic Survey, Controller of Publications, Delhi.
76. INDIA, GOVT. OF (1974) Fuel Policy Committee (Chairman : CHAKRAVARTI S), Manager of Publications, Delni.
77. INDIA, MINISTRY OF INFORMATION AND BROADCASTING (1982) India : A Reference Annual, Publications Division, Delhi, 322-326.
78. INDIA, PLANNING COMMISSION (1952) First Five Year Plan (1951-56), Manager of Publications, Delhi.
79. INDIA, PLANNING COMMISSION (1956) Second Five Year Plan (1956-61), Manager of Publications, Delhi.
80. INDIA, PLANNING COMMISSION (1981) Sixth Five Year Plan (1980-85), Manager of Publications, Delhi.
81. INDIA, PLANNING COMMISSION (1981) A Technical Note on Sixth Plan of India (1980-85), Manager of Publications, Delhi, 55-56.
82. INTERNATIONAL IRON AND STEEL INSTITUTE, COMMITTEE ON STATISTICS (1982) Steel Statistical Year Book, IISI, Brussels.
83. INTERNATIONAL IRON AND STEEL INSTITUTE, COMMITTEE ON ECONOMIC STUDIES (1972) World Steel Demand : Projection 85, IISI, Brussels.
84. JOHNSON WA (1966) The Steel Industry of India, Harvard University Press, Cambridge.
85. JOHRI CK and AGARWAL NC (1966) Inter Industry Wage Structure in India, 1950-1961, Indian Journal of Industrial Relations, 1(4), 377-414.
86. KENDRICK JW (1956) Productivity Trends : Capital and

Labour, Review of Economics and Statistics, 38(3), 248-257.

87. KENNEDY C and THIRLWALL AP (1972) Surveys in Applied Economics : Technical Progress, Economic Journal, 82(325), 11-72.
88. KLEIN LR (1950) Economic Fluctuations in the United States, 1921-1941, Cowles Commission for Research in Economics, Monograph No. 11, John Wiley and Sons, New York.
89. KLEIN LR (1973) An Introduction to Econometrics, Prentice Hall, New Delhi.
90. KLEIN LR (1975) A Textbook of Econometrics, Prentice Hall, New Delhi.
91. KMENTA J and GILBERT RF (1968) Small Sample Properties of Alternative Estimators of Seemingly Unrelated Regressions, Journal of American Statistical Association, 63(324), 1180-1200.
92. KOUTSOYIANNIS A (1975) Modern Microeconomics, Macmillan Press, London.
93. KOUTSOYIANNIS A (1977) Theory of Econometrics, Macmillan Press, London.
94. KRISHNA R and MEHTA SS (1968) Productivity Trends in Large Scale Industries, Economic and Political Weekly, 3(43), 1655-1660.
95. LEABO DA (1972) Basic Statistics, D.B. Taraporevala Sons, Bombay.
96. MAHALANOBIS PC (1953) Some Observations on the Process of Growth of National Income, Sankhya, 12(4), 307-312.
97. MAIZEL A (1963) Inustrial Growth and World Trade, Cambridge University Press, Cambridge.
98. MAJUMDAR DD (1967) Productivity of Labour and Capital in Indian Industry During 1951-1961, Arthanity, 10(1,2), 98-109.
99. MAKRIDAKIS S and WHEELWRIGHT SC (1978) Interactive Forecasting, Holden Day, San Francisco.
100. McFadden D (1963) Further Results on CES Production Function, Review of Economic Studies, 30, 73-83.
101. MEHTA SS (1974) Growth and Productivity in Indian Industries, Anvesak, 4(1), 1-11.
102. MEHTA SS (1976) Returns to Scale and Sources of Growth of Output in Large Scale Indian Industries, Indian Journal of Industrial Relations, 11(3), 339-350.

103. MORONEY JR and TRAPANI JM (1981) Factor Demand and Substitution in Mineral Intensive Industries, Bell Journal of Economics, 12(1), 272-284.
104. MUKERJI V (1963) A Generalized SMAC Function With Constant Ratios of Elasticities of Substitution, Review of Economic Studies, 30, 233-236.
105. MUKHERJEE M (1969) National Income in India : Trends and Structure, Statistical Publishing Co., Calcutta.
106. NADIRI MI (1970) Some Approaches to the Theory and Measurement of the Total Factor Productivity : A Survey, Journal of Economic Literature, 8(4), 1137-1177.
107. NADIRI MI (1982) Producers Theory, Chapter 1 in Handbook of Mathematical Economics, Volume II (Eds. ARROW KJ and INTRILIGATOR MD), North Holland, Amsterdam, 431-490.
108. NARSIMHAN GVL and FEBRYCY MZ (1974) Relative Efficiencies of Organized Industries in India, 1949-58, Journal of Development Studies, 10(2), 230-241.
109. NATIONAL COUNCIL OF APPLIED ECONOMIC RESEARCH (1960) Appraisal of Steel Demand, CSIR, New Delhi.
110. NATIONAL COUNCIL OF APPLIED ECONOMIC RESEARCH (1963) Reappraisal of Steel Demand (2 Volumes), NCAER, New Delhi.
111. NATIONAL COUNCIL OF APPLIED ECONOMIC RESEARCH (1968) Long Term Projections for Iron and Steel, NCAER, New Delhi.
112. NATIONAL COUNCIL OF APPLIED ECONOMIC RESEARCH (1971) Demand for Steel - 1975 and 1980, NCAER, New Delhi.
113. NATIONAL PRODUCTIVITY COUNCIL (1974) Productivity Trends in Iron and Steel Industry in India, NPC, New Delhi.
114. NATIONAL PRODUCTIVITY COUNCIL (1981) Rourkela Steel Plant Planning System : A Systems Dynamics Model, NPC, New Delhi.
115. NAYLOR TH, BALINTFY JL, BURDICK DS and CHU K (1966) Computer Simulation Techniques, John Wiley and Sons, New York.
116. NYLOR TH, BURDICK DS and SASSER WE (1967) Computer Simulation Experiments with Economic Systems : The

Problem of Experimental Design, Journal of American Statistical Association, 62(320), 1315-1337.

117. NAYLOR TH, WALLACE WH and SASSER WE (1967) Computer Simulation Model of the Textile Industry, Journal of American Statistical Association, 62(320), 1338-1364.
118. NAYLOR TH and VERNON JM (1969) Microeconomics and Decision Models of the Firm, Harcourt, Brace and World, New York.
119. NAYLOR TH (1971) Computer Simulation Experiments with Models of Economic Systems, John Wiley and Sons, New York.
120. NERLOVE M (1963) Returns to Scale in Electricity Supply, Chapter 7 in Measurement in Economics (Ed. CHRIST CF et al.), Stanford University Press, Stanford, California.
121. NICKELS RRD and JACOBSON JE (1982) The World Steel Outlook to 1990, Chase Econometric Associates, Bala Cynwyd, PA.
122. ORCUTT GH (1960) Simulation of Economic Systems, American Economic Review, 50(5), 893-907.
123. ORGANISATION FOR ECONOMIC CO-OPERATION AND DEVELOPMENT (1969) Steel Demand Forecasting in OECD Countries, OECD, Paris.
124. ORGANISATION FOR ECONOMIC CO-OPERATION AND DEVELOPMENT (1974) Forecasting Steel Consumption : Cross Section and Time Series Approaches, OECD, Paris.
125. PINDYCK RS (1979) Interfuel Substitution and the Industrial Demand for Energy : An International Comparison, Review of Economics and Statistics, 61(2), 169-179.
126. PINDYCK RS and RUBINFELD DL (1976) Econometric Models and Economic Forecasts, McGraw Hill Kogakusha, Tokyo.
127. RADER T (1972) Theory of Microeconomics, Academic Press, New York.
128. RAO P and Miller RL (1972) Applied Econometrics, Prentice Hall, New Delhi.
129. REDDY MGK and RAO SV (1962) Functional Distribution in the Large Scale Manufacturing Sector in India, Artha Vijnana, 4(3), 189-196.
130. REVANKAR NS (1971) A Class of Variable Elasticity of Substitution Production Functions, Econometrica, 39(1), 61-71.

131. ROWLEY CK (1969) Steel Prices and Public Policy, Applied Economics, 1(1), 51-78.
132. ROWLEY CK (1971) Steel and Public Policy, McGraw Hill, London.
133. RUIST E (1974) Some Statistical Problems in Testing of Models, Chapter 3 in Forecasting Steel Consumption : Cross Section and Time Series Approaches, OECD, Paris.
134. SAMUELSON PA (1947) Foundations of Economic Analysis, Harvard University Press, Cambridge.
135. SAMUELSON PA (1980) Economics, McGraw Hill, Auckland.
136. SANKAR U (1970) Elasticities of Substitution and Returns to Scale in Indian Manufacturing Industries, International Economic Review, 11(3), 399-411.
137. SARKAR AK (1965) Production Function for Indian Steel Industry, Indian Economic Journal, 12(3), 263-285.
138. SASTRY VSRK (1966) Measurement of Productivity and Production Functions in Sugar Industry in India : 1951-1961, Indian Journal of Industrial Relations, 2(1), 70-94.
139. SHARMA KD (1976) Programming in FORTRAN IV, Affiliated East West Press, New Delhi.
140. SHEPHARD RW (1953) The Theory of Cost and Production Function, Princeton University Press, Princeton, New Jersey.
141. SHONE R and FISHER HR (1958) Industrial Production and Steel Consumption, Journal of Royal Statistical Society, 121(3), 269-311.
142. SHUBIK M (1960) Simulation of the Industry and the Firm, American Economic Review, 50(5), 908-919.
143. SIDHU SS (1983) The Steel Industry in India : Problems and Perspective, Vikas Publishing House, New Delhi.
144. SIEGAL S (1956) Nonparametric Statistics for the Behavioral Sciences, McGraw Hill, Kogakusha, Tokyo.
145. SINHA JN and SAWHNEY PK (1970) Wages and Productivity in Selected Indian Industries, Vikas Publishing House, New Delhi.
146. SOLOW RM (1957) Technical Change and the Aggregate Production Function, Review of Economics and Statistics, 39(3), 312-320.
147. STEEL AUTHORITY OF INDIA LTD. (1983) Saga of Steel, Unpublished Report, SAIL, New Delhi.

148. THIRSK W (1974) Factor Substitution in Colombian Agriculture, American Journal of Agricultural Economics, 56(1), 73-84.
149. TIMES OF INDIA (1983) Directory and Year Book : 1982, Times of India, Bombay, 87-89.
150. UNITED NATIONS (Annual Publication, 1951-1978) Statistical Year Book, U.N., New York.
151. UNITED NATIONS (1953) European Steel Exports and Steel Demand in Non European Countries, UNECE, Geneva.
152. UNITED NATIONS (1959) Long Term Trends and Problems of European Steel Industry, UNECE, Geneva.
153. UZAWA H (1962) Production Functions with Constant Elasticities of Substitution, Review of Economic Studies, 29, 291-299.
154. UZAWA H (1964) Duality Principles in the Theory of Cost and Production, International Economic Review, 5(2), 216-220.
155. VARIAN HR (1978) Microeconomic Analysis, W.W. Norton and Co., New York.
156. VERNON JM, RIVES NW and NAYLOR TH (1969) An Econometric Model of the Tobacco Industry, Review of Economics and Statistics, 51(2), 149-158.
157. VINELL L (1973) Business Cycles and Steel Markets : Studies in Demand Variations and Firms' Short Term Behaviour in the Swedish Steel Market, Beckmans, Stockholm.
158. VINELL L (1974) A Theory of Steel Consumption, Chapter 3 in Forecasting Steel Consumption : Cross Section and Time Series Approaches, OECD, Paris, 43-61.
159. VLEMMINGS FAM (1974) The Use of A Global Model as a Base for Steel Forecasting, Chapter 4 in Forecasting Steel Consumption : Cross Section and Time Series Approaches, OECD, Paris, 64-84.
160. VON BERTALANFFY L (1950) The Theory of Open Systems in Physics and Biology, Science, 111, 23-29.
161. WHITMAN RH (1936) The Statistical Law of Demand for a Producer's Good as Illustrated by the Demand for Steel, Econometrica, 4, 138-152.
162. WILLIAMS M and LAUMAS P (1981) The Relation Between Energy and Non Energy Inputs in India's Manufacturing Industries, Journal of Industrial Economics, 30(2), 113-122.
163. WOODLAND AD (1976) Modelling the Production Sector of

an Economy : A Selective Survey and Analysis, Working Paper No. 0-04, University of British Columbia, Malbourne.

164. WOODWARD RD (1966) Economic Forecasting in the Steel Industry, Chapter 3 (Part 3) *in* How Business Economists Forecast (Eds. BUTLER WF and KAVESH RA), Prentice Hall, Englewood Cliffs, New Jersey, 334-350.

165. YEH YH (1966) Economies of Scale for the Indian Manufacturing Industries, The Econometric Annual of the Indian Economic Journal, 14(2), 275-291.

166. ZELLNER A (1962) An Efficient Method of Estimating Seemingly Unrelated Regressions and Tests for Aggregation Bias, Journal of American Statistical Association, 57(298), 348-368.

167. ZELLNER A and REVANKAR NS (1969) Generalized Production Functions, Review of Economic Studies, 36, 241-250.

APPENDIX - 1

A TRANSLOG MODEL OF INPUT SUBSTITUTION POSSIBILITIES IN INDIAN STEEL INDUSTRY[1]

A.1.1 INTRODUCTION

It has already been mentioned under sub-section 2.3.4 that the Transcendental Logarithmic (Translog) form introduced by Christensen, Jorgenson and Lau (25) *[2] is the most flexible form to analyse the production structure of a firm or an industry. The translog cost or production function does not impose prior restrictions on the elasticities of substitution between different inputs except those which arise from their definition and from assumptions of optimising behaviour. The translog form is capable of analysing the elasticities of substitution in a dynamic framework while the specification of production structure used in Chapter V of the present study, which is similar to the one used by Thirsk (148), estimates overall average values of elasticities of substitution between different inputs during the period under consideration. One of the limitations of using the translog form is that only input share equations can be estimated and not the input demand (in real terms) equations. This is the main reason of not using this form in the analysis of the production structure of Indian steel industry in the present study.

----

1. Part of this Appendix has been published in 15th Annual Convention of ORSI, Kharagpur, December, 1982.

2. * Numbers in parentheses indicate references at the end of the thesis.

Since 1973, a number of attempts have been made to analyse the production structure of various industries using a translog form. Chakrabarty (19) has reported an extensive literature review of translog production function. Some of the attempts have used the translog cost function approach while the others have used the translog production function approach to analyse the production structure and input substitution possibilities in different industries. The present study uses the translog cost function approach to analyse input substitution possibilities in Indian steel industry.

A 1.2 ESTIMATION OF INPUT SHARE EQUATIONS IN INDIAN STEEL INDUSTRY

A 1.2.1 Selecting a Translog Form and the Corresponding Input Share Equations

The translog form (production function or cost function) is quite flexible and is capable of analysing a non-homothetic production function (127). Every homogeneous production function is homothetic, but the homothetic family contains non-homogeneous production functions as well (167).

Most of the studies which have used the translog form to estimate the input share equations and analyse the substitution possibilities have made the following two restrictive assumptions:

i. Production function is linearly homogeneous, i.e. there are constant returns to scale. The assumption of homotheticity is, thus, implicit; and
ii. There is a neutral technical change.

The concepts of homogeneity and technical change have already been explained in Section 5.3.

The present study does not make these assumptions on a priori basis. In fact, it has been concluded in Chapter V that the production function in Indian steel industry is non-homogeneous and that there is a non-neutral (biased) technical change in this industry.

The one-output translog cost function as suggested by Nadiri (107) has been considered in the present Appendix as it represents one of the most flexible translog forms. The corresponding input share equations are specified as follows :

$$S_i(t) = \alpha_i + \sum_{j=L,K,F} \gamma_{ij} \ln P_j(t)$$

$$+ \gamma_{iQ} \ln Q(t) + \theta_{it} \ln t \qquad \text{(A 1.1)}$$

for i = L, K and F.

where,

$S_i(t)$ = cost share of the ith input in the total cost of L, K, and F during the year t ;

$P_j(t)$ = price of jth input during the year t ;

$Q(t)$ = output during the year t ; and

α_i, γ_{ij}, γ_{iQ} and θ_{it} are the parameters to be estimated.

The duality theory and the translog approximation require the following prior restrictions to be imposed on the specification given in equation (A 1.1) :

Firstly, the cost function must be linearly homogeneous in factor (input) prices. This implies that :

$$\sum_i \alpha_i = 1 \qquad \text{(A 1.2)}$$

$$\sum_j \gamma_{ij} = 0 \qquad \text{(A 1.3)}$$

$$\sum_i \gamma_{iQ} = 0 \qquad \text{(A 1.4)}$$

This is known as the Homogeneity Restriction.

Secondly, the Symmetry Restriction requires that :

$$\sum_i \gamma_{ij} = \sum_j \gamma_{ji} \tag{A 1.5}$$

or that

$$\gamma_{ij} = \gamma_{ji} \text{ for all } i \neq j \tag{A 1.6}$$

The technical change in the production structure of Indian steel industry is non-neutral (biased) if $\theta_{it} \neq 0$ for all i. Biased technical change affects the cost shares ; it saves (uses) the ith input if

$\theta_{it} < 0$ ($\theta_{it} > 0$).

The production function corresponding to the specification of input share equations given in equation (A 1.1) is homothetic if $\gamma_{iq} = 0$ for all i and non-homothetic otherwise.

The translog function does not assume separability of various inputs. Separability conditions should rather be tested. It is, however, assumed in this study that the inputs labour, capital and fuels, as a group, are weakly separable from the fourth input, viz. raw-materials. This assumption has been tested and found valid in Section 5.7.

If the two restrictive assumptions of constant returns to scale and neutral technical change are made, the specification of input share equations given in equation (A 1.1) reduces to the following form :

$$S_i(t) = \alpha_i + \sum_{j=L,K,F} \gamma_{ij} \ln P_j \tag{A 1.7}$$

for i = L,K and F,

as γ_{iQ} and θ_{it} become zero for all i.

A 1.2.2 Estimating the Input Share Equations

While estimating the three input share equations corresponding to the specification given in equation (A 1.1) or in equation (A 1.7), the restrictions of homogeneity and symmetry, as given in equations (A1.2), (A 1.3), (A 1.4) and (A 1.6) are pre-imposed. In fact, the imposition of restriction given in equation (A 1.3) automatically imposes the two restrictions given in equations (A 1.2) and (A 1.4). Thus, only two restrictions, given in equations (A 1.3) and (A 1.6), are to be imposed on the estimation procedure. It has been shown that, under such restrictions, the estimation of the parameters of any two share equations implicitly estimates the parameters of the third share equation. All the three equations cannot be simultaneously estimated because of the nature of restrictions imposed. Thus, one can arbitrarily drop any one equation and test the validity of the two restrictions given in equations (A 1.3) and (A 1.6) with regard to the remaining two equations. If the restrictions are found to be valid, the two equations are simultaneously estimated using the same technique as is used to estimate the input demand equations in Section 5.7; the two restrictions are pre-imposed on the estimation procedure.

To begin with, the validity of the two restrictions given in equations (A 1.3) and (A 1.6) is tested with regard to the specification of input share equations given in equation (A 1.7) as per the procedure mentioned in Section 5.7. The data used are for the years 1951 through 1977. The F^*-value is estimated to be 6.83 with $n_1=3$ and $n_2=46$. The critical F-value (at $n_1=3$, $n_2=46$) is 2.81 at 5 per cent level of significance and 4.24 at 1 per cent level of significance. The F^*-value is greater than the critical F-value even at 1 per cent level of significance. It may, thus, be concluded that the restrictions given in equations (A 1.3) and (A 1.6) are not true with regard to the specification of input share equations mentioned in equation (A 1.7), which is, therefore, not a theoretically acceptable specification.

Next, the two restrictions given in equations (A 1.3) and (A 1.6) are tested with regard to the specification of input share equations given in equation (A 1.1). The data used are for the years 1951 through 1977. The F^*-value is estimated to be 0.55 ($n_1=3$, $n_2=42$). The critical F-values are 2.83 and 4.29 at 5 per cent and 1 per cent levels of significance, respectively. The F^*-value is less than the critical F-value (even at 5 per cent level of significance). Thus, the restrictions given in equations (A 1.3) and (A 1.6) are found to be true when tested with regard to the specification of input share equations given in equation (A 1.1), which is, therefore, a theoretically acceptable specification.

The estimated input share equations, when the two restrictions given in equations (A 1.3) and (A 1.6) are imposed on the specification given in equation (A 1.1), are given as follows :

$$S_L(t) = 0.9112 + \underset{(7.90)}{0.1669} \ln P_L(t) - \underset{(-10.01)}{0.1128} \ln P_K(t)$$
$$- \underset{(-2.66)}{0.0541} \ln P_F(t) - \underset{(-1.88)}{0.0124} \ln t - \underset{(-3.76)}{0.0758} \ln Q(t) \qquad \text{(A 1.8)}$$

$$S_K(t) = 0.3716 - \underset{(-10.01)}{0.1128} \ln P_L(t)$$
$$+ \underset{(13.32)}{0.1740} \ln P_K(t)$$
$$- \underset{(-5.37)}{0.0612} \ln P_F(t) + \underset{(4.29)}{0.0485} \ln t + \underset{(3.23)}{0.0734} \ln Q(t) \qquad \text{(A 1.9)}$$

$$S_F(t) = -0.2828 - \underset{(-2.66)}{0.0541} \ln P_L(t)$$
$$- \underset{(-5.37)}{0.0612} \ln P_K(t)$$
$$+ \underset{(4.88)}{0.1152} \ln P_F(t) - \underset{(-3.60)}{0.0360} \ln t + \underset{(0.11)}{0.0024} \ln Q(t) \qquad \text{(A 1.10)}$$

Weighted R^2 for the System = 0.91

Weighted Mean Square Error (MSE) for the System = 1.2473

The estimated coefficients of all the variables in equations (A 1.8), (A 1.9) and (A 1.10) are statistically significant. These estimates also put forward the evidence that it would have been wrong to assume constant returns to scale ($\gamma_{iQ} = 0$) and neutral technical change ($\theta_{it} = 0$), as implied in the specification given in equation (A 1.7). Thus the specification given in equation (A 1.1) is meaningful in Indian steel industry and is accepted on its own merits and strength.

The corresponding production function is, therefore, non-homothetic (and also non-homogeneous) and there is a biased technical change which saves labour and fuels but uses capital.

A 1.3 PRICE ELASTICITIES OF INPUT DEMANDS AND PARTIAL ELASTICITIES OF SUBSTITUTION BETWEEN INPUTS

The price elasticities of input demands (η_{ij}) and partial elasticities of substitution between inputs (σ_{ij}) have been defined in Section 7.3 of the present thesis. The elasticity values, as computed under Section 7.3 and specified in Table 7.4, are the average elasticity values over the period of analysis. In case of a translog form (being used in this Appendix), the dynamic behaviour of these elasticities during the period of analysis can be studied.

The computed η_{ij} and σ_{ij} values for some selected years during the period of analysis (using the estimated values of $S_i(t)$'s and $S_j(t)$'s) are reported in Table A 1.1.

TABLE A 1.1

Price Elasticities of Input Demands and Partial Elasticities of Substitution Between Inputs of Labour, Capital and Fuels in Indian Steel Industry for Some Selected Years 1951-1977

Type of Elasticity	1951	1956	1961	1966	1971	1977
n_{LL}	-0.18	-0.12	-0.15	-0.17	-0.18	-0.18
n_{KK}	-0.14	-0.13	-0.16	-0.16	-0.11	-0.13
n_{FF}	-0.29	-0.11	-0.24	-0.29	-0.31	-0.32
n_{LK}	0.06	0.16	0.11	0.08	0.02	0.00
n_{KL}	0.08	0.08	0.08	0.06	0.03	0.00
n_{KF}	0.06	0.05	0.08	0.10	0.08	0.13
n_{FK}	0.08	0.18	0.19	0.17	0.08	0.12
n_{LF}	0.12	-0.04	0.04	0.09	0.16	0.18
n_{FL}	0.21	-0.07	0.06	0.12	0.23	0.20
σ_{LK}	0.18	0.28	0.24	0.19	0.08	0.00
σ_{KF}	0.24	0.31	0.39	0.41	0.27	0.40
σ_{LF}	0.49	-0.26	0.18	0.36	0.55	0.54

A 1.4 A CHECK ON THE BEHAVIOUR OF TRANSLOG COST FUNCTION

It is necessary to check whether the estimated translog cost function is well behaved or not. For a cost function to be well behaved it should be concave in input prices and its input demand functions should be strictly positive (11). The translog cost function does not satisfy these conditions globally. The positivity and concavity of the estimated translog cost function must be checked for each annual observation during the period of estimation (1951 to 1977). It is found that positivity condition is satisfied as the estimated cost shares of labour, capital and fuels are all positive. Concavity condition is satisfied if the Hessian matrix based on the parameter estimates of equations (A 1.8), (A 1.9) and (A 1.10) is negative semi-definite. This condition is also satisfied for each annual observation. Thus, the KLF translog cost function corresponding to the estimated input share equations (A 1.8), (A 1.9) and (A 1.10) is well behaved in the region including the data on Indian steel industry for the period 1951 to 1977.

A 1.5 CONCLUDING REMARKS

Several important conclusions emerge from the analysis of Table A 1.1. The partial elasticity of substitution between labour and capital has been declining in the post-1956 period and becomes almost insignificant from 1971 onwards. It implies that the scope of substitution between labour and capital has gone down since 1956 and is almost zero in 1977. The partial elasticity of substitution between capital and fuels has been rising since 1951 and that between labour and fuels has been rising since 1956. These elasticities are the short term elasticities and have exhibited wide annual fluctuations. while the ones estimated in Section 7.3 are the average long run elasticity values.

The own price elasticities (η_{ii}) estimated in this Appendix are roughly of the order of -0.16 in case of labour, -0.14 in case of capital and -0.26 in case of fuels. These values are much in agreement with η_{ii} -values estimated under Section 7.3 and given in Table 7.4 (η_{LL} = -0.21 ; η_{KK} = -0.10 ; and η_{FF} = -0.27). The cross-price elasticities (η_{ij} have, however, exhibited wide fluctuations from time to time during the period of analysis.

The production function corresponding to the estimated input share equations (A 1.8), (A 1.9) and (A 1.10) is non-homogeneous and there is a non-neutral (biased) technical change which saves labour and fuels but uses capital. These findings are similar to those obtained in the analysis of Section 5.7.

In general, the results of this Appendix are much in agreement with the ones obtained in the analysis of production function during the course of the present study.

There is a wide scope to analyse the substitution possibilities in Indian Iron and steel industry by adopting still more finer and disaggregated forms of the translog approach.

APPENDIX-2

TABLES OF RAW DATA

TABLE A1
Data on Labour Used in Indian Iron and Steel Industry (1951-1977)

Year	Direct Workers (Number)	All Workers : Direct + Contract (Number)	All Employees (Number)
1951	56797	66205	79034
1952	56525	65491	78466
1953	56367	63664	77054
1954	61756	69566	85634
1955	61928	72654	89226
1956	61589	71688	88027
1957	63456	73651	90184
1958	64228	75997	93283
1959	NA	70799	88574
1960	61696	73734	89959
1961	65310	75858	92962
1962	110510	130793	164007
1963	110606	125732	165181
1964	125631	139792	178073
1965	111639	127262	173112
1966	120274	135988	182063
1967	NA	NA	NA
1968	128988	144152	194995
1969	137628	152524	203034
1970	130643	146369	196353
1971	140007	159761	209785
1972	NA	NA	NA
1973	NA	161116	212229
1974	NA	143513	182282
1975	NA	167657	227448
1976	NA	165316	226448
1977	NA	171072	242651

TABLE A1 cont...

Year	Lakh Hours (Direct workers)	Lakh Hours (All workers)	Lakh Hours (All employees)
1951	1487	NA	NA
1952	1428	NA	NA
1953	1455	NA	NA
1954	1606	NA	NA
1955	1612	NA	NA
1956	1656	NA	NA
1957	1656	NA	NA
1958	1634	NA	NA
1959	NA	1694	NA
1960	NA	1949	NA
1961	NA	1988	NA
1962	NA	3626	NA
1963	NA	3300	NA
1964	NA	3714	NA
1965	NA	3464	NA
1966	NA	3624	NA
1967	NA	NA	NA
1968	NA	3715	NA
1969	NA	3809	NA
1970	NA	3716	NA
1971	NA	4179	NA
1972	NA	NA	NA
1973	NA	4033	NA
1974	NA	3884	NA
1975	NA	4570	NA
1976	NA	NA	6248
1977	NA	NA	6728

Sources : 1. CMI Series (72)
2. ASI Series (73)

TABLE A2

Depreciated Book Values (Rs. lakh) of Fixed Capital, Components of Fixed Capital and Reported Depreciation, and Price Indices for Components of Fixed Capital (1950-1977)

Year	(1) Fixed Capital (Total)	(2) Structures and Cons-tructions	(3) Plant, Machi-nery and Other Assets	(4) Reported Deprecia-tion (Total)	(5) Price Index for Cons-truction	(6) Price Index for Machi-nery and Equipment
1950	2816	655	2161		80.2	72.7
1951	2662	656	2006	225	79.9	83.0
1952	2553	646	1907	214	80.8	89.4
1953	2890	580	2310	248	81.2	87.6
1954	3590	821	2769	305	81.3	86.7
1955	4088	838	3250	354	82.8	87.1
1956	5290	944	4346	466	87.1	88.5
1957	8106	1309	6797	728	91.7	91.0
1958	13106	1341	11765	1224	95.5	92.9
1959	17364	1562	15802	1452	95.1	95.1
1960	17798	2174	15624	1132	100.0	100.0
1961	17950	2339	15611	1752	105.1	102.2
1962	68169	8884	59285	5264	107.9	105.4
1963	71070	10434	60636	4565	110.6	110.9
1964	73216	12210	61006	4576	116.1	114.4
1965	74970	13944	61026	5826	124.2	121.4
1966*	87918	15856	72062	6090	133.1	133.8
1967	90155	16241	73914	6800	142.3	135.0
1968	92391	16626	75765	7509	150.3	136.0
1969	89114	16676	72438	8230	161.9	139.4
1970	84365	16860	67505	8697	172.4	151.1
1971**	79322	16945	62377	9534	185.0	159.1
1972	80746	17485	63261	9154	199.6	169.3
1973	82169	18345	63824	8774	229.4	185.3
1974	74553	17178	57375	7876	277.9	236.3
1975	160372	38175	122197	7828	301.9	260.7
1976	178009	43823	134186	10324	313.7	256.9
1977	195243	49769	145474	12089	326.7	260.7

* Figures in various columns (except price indices) are average values of the preceding and succeeding years. The data for price indices were available for all the years.

** Figure of fixed capital is the average of corresponding figures in preceding and succeeding years.

Note: For the years 1973 to 1977, the data are available only for fixed capital (total). The method used to split the figure of each year into two components is explained in sub-section 3.5.3 of this book.

Sources: 1. CMI Series (72) ; 2. ASI Series (73) ; 3. National Accounts Statistics (74); 4. Chandhok (21) ; 5. Dholakia (33).

TABLE A3
Quantities of Various Fuels Consumed in Indian Iron and Steel Industry (1951-1971)

Year	Coal (Thousand tonnes)	Coal (Rs. lakh at current prices)	Coke (Thousand) tonnes)	Coal Gas (Thousand cubic metres)
1951	3580	702	255	67923
1952	3565	728	176	70115.
1953	3205	684	145	52910
1954	2694	601	237	2
1955	2593	587	249	17
1956	2356	595	243	10
1957	2424	701	294	6
1958	2499	784	292	6
1959	2904	912	88	NA**
1960	3109	1017	212	28
1961	3208	1132	413	6
1962	6786	2535	289	-*
1963	6612	3335	400	-
1964	4910	2589	344	-
1965	5804	2894	306	89
1966	5183	2932	239	9250
1967	NA	NA	NA	NA
1968	5895	3861	98	33190
1969	5267	3808	323	15424
1970	5262	3897	377	15749
1971	4207	4039	336	2912

* Value less than 0.5
** Not Available

TABLE A3 cont...

Year	Firewood (Thousand tonnes)	Charcoal (Thousand tonnes)	Motor Spirit (Thousand litres)	Diesel Oil (Thousand litres)
1951	5	-	NA	NA
1952	5	-	NA	NA
1953	3	-	NA	NA
1954	54	22	NA	NA
1955	50	22	NA	NA
1956	55	23	NA	NA
1957	47	23	NA	NA
1958	45	28	NA	NA
1959	NA	NA	NA	NA
1960	38	30	717	NA

1961	52	46	741	NA
1962	43	39	564	NA
1963	32	43	2485	NA
1964	19	44	3204	NA
1965	14	43	19319	NA
1966	15	39	12618	18295
1967	NA	NA	NA	NA
1968	12	33	8173	20921
1969	13	29	8954	27149
1970	14	32	9132	30392
1971	18	40	10904	33622

TABLE A3 contd...

Year	Other Fuel Oils (Thousand litres)	Electricity Purchased (Thousand KWH)	Others (Rs. Thousand at current prices)
1951	6313	140564	1828
1952	6204	154457	1695
1953	6349	148810	1407
1954	8837	263066	846
1955	10956	317744	981
1956	13189	383896	1419
1957	24349	533523	3570
1958	83146	589138	4830
1959	NA	685601	24248
1960	80050	784950	9102
1961	91061	753349	2202
1962	97693	1088583	2752
1963	151281	1240143	3103
1964	140855	1522215	3317
1965	143880	1579558	3026
1966	158646	1607407	3277
1967	NA	NA	NA
1968	120852	1064134	3808
1969	215210	2228044	4966
1970	212838	2449217	15483
1971	218565	2683603	14862

Sources: 1. CMI Series (72)
2. ASI Series (73)

TABLE A4

Coal Replacement of Different Fuels

S. No.	Fuels	Units	Coal Replacement in million tonnes
1.	Coal (Coking and non-coking used in steam generation)	1 million tonnes	1.0
2.	Hard Coke	-do-	1.3
3.	Soft Coke	-do-	1.5
4.	Fire Wood	-do-	0.95
5.	Charcoal	-do-	1.0
6.	Oil Products, Black Products (i.e. Fuel oil, Furnace oil, Refinery fuels, etc.)	-do-	2.0
7.	Kerosene and LPG	-do-	8.3
8.	High Speed Diesel Oil and Low Speed Diesel Oil	-do-	9.0
9.	Motor Spirit and Jet Fuel	-do-	7.5
10.	Natural Gas	10^9 metre^3	3.6
11.	Electricity	10^9 KWH	1.0

Source : Fuel Policy Committee Report (76).

TABLE A5

Specific Gravity of Different Liquid Fuels (at 15° C)

S. No.	Liquid Fuel	Specific Gravity
1.	Motor Spirit	0.92
2.	Diesel Oil	0.73
3.	Other Fuel Oils	0.89

TABLE A6
Quantities and Values of Major Raw-Materials Used in Indian Iron and Steel Industry (1951-1971)

Year	Iron Ore		Lime Stone	
	Thousand tonnes	Rs. Thousand at current prices	Thousand tonnes	Rs. Thousand at current prices
1951	2939	27121	884	9286
1952	3013	35761	894	12353
1953	2900	39483	742	11242
1954	3225	43272	934	13232
1955	3168	44243	915	13366
1956	3228	48407	979	15818
1957	3262	54947	1039	17609
1958	3518	65768	1095	21841
1959	4465	101954	NA	NA
1960	4741	95123	1346	30037
1961	4958	111495	1497	37539
1962	10089	227120	3159	78638
1963	11735	261522	3201	82503
1964	11671	295682	3303	94277
1965	11492	303509	3410	95673
1966	11871	324025	3212	99244
1967	NA	NA	NA	NA
1968	11777	390344	3465	138664
1969	12100	476618	3617	138404
1970	11599	467872	3475	133082
1971	11403	390151	3434	129551

TABLE A6 cont...

Year	Scrap, Pig Iron, Steel, etc.		Aluminium	
	Thousand tonnes	Rs. Thousand at current prices	Thousand tonnes	Rs. Thousand at current prices
1951	742	113247	0.27	701
1952	810	122755	0.28	871
1953	709	114595	0.25	733
1954	468	112755	0.28	756
1955	544	143797	0.26	700
1956	671	223618	0.26	722
1957	582	226397	0.42	1313
1958	627	265025	0.27	970
1959	362	178465	NA	NA
1960	875	378944	0.34	1482
1961	863	380923	0.35	1597
1962	1150	415709	0.50	2075

1963	1425	607112	0.71	2825
1964	1507	715610	1.13	4552
1965	1131	646870	1.30	6053
1966	1350	717728	1.47	7357
1967	NA	NA	NA	NA
1968	1572	863245	1.64	8792
1969	1607	948204	1.84	10566
1970	1378	995685	1.67	11263
1971	1818	1531424	1.61	11022

ABLE A6 cont...

	Tin		Spelter (Zinc)	
Year	Thousand tonnes	Rs. Thousand at current prices	Thousand tonnes	Rs. Thousand at current prices
1951	1.16	16181	6.50	12195
1952	1.16	14655	9.95	30353
1953	0.99	11462	8.16	16442
1954	1.13	9707	11.74	14396
1955	1.24	10728	11.50	13613
1956	1.28	11096	12.27	16567
1957	1.16	10073	13.66	19240
1958	1.04	10560	12.17	14413
1959	NA	NA	NA	NA
1960	1.28	12905	10.69	12853
1961	1.30	13059	11.41	15743
1962	1.35	13460	12.58	17941
1963	1.70	20448	12.37	15113
1964	1.76	25487	12.91	17956
1965	1.50	33619	10.68	17797
1966	1.32	41496	4.73	11493
1967	NA	NA	NA	NA
1968	1.49	50373	13.06	35577
1969	1.44	45584	9.30	31427
1970	1.66	61910	8.64	29406
1971	1.31	50018	17.04	68706

TABLE A6 cont ...

	Magnesite		Coal	
Year	Thousand tonnes	Rs. Thousand at current prices	Thousand tonnes	Rs. Thousand at current prices
1951	8.09	1648	NR	NR
1952	8.18	1870	NR	NR
1953	8.49	1642	NR	NR
1954	9.36	2028	NR	NR
1955	8.48	1932	NR	NR

1956	10.59	2108	NR	NR
1957	8.24	1189	NR	NR
1958	9.90	3045	NR	NR
1959	NA	NA	NR	NR
1960	11.76	1749	1961	57571
1961	7.98	1394	2143	66065
1962	19.70	2651	4095	134642
1963	16.72	3464	4205	150927
1964	19.53	3505	5509	228705
1965	18.98	3724	5809	255439
1966	20.47	3818	6339	348238
1967	NA	NA	NA	NA
1968	19.97	3772	4680	454847
1969	19.22	3826	6984	512568
1970	29.49	11848	6949	510211
1971	31.57	17859	6948	520233

* Not Reported

TABLE A6 contd...

Year	Chemicals Rs. Thousand at current prices	Total Expenditure on Major Raw-Materials Rs. Thousand at current prices
1951	3477	183856
1952	5406	224024
1953	3737	199336
1954	4133	200279
1955	4126	232505
1956	4171	322507
1957	4774	335542
1958	4746	386368
1959	NA	NA
1960	3760	594424
1961	6405	634220
1962	14612	906848
1963	22933	1166847
1964	20059	1405833
1965	28856	1391540
1966	35917	1589316
1967	NA	NA
1968	38793	1984407
1969	50314	2217511
1970	56225	2277502
1971	80737	2799701

Sources: 1. CMI Series (72)
2. ASI Series (73).

TABLE A7
Price Indices of Chemicals and Fuels Used in Indian Iron and Steel Industry (1951 to 1971)
Base 1970-71 = 100

Year	Chemicals (Industrial)	Fuels, Power, Light and Lubricants
1951	53.4	47.5
1952	55.9	50.7
1953	51.0	50.5
1954	53.3	50.5
1955	53.1	49.3
1956	50.7	52.9
1957	52.4	57.6
1958	61.1	59.0
1959	62.2	59.6
1960	53.8	61.2
1961	52.8	62.3
1962	59.3	64.4
1963	60.4	73.7
1964	61.9	74.9
1965	65.4	77.2
1966	73.8	83.2
1967	82.3	88.0
1968	87.9	92.2
1969	96.1	96.1
1970	100.1	100.0
1971	106.3	105.9

Source : Chandhok (21)

TABLE A8
Price Indices of Major Raw-Materials and Fuels Used in Indian Iron and Steel Industry (1971-77)
(Base 1970-71 = 100)

Year	Iron Ore	Lime Stone	Steel	Aluminium	Tin
1971	97.8	100.0	104.1	99.6	89.6
1972	93.7	100.0	115.4	106.3	94.3
1973	100.1	176.4	132.1	107.5	120.7
1974	93.3	183.4	167.2	123.4	201.4
1975	124.5	187.2	181.6	190.0	228.1
1976	163.2	187.2	186.6	229.4	205.9
1977	176.4	187.2	187.6	228.0	278.2

TABLE A8 cont...

Year	Zinc (Industrial)	Chemicals	Magnesite	Coal	Fuels, Power, Light and Lubricants
1971	104.6	106.3	102.4	100.0	105.9
1972	117.1	110.1	113.0	110.3	110.1
1973	199.6	119.2	116.1	119.0	130.6
1974	342.7	180.2	164.5	138.3	198.3
1975	279.4	201.5	214.4	170.7	219.2
1976	284.6	191.6	217.2	197.6	230.8
1977	247.7	190.9	217.2	197.6	234.2

Source : Chandhok (21)

TABLE A9
Money Value of Fuels and Raw-Materials Used in Indian Iron and Steel Industry (1973-1977) (Rs. lakh at current prices)

Year	Fuels	Raw-Materials
1973	10999	51635
1974	16204	59444
1975	23832	77381
1976	26119	81875
1977	22665	99947

Source : ASI Series (73)

TABLE A10
Value of Costs of Different Inputs Used in Indian Iron and Steel Industry (1951-1977) (Rs. lakh at current prices)

Year	Labour (Total emoluments)	Capital (Gross quasi rent)	Fuels	Raw-Materials	Total
1951	1583	1293	916	2302	6094
1952	1692	1581	921	2859	7053
1953	1649	2072	867	2677	7265
1954	1813	2739	882	3082	8516

1955	1909	2910	896	3523	9238
1956	2037	3940	961	4433	11371
1957	2131	3738	1198	4624	11691
1958	2277	3812	1451	5322	12862
1959	2557	3729	1540	7331	15157
1960	2690	3104	1818	8537	16149
1961	2814	3775	2172	9143	17904
1962	4468	6508	3771	14355	29102
1963	5016	8319	4966	16876	35177
1964	5991	10376	4430	19787	40584
1965	6668	10809	4947	19626	42050
1966*	7644	9616	5288	22824	45372
1967*	8656	10055	6079	26310	51100
1968	9668	10493	6883	29795	56839
1969	10278	9610	7437	32227	59552
1970	11854	10386	7980	34237	64457
1971	13229	8159	8574	43229	73191
1972	15154	11409	8762	47432	82757
1973	17079	14659	10999	51635	94372
1974	18628	24464	16204	59444	118740
1975	24269	26319	23832	77381	151801
1976	24502	27778	26119	81875	160274
1977	28425	21488	22665	99947	172525

* The values in these years are averages of the corresponding preceding and succeeding years.

Sources: 1. CMI Series (72); 2. ASI Series (73)

Index